The Explosive
Sixties

William B. Mead

A

BOOK

BASEBALL'S DECADE OF EXPANSION

The Explosive Sixties

UMPIRES 20 15 6 11   AT BAT
CHI   30 DH   23
CLEV   31 JUNE 1

May 28, 1967, was a good Sunday to be a Tiger fan. Detroit was neck-and-neck with Minnesota atop the American League standings, the last-place Senators were in town, and best of all, it was Bat Day.

The Greatest Sacrilege

"I give the man a point for speed. I do this because Maris can run fast. Then I give him a point because he can slide fast. I give him another point because he can field. He is very good around the fences—sometimes on top of the fences. Next I give him a point because he can throw. A right fielder has to be a thrower or he's not a right fielder. So I add up my points, and I've got five for him before I even come to his hitting. I would say this is a good man."

Casey Stengel

Roger Maris got off to a slow start in 1961. He hit only one home run in the Yankees' 25 spring training games, and when the season started he went ten games before connecting off Detroit's Paul Foytack. His teammate Mickey Mantle homered twice that day and led the league with seven.

In 1960, his first season with the Yankees, Maris had hit 39 homers, second in the American League to Mantle's 40. He led the league in runs batted in with 112, played superbly in right field, and ran the bases with skill and daring. He was voted the league's Most Valuable Player as the Yankees won the pennant after a disappointing third-place finish in 1959.

But now, in late April of 1961, he was hitting under .200. "I was pressing and feeling for the ball instead of swinging at it," he said. "Nothing was going right." Maris, so often portrayed as a man immune to human pleasantry, was called into the Yankee front office. "They said they didn't want me to be concerned, because they weren't. They told me to swing and not to worry about my batting average. I quit pressing, and the homers started to come."

Roger Maris (opposite) watches his 61st home run sail into Yankee Stadium's right field stands on October 1, 1961. Maris took 161 games to break Babe Ruth's record of 60 home runs, hit in 151 games in 1927.

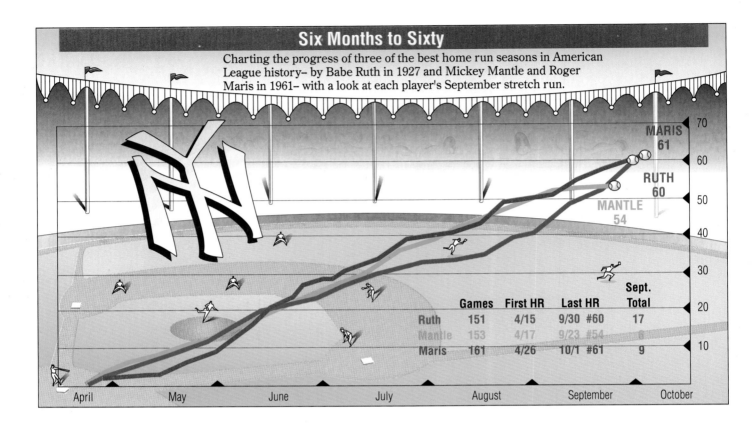

Six Months to Sixty

Charting the progress of three of the best home run seasons in American League history– by Babe Ruth in 1927 and Mickey Mantle and Roger Maris in 1961– with a look at each player's September stretch run.

MARIS
61

RUTH
60

MANTLE
54

	Games	First HR	Last HR	Sept. Total
Ruth	151	4/15	9/30 #60	17
Mantle	153	4/17	9/23 #54	6
Maris	161	4/26	10/1 #61	9

April   May   June   July   August   September   October

Indeed they did. By May 31 at Fenway Park, against Boston's Billy Muffett, Maris hit his 12th homer and Mantle hit his 14th. On July 17 Maris lost a homer; his first-inning blast against the Orioles didn't count because the game was rained out before five innings were completed. Against the White Sox on July 25, Maris hit two homers in the first game of a doubleheader and two more in the second; the Yankees swept the day and edged past Detroit into first place. Maris had 40 homers. Mantle had 38. On the same date back in 1927, Babe Ruth had 31.

It wasn't the first time a player or two had been ahead of Ruth's record pace. The Babe hit his 60 with a hot September of 17 homers, and many a challenger had faded in the stretch. Nevertheless, the count was on. Sportswriters began to bore in on the "M&M Boys," as they were called. Maris' hometown of Fargo, North Dakota, named a street after its heroic native son, and the state's senior senator, Milton Young, who rarely spoke on the Senate floor on subjects unrelated to wheat farming, rose to tell his colleagues that Roger Maris had hit another homer.

Back in New York, things weren't as rosy.

"Roger," asked Joe Trimble of the New York *Daily News,* "do you think you can break Babe Ruth's record?"

"How the ____ do I know?" Maris replied.

"He doesn't take surly pills," Trimble wrote. "He only acts that way."

Writers began lining up three deep around Maris' locker before and after games. He answered question after question, day after day. But he did not enjoy it or pretend to, and he lacked the sophistication of a Reggie Jackson or the personality of a Pete Rose. His repetitive answers (to repetitious questions) weren't widely quoted, but his occasionally intemperate replies

Mickey Mantle was the fans' choice to break Ruth's record, but the great switch-hitter fell seven homers short in 1961.

Maris, like Ruth, was an excellent right fielder whose power overshadowed his defensive ability. The home run porch that each bombarded—296 feet from home plate—was also the one each had to defend.

were. He became typecast as a villain, and some writers goaded him in search of an ill-tempered quote.

"What's a .260 hitter like you doing hitting so many home runs?" one writer asked.

"You've got to be a damned idiot," Maris replied.

There was a time when Yankee fans used to boo Mickey Mantle, finding him an imperfect heir to the great Joe DiMaggio. Writers focusing on Mantle found him a churlish interview. But in 1961 Mantle became the true Yankee, Maris the interloper. With the pressure shifted to Maris, Mantle became more cheerful and quotable. The fans cheered him, openly rooting for him to beat out Maris in their pursuit of Ruth. The press heaped scorn on Maris, and the fans followed suit.

Maris got along well with his teammates, but he was still an outsider. Among regulars, only Maris and third baseman Clete Boyer had not come up through the Yankee farm system. So the players, too, tended to hope Mantle would break the record.

There was, in the meantime, a pennant race. The 1961 Yankees were a great team, the cream of their era, a team good enough to compare to the historic Yankee teams of 1927, when Ruth and Gehrig led "Murderers' Row," and 1936, when DiMaggio was making his sensational debut and Gehrig was still in his prime. The 1961 Yankees hit 240 home runs, a record that still stands. Bill "Moose" Skowron hit 28 homers, drove in 89 runs, and was just good enough to bat seventh in the order. John Blanchard hit 21 homers and batted .305; he was the Yankees' top pinch-hitter—the designated hitter wasn't dreamed of in the 1960s—fifth outfielder, and third-string catcher.

Elston Howard was the league's best catcher. The infield of Skowron,

Known as "The Chairman of the Board," Whitey Ford was the winningest pitcher in Yankee history. After learning to throw a slider from pitching coach Johnny Sain, Ford went from 12–9 in 1960 to 25–4 in 1961. Under Casey Stengel, Ford was saved to face the opposition's best pitcher, but in 1961 new manager Ralph Houk started Ford every fourth day.

Triple Tandems

In 1961 Roger Maris and Mickey Mantle combined for more home runs in a season than any two teammates in history. That year was also the first time teammates from *three* teams each hit 40 or more home runs in the same season.

Year	Team	Teammates / HRs			
1961	New York	Maris	61	Mantle	54
	Detroit	Colavito	45	Cash	41
	San Francisco	Cepeda	46	Mays	40
1954	Cincinnati	Kluszewski	47	Post	40
1955	Brooklyn	Hodges	42	Snider	40
1931	New York	Ruth	46	Gehrig	46
1930	New York	Ruth	49	Gehrig	41
1927	New York	Ruth	60	Gehrig	47

Bobby Richardson, Tony Kubek and Boyer was good offensively and superb defensively. Whitey Ford had his best season, 25–4. Ralph Terry was 16–3 and reliever Luis Arroyo was 15–5 with 29 saves. Arroyo had been languishing in the minors for years until the Yankees discovered him in 1960. "Who'd ever think a guy like that would be lying around dead somewhere?" Casey Stengel said.

The grouchy Stengel was gone in 1961, and the Yankee players responded enthusiastically to the pat-on-the-back managing style of Ralph Houk. This was a team that should win in a walk.

The Yankees did win, but the Detroit Tigers gave them a run. The Tigers, too, were a team of explosive power. Rocky Colavito hit 45 homers and drove in 140 runs, only two fewer than Maris. Norm Cash had the only .300 season of his 17-year career and made it a dilly: .361, 41 homers, 132 runs batted in. Al Kaline hit .324 with 19 homers.

The Tigers actually scored more runs than the Yankees, 841 to 827. In 1927 the Yankees stood alone, outscoring their nearest competitor by 130 runs—almost a run a game—and the Yankees of 1936 did even better, outscoring the league's second most productive team by a whopping 144. But in 1961 two powerhouse teams were competing, both led by sluggers having the best years of their careers.

The Tigers came to New York September 1, trailing by only a game and a half. Ford, Bud Daley and Arroyo outdueled Detroit's Don Mossi, 1–0. The next day, Maris doubled and hit his 52nd and 53rd homers of the season to beat the Tiger ace and Yankee nemesis Frank Lary. In the third and final game of the series, Howard hit a three-run homer and Mantle,

As much a legend as the M&M Boys, sportscaster Red Barber spent 28 years on the New York airwaves—15 with the Brooklyn Dodgers and 13 with the New York Yankees.

5'11" 193 lbs.   b 8/9/19
BR TR

RALPH HOUK
Manager

"I am not Casey Stengel. I am Ralph Houk!" In 1961, that was the battle cry of the New York Yankees' rookie manager. With the possible exception of Joe McCarthy, no Yankee manager ever unified a team as well as the "Major." Houk appointed Mickey Mantle unofficial team captain and was capable of convincing backup catcher Johnny Blanchard that he belonged in the big leagues.

"He's fresh out of the ranks, himself," said Yankee third baseman Clete Boyer. "He never was a great hitter. He knows what bad times are."

In World War II, through combat promotion, Houk rose from private to major, hence the nickname. As Yankee backup catcher from 1947 to 1954, Houk played just 91 games. But he spent his ample bench and bullpen time studying the game.

Houk learned well. In his first season as manager, New York won 109 games en route to back-to-back world championships—against the Cincinnati Reds and the San Francisco Giants—and three straight pennants.

Following two years as Yankee general manager, Houk came back to manage the team in 1966, remaining through the 1973 season. In all, Ralph Houk managed in the major leagues for 20 seasons, including 1974–1977 with the Detroit Tigers and 1981 to 1984 with the Boston Red Sox. Among managers, Houk ranks third on the all-time list with 3,156 games, 1,619 wins, and 1,531 losses.

playing with a painfully injured arm, hit his 49th and 50th. The Tigers were beaten, and to make sure, the Yankees ran their winning streak to 13 straight games.

The American League had expanded from eight to ten teams in 1961 and was playing a 162-game schedule for the first time. Writers and fans were conscious of the change, and so was Ford Frick. Frick was commissioner of baseball, but in 1927 he had been a New York sportswriter. He was a ghostwriter for Ruth, a friend who remained close to the Babe until Ruth's death in 1948.

As Maris and Mantle chased the record, Frick established this rule: "Babe Ruth's mark of 60 home runs, made in a schedule of 154 games in 1927, cannot be broken unless some batter hits 61 or more within his club's first 154 games."

Mantle hit his 53rd homer on September 10, but his legs and arm were hurting. He caught cold and got a shot in the hip from a doctor recommended by Mel Allen, the Yankees' broadcaster. The hip got infected and abscessed. Mantle's run was over. The writers concentrated even more on Maris, played up his petulance, and fanned the resentment among Yankee fans. Some didn't want Ruth's record broken at all; others wanted it reserved for another try by Mantle. Maris was so troubled that his hair fell out in clumps, but he kept hitting home runs.

The Yankees played their 154th game of the season against the Orioles in Baltimore. Maris needed two homers to tie Ruth. Sitting by his locker before the game, Maris began to shake. He walked into Houk's office, tears running down his cheeks. "I can't stand it anymore," he said. "All those goddamn questions." Houk closed the door and calmed his star. The Yankees needed

Maris hit the record-breaking homer, Sal Durante retrieved it and the $5,000 reward that was offered. Durante used the money to finance his honeymoon.

It was a golden moment for a reluctant hero, as Maris took a then-rare curtain call after breaking Babe Ruth's home run record. In 1961 he led the league in homers, RBI and runs scored, and although he hit 33 homers the next year, he was never again a league-leader in any offensive category.

only one more win to clinch the pennant, and Maris said, "If I can help win the game with a bunt, Skip, would you mind if I bunted? It wouldn't make me look bad, would it?" Houk replied, "No, it would make you a bigger man than ever."

Maris, composed, hit his 59th homer in the third inning. He came up in the ninth against Hoyt Wilhelm, and tapped a knuckle ball weakly toward first base. The Yankees won, 4–2, but Ruth's record, as defined by Frick, was safe.

Maris thought the pressure was off, but the writers kept after him, and the newspapers, radio and television continued to play up the pursuit of Number 60. Back in New York, Maris caught a curveball thrown by Baltimore's Jack Fisher and hit it so high and hard that he could comfortably lean on his bat, watching his 60th home run sail into the upper right field stands. His teammates enthusiastically congratulated him, and the fans cheered insistently until he stepped out of the dugout and tipped his cap.

The next day, to everyone's amazement, Maris took the day off. That left him three games to hit one home run. He didn't connect the next day, the day after, or his first time up in the season's final game. But in the fourth inning he drove Boston rookie Tracy Stallard's pitch into the right field stands, which were jammed with fans anxious for a chance at $5,000 offered by a California restaurateur for the ball that became Number 61. Sal Durante, a young man from Brooklyn, got the ball in a wild melee and hung on until rescued by stadium police.

Maris was wildly applauded, and his teammates wouldn't let him in the dugout, forcing him to take repeated curtain calls. Stallard had nothing to be ashamed of; he yielded only five hits, and Maris' homer was the only run of the game. Maris had his 61. Public legend to the contrary, it is not marked

Outs were all too frequent for the Reds in the 1961 World Series against New York. Cincinnati hit just .206 as a team, and Frank Robinson and Vada Pinson went five for 37. The Yankees won in five as Bobby Richardson hit .391, Johnny Blanchard hit two homers, and Hector Lopez drove in seven runs in nine at-bats.

in the record books with an asterisk. For example, *The Complete Baseball Record Book,* published by *The Sporting News,* lists the record this way:

Most Home Runs, Season
A.L. (162-game season)—61—Roger E. Maris, New York, 161 games, 1961.
A.L. (154-game season)—60—George H. Ruth, New York, 151 games, 1927.
N.L. (154-game season)—56—Lewis R. Wilson, Chicago, 155 games, 1930.
N.L. (162-game season)—52—Willie H. Mays, San Francisco, 157 games, 1965; George A. Foster, Cincinnati, 158 games, 1977.

Maris' misery was not over. Just as Ruth, in his day, had been disparaged by traditionalists who insisted that Ty Cobb's slash-and-run game was superior to the Ruthian style of home run baseball, Maris was criticized as an unqualified usurper. "They just decided they had the wrong hero thrown at them," Maris said.

Rogers Hornsby, who won two Triple Crowns and seven National League batting championships in the 1920s, had a habit of running down modern ballplayers—Ty Cobb used to do the same thing—and in spring training of 1962 Hornsby had a new platform: the brand-new expansion New York Mets had hired him as a coach. Hornsby said the only thing Maris could do as well as Ruth was run. Maris was asked to pose with Hornsby for a picture—and declined. Hornsby called Maris "a little punk ballplayer . . . a

It was a familiar get-together for the 1961 Tigers, as Rocky Colavito (7) was greeted by Al Kaline (6), Norm Cash (25), and Bill Bruton (38). The Tigers led the AL in runs scored that year, won 101 games, and still finished eight games behind the Yankees.

swelled-up guy . . . a bush leaguer." Sportswriters again lit into Maris, and the Yankees stonewalled him in contract negotiations, finally paying him $72,500, a raise of $30,000.

Maris hit 33 homers in 1962, 23 in 1963, and 26 in 1964. He was not a Babe Ruth. He had never claimed to be, but his well-rounded game continued to contribute to the team's success. In May of 1965 he injured his hand while sliding home. The hand got worse, and Maris didn't play the last three months of the season, although the Yankees kept saying he was "day to day" and kept urging him to take batting practice.

He did, but it hurt. In September he learned that the hand was broken, and he had reason to believe that Houk and other Yankee officials had known that all along. The hand never healed thoroughly, and Maris could no longer pull the ball with power. The New York fans kept on him, and after a disappointing 1966 season the Yankees traded Maris to the St. Louis Cardinals for a journeyman infielder named Charley Smith.

The St. Louis players and fans had read all about Maris, and they were pleasantly surprised by his hustling, unselfish, all-around play. He helped the Cardinals win pennants in 1967 and 1968, and then retired; August A. Busch, Jr., the Cardinals' chairman, awarded him a Budweiser distributorship in Gainesville, Florida. Maris never came close to election to the Baseball Hall of Fame. He died of cancer in 1985, at the age of 51.

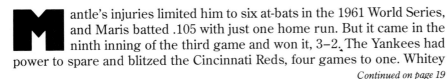

Mantle's injuries limited him to six at-bats in the 1961 World Series, and Maris batted .105 with just one home run. But it came in the ninth inning of the third game and won it, 3–2. The Yankees had power to spare and blitzed the Cincinnati Reds, four games to one. Whitey

Continued on page 19

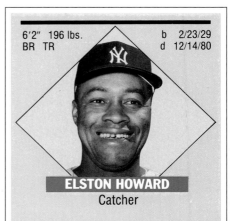

6'2" 196 lbs.	b 2/23/29
BR TR	d 12/14/80

ELSTON HOWARD
Catcher

Elston Howard broke in with the Yankees in 1955. Not only was he the first black player in Yankee history, he was expected to measure up to the legendary catchers who preceded him, Bill Dickey and Yogi Berra. Dickey, who had coached young Berra in 1946, became Howard's teacher. "I worked hard," Howard recalled. "Dickey worked harder."

After five seasons as a part-time outfielder and Berra's backup, Howard became New York's number one receiver in 1960. By the time he retired in 1968, Elston Howard was recognized as one of the game's finest all-around catchers.

Always dependable at the plate, Howard hit .290 with ten home runs in 97 games as a rookie. A .274 lifetime hitter, he hit over .300 three times, with a career-high .348 in 1961. As the American League's Most Valuable Player in 1963, Howard led the Yankees with 28 home runs and a .287 batting average.

In his 14-year big-league career, Howard played 54 games in ten World Series. Only Mickey Mantle and Yogi Berra have appeared in more World Series games.

Traded to the Red Sox during the 1967 pennant stretch, he ended his playing career in Boston the following year, rejoining the Yankees in 1969 as the American League's first black coach. Elston Howard died on December 14, 1980, five years to the day before the death of his former teammate, Roger Maris.

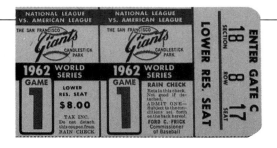

One Swing

After six games and four rain postponements, the 1962 World Series had come down to Jack Sanford and Ralph Terry. Again. For the third time in the Series, the Giants and Yankees sent their aces to the mound.

The last time these two teams had met in the World Series was 1951. In Joe DiMaggio's final season, the Yankees won in six, taking some of the glow from the Miracle of Coogan's Bluff and Bobby Thomson's pennant-winning homer. Eleven years and three time zones later, the Giants were primed for revenge. In fact, their entire 1962 season seemed to have been scripted in Hollywood. As in 1951, the Giants had come from behind to catch the Dodgers, taking the pennant in a three-game play-off. Now they were playing catch-up against New York. The Giants had that look of destiny.

If justice ruled baseball, Willie Mays should have been cast as the hero of Game 7. Since the Giants moved to San Francisco in 1958, Mays had never hit under .304, and he drove in at least 100 runs in each of five seasons. In 1962 he led the National League with 49 home runs. Despite five great seasons the locals wanted more. There were frequent boos. "For the first time in my career," Mays recalled years later, "I felt like an incomplete ballplayer."

Then there was Sanford. A workhorse pitcher throughout his career, Jack Sanford had been the Giants' stopper all season, winning a career-high 24 games while losing just seven. He had been nearly perfect in Game 2, stifling New York and Terry 2–0 with a two-hit shutout. In Game 5 he struck out ten in 7 1/3 innings. Sanford was ready.

Joe DiMaggio said that Game 7 was "the best-pitched World Series game I have ever seen." Terry pitched perfect ball through 5 2/3 innings, when Sanford singled for the Giants' first hit. On the mound, Sanford's only trouble came in the fifth. After walking Terry to load the bases, he got Tony Kubek to hit into a double play, allowing Bill Skowron to score from third. New York took that 1–0 lead into the bottom of the ninth.

Matty Alou, pinch-hitting for pitcher Billy O'Dell, beat out a bunt. Terry then struck out Felipe Alou and Chuck Hiller. Mays followed and promptly doubled down the right field line. Roger Maris fielded the ball in the corner and fired to the cut-off man, second baseman Bobby Richardson. Alou was hell-bent for third and had a notion to come home, but third-base coach Whitey Lockman held him up.

With runners on second and third, two out in the bottom of the ninth of Game 7 of the 1962 World Series, Yankee manager Ralph Houk slowly made his way to the mound. Willie McCovey was the next batter, and most of the 43,948 fans in Candlestick Park had to be thinking *intentional walk*. The right-handed hitting Orlando Cepeda was on deck, and Cepeda had done nothing all day. McCovey was in a groove against Terry, having tripled in the seventh after homering, a tape-measure shot, in Game 2. Two years before, in a similar situation, Ralph Terry had given up a Series-winning homer to Bill Mazeroski. This, too, was in the air. Houk left the decision up to his pitcher.

Terry's first pitch was good enough to hit, and McCovey hit it long and far and foul down the right field line. A single meant two runs and the Series. McCovey took the next pitch for a strike. Terry delivered his next pitch, and McCovey hit a shot—he said later it was the hardest ball he ever hit, no small claim for a man who hit 521 home runs. But this one was a bullet right at Richardson on the edge of the outfield grass. He caught it cleanly. New York, and Ralph Terry at last, four games to three.

San Francisco Giants' right-hander Juan Marichal (27, above) ran down Tony Kubek in Game 4 of the 1962 World Series as teammates Tom Haller (5) and Chuck Hiller looked on. Marichal left with an injury after four innings, but Hiller, who hit just three home runs in the regular season, gave the Giants a 7–3 win with the National League's first Series grand slam.

For a while it looked like they'd never play, as the 1962 Series was deluged with rain on both coasts and took 13 days to complete. San Francisco led New York in rain delays, 3–1, but Ralph Terry's shutout in Game 7 gave the Yankees their 20th world championship.

Sandy Koufax (above) had 306 strikeouts for Los Angeles in the 1963 regular season, and then fanned a World Series record 15 in Game 1, including the first five Yankee batters he faced. He also fanned the last, pinch-hitter Harry Bright (above), to break a record Brooklyn Dodger Carl Erskine had set ten years to the day earlier, also against the Yankees.

Broadcaster Mel Allen (right), known simply as "The Voice," called Yankee games for 25 years, including 20 World Series. Caught in a budget squeeze when the radio sponsor Ballantine Beer fell on hard times, Allen was let go in 1965.

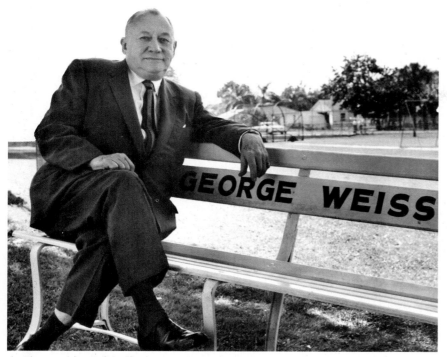

A prime architect of the Yankee dynasty, general manager George Weiss was as shrewd and workmanlike as his favorite manager—Casey Stengel—was shrewd and colorful.

Harmon Killebrew, who stole a total of 19 bases in his career, made his major league debut with the Washington Senators in 1954 as a pinch-runner. And for the next four seasons, Killebrew filled the role of reserve player. Through the 1958 season, the man who would become known as "Killer" hit a grand total of 11 home runs.

Then came 1959. In his first year as a Washington Senators' regular, Killebrew hit a league-leading 42 home runs, one of six times he led the American League in homers. From 1959 to 1972 Killebrew averaged 38 home runs a season with the Senators and Twins, eight times hitting 40 or more, including a career-high 49 in 1964 and 1969.

Killebrew's lifetime total of 573 homers, an AL record for a right-handed hitter, is the fifth highest of all time. His career home run percentage of 7.0 ranks third behind Babe Ruth's 8.5 and Ralph Kiner's 7.1.

The 1969 American League Most Valuable Player, Killebrew drove in 100 or more runs nine times, leading the league in 1962, 1971, and in 1969, when he established a career high of 140 RBI.

A career .256 hitter, Killebrew had 1,559 walks and 1,699 strikeouts, ranking tenth and ninth, respectively, on the all-time list. Having spent 21 of 22 years with the Senators and Twins, Killebrew retired after playing the 1975 season as a designated hitter with the Kansas City Royals.

Ford pitched 14 scoreless innings, running his string of consecutive scoreless World Series innings to 32. Babe Ruth had held the old record of $29\frac{2}{3}$ innings, earned when he was the ace pitcher of the Boston Red Sox back in 1918. "This sure wasn't a very good year for the Babe," Ford said.

The Yankees had themselves another dynasty. Under Houk, they fended off challenges from the Minnesota Twins and Los Angeles Angels in 1962 to win their third straight pennant. Injuries kept both Mantle and Maris out of the lineup through much of 1963, but the reliably superior Yankee farm system filled the gap with youngsters Joe Pepitone, Tom Tresh, Phil Linz, Jim Bouton and Al Downing. The Yankees won with ease. They won again in 1964, coming from behind to edge the White Sox and Orioles.

That made five straight pennants, tying the Yankees' own record and bringing their totals to 29 pennants and 20 world championships in 44 years. The American League had long since become Yankee property. Of every ten fans who came to see an American League game, four came to see the Yankees, either at home or on the road. Even outside New York, many baseball officials felt that a strong Yankee team was essential to continued fan interest and league prosperity.

But ragged edges were apparent as early as 1959. After the Yankees finished third that year, Dan Topping and Del Webb, who owned the team, decided to get rid of Stengel. He was showing his age, and they wanted to give Houk, their bullpen coach, a shot at managing before another team grabbed him. So they told Stengel, 71, that he would be out after the 1960 Series, and talked him into giving a peaceful retirement speech.

A sportswriter ruined the plot by asking Stengel if he had been fired. "You're goddamn right I was fired," Stengel replied.

The press conference became a forum for Stengel's anger. "I'll never make the mistake of being 70 again," he said. The Yankee management was portrayed as the heartless executioner of a kind, witty man who had managed the team to ten pennants.

A month later Topping and Webb pushed George Weiss into retirement. Weiss had been hired by the Yankees 29 years before to set up a farm system modeled after the one Branch Rickey established for the Cardinals. Helped by Yankee money, Weiss out-Rickeyed Rickey, and the rich Yankee farm system fed one dynasty after another. Weiss became general manager of the Yankees, and he ran the organization with a tight, workaholic efficiency that kept the team on top.

But Topping's health declined, and in 1962 he and Webb decided to sell the Yankees. With no stake in the team's future, they cut back on spending for young talent. In the meantime, the Mets were born. Capitalizing on the Yankees' public relations gaffes, the Mets hired Weiss as president and Stengel as manager. An astounding number of New York fans picked the Mets' comedy act over Yankee proficiency.

Anxious to find a manager whom the patrons would love, the Yankees gave the job to Yogi Berra in 1964, promoting Houk to general manager. Berra's Yankees won the pennant, but before the season was over the Yankee brass had decided to get rid of him. They fired Berra after the World Series— another embarrassment—and hired Johnny Keane, who, as the Cardinals' manager, had just beaten the Yankees in the 1964 World Series.

Two months earlier, in August of 1964, Topping and Webb had sold the team to CBS. The Yankees, long accused of possessing a cold corporate heart, now were possessed by a cold corporate owner. There was much ado

The glory and gloom of the Yankees merged in 1969 as Mickey Mantle and Elston Howard, now coaches, shared a clubhouse with newcomers Mel Stottlemyre and Thurman Munson. Stottlemyre won 20 games three times for bad to mediocre Yankee teams, while Munson was central to the team's resurgence in the late 1970s.

Ralph Houk (35, opposite) should have stayed home. After managing the Yankees to three pennants and two world championships in 1961–63, Houk returned to pinstripes in 1966 and managed the Yankees to their first last-place finish in 54 years. In 17 subsequent seasons managing the Yankees, Tigers and Red Sox, Houk never won another pennant.

Fans sitting in the third deck in Yankee Stadium's right field stands were targets for all-time greats like Lou Gehrig, Ruth, Maris and Mantle. Constructed in 1923, The House That Ruth Built has hosted 31 World Series, 22 of which the Yankees won. When the stadium was renovated in 1976, the overhanging facade shown here was moved and hung beyond the center field bleachers.

Gehrig (above, left) and Ruth established baseball's tradition of a murderer's row. Together they led the Yankees to three world championships between 1927 and 1932. Their styles contrasted sharply, with Ruth a champion of flamboyant excess and Gehrig a study in moderation.

Casey Stengel managed the Yankees to 10 pennants and seven world championships in 12 years. One of the game's great personalities, he worked in professional baseball from 1910 until his death in 1975. Sportswriter Red Smith wrote of Stengel: "It is erroneous and unjust to conceive of Casey Stengel merely as a clown. He is something else entirely—a competitor who always had fun competing, a fighter with the gift of laughter."

in the press and in Congress about the unhealthy mix of a baseball team and a communications company, but nothing came of it.

Still, the Yankees won. And few doubted that they would win again in 1965. But the farm system was no longer producing, and as Jim Bouton told author Peter Golenbock, "about 12 guys got old one day." One was Mantle, who after 1964 never batted .300 or hit more than 23 homers. Another was Maris. Whitey Ford was 38, Elston Howard 36. Bouton, a sensational young fastball pitcher, lost his career to a sore arm.

The Twins, Tigers, White Sox, Indians and Orioles got off to good starts in 1965, but they were looking over their shoulders at the Yankees. The Yankees came to Minnesota for four games just before the All-Star break, and the series was viewed as the Yankees' opportunity to start their inevitable pennant drive by cutting the Minnesota lead, which stood at $4^1/_2$ games.

The Twins won two of the first three games, as Dave Boswell outpitched Jim Bouton and Jim Perry bested Whitey Ford. But Minnesota trailed 5–4 in the ninth inning of the finale. Two were out, a runner was on first, and the count ran to three and two on Harmon Killebrew, the great Minnesota slugger. He homered. The Twins were on top to stay, and people began to notice that the Yankees looked at home in the second division.

They finished sixth, and the next season they came in dead last. The Mets had become the city's darlings even before the Yankee decline, outdrawing the 1964 pennant winners. "CBS bought a pig in a poke," said Mike Burke, the CBS executive who became Yankee president. The Yankees did not win another pennant until 1976. The dynasty was dead. ◗

Maris' Misery

Roger Maris got more grief than glory for breaking Ruth's home run record. Writing for The Los Angeles Times, *columnist Jim Murray looked back on Maris' long ordeal. This column was written during spring training, 1967, following Maris' trade to the St. Louis Cardinals.*

Maris' Big Mistake—He Hit Two Too Many

All Roger Maris did was break Babe Ruth's record. He would have been better off wallpapering over the Sistine Chapel ceiling, taking a hammer to Michelangelo's best statue, talking out loud during a Rachmaninoff concert, or drawing whiskers on the Mona Lisa. It was like casting a baggy pants comic in "King Lear," or putting Jayne Mansfield in a role made famous by Sarah Bernhardt.

Even before Maris broke the record, the commissioner of baseball announced he would never forgive him. The rest of baseball was more patient: they waited till the day after. He crept into the hearts of his countrymen the same way John Wilkes Booth did. People on the way to the electric chair get a better press. He would have been better off setting a trap for Santa Claus—or lighting the fireplace at quarter to 12 on Christmas Eve.

Maris had the good sense not to compound his error. He not only stopped hitting home runs, but stopped hitting, period. He became a jewel of inconsistency. The year he hit 61 home runs, he made only 98 other hits, but there was one year when he didn't even get 61 hits.

Roger was about as well-equipped for fame as a forest ranger. He came to the ball park every day as if it was a prisoner-of-war camp and it was his turn on the fingernail pull. "Hey, Maris, whose record you gonna break this year—Maury Wills?" the fans would shout. And then double up with laughter. The booing would start before he got his cap on. The press would try to be tactful, but at least one writer began to refer to his record as "The Great Mistake of 1961." It began to rank in the public mind with other great cataclysms like the Johnstown Flood or the explosion of the Hindenburg, or the sinking of the Titanic.

Baseball wasn't a game anymore for Maris, it was a sentence. Five years at hard labor and no time off for good behavior. Roger became defiant. "I ain't going to crash into no walls," he growled in the 1962 World Series. "They don't pay me to fracture my skull." A few games later, they had to carry him off the field anyway—he collided with a wall chasing a home run into the front row of seats. He quarreled with reporters, which, in New York, makes about as much sense as writing nasty things about the warden on your cell block in Death Row. Or putting the knock on your parole board.

Roger Maris' feat ranks as one of the stupendous athletic achievements of his generation, but the plain facts of the matter are, he would have been wiser sitting out the last half of the season. He hit two homers too many. Overlooked was the fact that he was one of the superior fielding players in the game. Coupled with his natural home-run stroke, as smooth as a Sam Snead backswing, it made him a favorite of *The Sporting News* readers. For all his genius, Babe Ruth never had to contend with the slider, night baseball and, as a matter of historical fact, one-fifth of the population was disenfranchised from the major leagues when the Babe played. Fact of the matter is, he never had to try to put one of Satchel Paige's Sunday pitches into the seats. Lefty Grove wasn't easy. But neither is Bob Gibson.

Success didn't spoil Roger Maris, but Roger Maris spoiled success. He wasn't his own worst enemy, but he had plenty of better friends than Roger Maris. There were days when he should have avoided himself.

They paid him $75,000 a year, but there's not enough money in the world to make up for being miserable in your work. Roger Maris got so he would rather wash elephants for a living—or ride sharks. The Yankees didn't really trade him, they uncaged him.

The Yankees had so little of his affection left they were glad enough to get a player named "Smith," if that's his real name, for him. Some say they didn't even ask the fellow's first name.

Roger Maris looked like a man who has just escaped a locked trunk as he stood around a Florida batting cage the other day. "This," he said evenly, "is the only place I would play. This is the only league." A rare expression crossed his face—a smile.

He stepped into the batting cage, idly timed a fast ball, and ripped it over the right field fence. Fortunately, no one told him that the National League homer record is 56 and was set by Hack Wilson in 1930. Hopefully, no one ever will.

Squeezing the Sluggers

aris' home run splurge shocked the baseball establishment for much the same reason it offended many writers and fans. A relative nobody had come from nowhere to break the most hallowed of records. Maris had never before even led the league in homers, whereas Babe Ruth had practically invented the home run, setting a record of 29 in 1919 and then breaking it with 54 in 1920 and 59 in 1921. When he hit 60 in 1927, there was little reason to doubt that he might hit 61 or 62 the next year (actually, he hit 54).

Ruth was Superman—no other American League *team,* let alone a mere player, matched his 60 homers in 1927—but in 1961 Maris was just the best of many in a new generation of sluggers. Eight players hit 40 or more home runs: Detroit's Rocky Colavito and Norm Cash, Jim Gentile of Baltimore, Harmon Killebrew of Minnesota, and Orlando Cepeda and Willie Mays of San Francisco, as well as Maris and Mantle.

Even more homers were hit in 1962—a record-breaking 3,001—although individual performances were not as dramatic. Commissioner Ford Frick was among those who believed that the delicate balance between baseball's offense and defense was out of whack. "I would even like the spitball to come back," he said. "Take a look at the batting, home run and slugging records for recent seasons and you become convinced that the pitchers need help urgently."

The return of the spitball was actually considered by the Official Baseball Playing Rules Committee, but only one member—Cal Hubbard,

In 1960, the legendary Ted Williams (9) ended a 19-year-career by homering in his final at bat. Williams' teammate Pete Runnels (3), a 32-year-old singles hitter, won the first of two batting titles that year with a .320 average.

Brooklyn-born Tommy Davis (right) took Los Angeles and the National League by storm in 1962, leading the league with 230 hits, 153 RBI, and a .346 average. In 1963, after the strike zone was enlarged, Davis' average dropped 20 points, yet he still led the league in hitting. By 1964 Davis' average had dipped to .275. Three years later, he was with the Mets, one of 12 teams he played with over the next ten seasons.

In 1963, when the Braves still called Milwaukee home, Henry Aaron (above) was nearly 400 home runs away from Babe Ruth's all-time career home run record of 714. Aaron finished the '63 season, his tenth in the majors, in typical fashion, hitting .319 and leading the league with 44 homers and 130 RBI.

head of umpires for the American League—favored it. Instead, the committee expanded the strike zone.

Like many baseball institutions, the strike zone had remained unchanged for many years. From 1887 until 1950, a strike was a pitch over the plate, between the batter's shoulders and knees. Home run production jumped after World War II, and so did attendance, so baseball moved to encourage slugging by tightening the strike zone. The new boundaries were from the batter's armpits to the tops of his knees. It worked; the home run became the centerpiece of offensive strategy for virtually every team. (The width of the strike zone is less subject to whim. Home plate is 17 inches wide and has been since 1900.)

In 1963 the Rules Committee made the strike zone larger—even a little larger than it had been before 1950. The new zone extended from the shoulders to the *bottoms* of the knees. Not only were pitchers given back the high, hard one—the hopping, shoulder-high fastball that pitchers like Sandy Koufax, Bob Gibson, Jim Palmer and Sam McDowell used with such devastating effect—they were also given the borderline low pitch.

The low strike fit neatly with the brushfire spread of the slider, a pitch that looks like a fastball but breaks slightly down and away. In addition, skillful pitchers were learning to disguise the spitball and the greaseball. Tony Kubek, the Yankee shortstop, recalls that Whitey Ford wouldn't let Yankee infielders oil their gloves, because a dry ball with a dab of grease, applied by Ford, did more tricks than a ball tainted with oil from infielders' gloves. The spitter and its cousins spread; in 1967 *Sports Illustrated* reported that "almost 25 percent of all major league pitchers are throwing the spitter, while 100 percent of all major league umpires, unable to enforce the rule against it, look

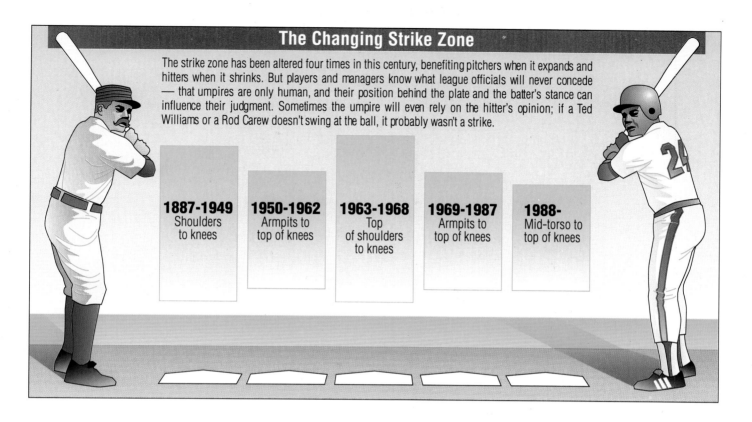

The Changing Strike Zone

The strike zone has been altered four times in this century, benefiting pitchers when it expands and hitters when it shrinks. But players and managers know what league officials will never concede — that umpires are only human, and their position behind the plate and the batter's stance can influence their judgment. Sometimes the umpire will even rely on the hitter's opinion; if a Ted Williams or a Rod Carew doesn't swing at the ball, it probably wasn't a strike.

1887-1949
Shoulders to knees

1950-1962
Armpits to top of knees

1963-1968
Top of shoulders to knees

1969-1987
Armpits to top of knees

1988-
Mid-torso to top of knees

the other way." The larger strike zone gave pitchers an unprecedented assortment of weapons. Members of the Rules Committee had not just applied the brakes to slugging; they had thrown the game into reverse. In 1963 the number of runs declined by 12 percent, the number of homers by 10 percent, and overall batting averages by 12 points.

In fact, the pitchers had been doing all right even before the strike zone was expanded. In his *Historical Baseball Abstract,* Bill James argues that trends had been favoring the pitcher since 1931. He points out that batting averages had been declining and strikeouts increasing, and says hitters began swinging for home runs because it had become so hard to score runs by stringing three or four hits together. Others contend that batting averages declined—and strikeouts increased—*because* more players were swinging from the heels for homers.

Whether homers were the cause or the effect, more of them were being hit, and the numbers posted by Maris and others gave the illusion that the hitters were overpowering the pitchers. More likely, the slugging of 1961 and 1962 merely marked the kind of high tide that comes along once in a while. The Yankees, to take the most prominent example, scored an average of 5.07 runs a game in 1961 and 5.04 in 1962—very good, but well below the same team's 5.56 runs per game in 1956, not to mention their 6.29-run average of 1927 or their 6.87 of 1936, neither of which aroused the rules makers.

You could run these statistics forever. In 1940 the Yankees scored 5.27 runs per game and finished in third place; in 1947 the New York Giants averaged 5.35 runs and finished in fourth place. The point is that the scoring of runs had not really exploded out of control in 1961 or in 1962, so the taller strike zone installed for 1963 was a dole to pitchers who were not really hungry.

*The St. Louis Cardinals'
Busch Stadium (left) is
typical of the bowl-shaped
ballparks of the 1960s.
Longer foul lines,
expansive outfields, and
circular banks of glaring lights
made new demands on batters.*

*Boston's Carl Yastrzemski
(right) made history in
1968. As the AL's lone
.300 hitter, his .301
average was the lowest
ever to lead either
league in hitting.*

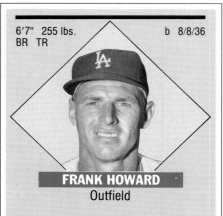

6′7″ 255 lbs.   b 8/8/36
BR TR

FRANK HOWARD
Outfield

They called him "Hondo" and, in Washington, "The Capital Punisher." Ted Williams called him "the strongest man I've ever seen in baseball." At 6′7″ and never less than 255 pounds, Frank Howard may well have been the strongest man ever to play baseball.

A basketball and baseball star at Ohio State University, Howard was Rookie of the Year with the Dodgers in 1960, hitting .268 with 23 home runs and 77 RBI. Two years later he enjoyed his finest year in Los Angeles, hitting .296 with 31 home runs and 119 RBI.

Traded to the Senators in 1964, Howard became an immediate folk hero in Washington. He was large and lovable, and he could hit. A career .273 hitter, Howard batted .280 for the Senators and averaged 34 homers a year. His 44 home runs led the league in both 1968 and 1970, and in 1969 he hit a career-high 48 homers. Three times he had more than 100 RBI in a season, including a league-leading 126 in 1970.

Howard's lifetime total of 382 home runs ranks 25th on the all-time list. An American League All-Star outfielder from 1968 to 1971, Howard homered in the 1969 All-Star Game in Washington. His ten homers in a single week is a major league record.

Traded to the Detroit Tigers in 1972, Howard retired following the 1973 season with Detroit. He managed the Padres in 1981 and the Mets in 1983.

More and more games were being played at night; hitters prefer daylight. Fielding had improved. Gloves and mitts were much larger—they were veritable baskets compared with those of 20 years before. Bats hadn't changed, although most players were switching to lighter bats, having learned that a light bat with a thin handle is easier to whip around in a home run swing. Groundskeeping improved, so fielders got fewer bad bounces. Warning tracks and padded fences were installed, allowing outfielders to take more risks and catch more balls. The pitcher's mound was supposed to be 15 inches high, but umpires had no way to measure it and no way to stop a groundskeeper from building it higher.

Eleven new ballparks were built during the 1960s, and most of them tended to help the defense at the expense of the offense. Many of the old parks were constricted in size and shape because, when built, they had to be crammed within the confines of city streets. The old parks seated fans close to the field—so lots of pop fouls drifted into the stands, out of fielders' reach. Some old parks offered a short home run to right field, left field or both. Whether viewed as oddities or charming eccentricities of architecture, these features helped hitters.

New ballparks were—and are—quite different. None give cheap home runs. Most are symmetrical, with virtually identical distances to left and right, so the home team cannot pile up homers by stacking its lineup with right- or left-handed pull-hitters. Most are roundish, with ample foul ground, allowing fielders more room to chase down foul pop-ups and fly balls. Bullpens in most newer parks are tucked behind barriers, so fielders no longer trip on bullpen mounds. The Houston Astrodome opened in 1965, and artificial turf was born a year later.

Continued on page 34

Good-Bye to The Man

There were no ninth-inning heroics. There was no game-winning homer, no spotlight, stop-time, home run trot. The game needed no emblem beyond the date: September 29, 1963, Stan Musial's last game.

"The Man" went out the way he broke in in 1941: a couple of hits before a St. Louis crowd. "I'm a singles hitter," joked Musial after the game. "It seemed appropriate that I should go out with a pair of them."

Of course, Musial was anything but a singles hitter; his nickname told you that. In 22 major league seasons, all with the Cardinals, Musial had accomplished everything imaginable, and then some. He won seven batting titles, hit .331 lifetime with 475 home runs and 3,630 career hits—1,815 on the road. He once hit five home runs in a doubleheader, and in 1948 he had four five-hit games. He won three MVP awards, and in 24 All-Star games he hit .317 with 20 hits and six home runs.

But Musial's career cannot be summed up in numbers. His retirement signified the end of an era in which three players—Joe DiMaggio, Ted Williams and Musial—completely dominated every aspect of the game. They were sluggers who hit for high averages and, in the case of DiMaggio and Musial, who could field and run. Of the three, Musial was the most versatile, an All-Star both at first base and in the outfield. He was probably the most gifted natural athlete of his generation. He was The Man.

A champion schoolboy gymnast, Musial turned down a basketball scholarship at the University of Pittsburgh to sign as a pitcher/outfielder with the Cardinals in 1938. In 1940 Musial compiled an 18–5 record with Daytona Beach of the Florida State League. That same season he permanently injured his throwing arm in an attempt to make a circus catch in the outfield. His career as a pitcher was all but over. Instead, he became the greatest hitter in Cardinal history and one of the greatest ever to play the game.

With his peekaboo, corkscrew batting stance, Musial did not so much hit a pitch as uncoil himself upon it. His inimitable stance and swing were as firmly identified with Musial as the number he wore on his back. The Babe was Number 3. Joltin' Joe was Number 5. Stan the Man was Number 6. You didn't have to be a fan of the St. Louis Cardinals to know that no one in either league would ever wear that number quite the way Stan Musial did. No one.

Despite his quirky stance, Stan Musial's swing was classic throughout his career. The 43-year-old Musial had two hits off Cincinnati's 23-game winner, Jim Maloney, in his final game. No other Cardinal player has ever been so popular in St. Louis, or as admired around the National League, as Musial. Brooklyn fans, as a measure of their respect for the Cardinal outfielder, bestowed on him the nickname The Man.

STAN MUSIAL

Outfield, First Base
St. Louis Cardinals 1941–1963
Hall of Fame 1969

GAMES	**3,026**
AT BATS	**10,972**
BATTING AVERAGE	
Career	**.331**
Season High	**.376**
SLUGGING AVERAGE	
Career *(9th all time)*	**.559**
Season High	**.702**
BATTING TITLES	**1943, 1946**
1948, 1950–1952, 1957	
HITS	
Career *(4th all time)*	**3,630**
Season High	**230**
DOUBLES	
Career *(3rd all time)*	**725**
Season High	**53**
TRIPLES	
Career	**177**
Season High	**20**
HOME RUNS	
Career	**475**
Season High	**39**
TOTAL BASES	**6,134**
(2nd all time)	
EXTRA BASE HITS	**1,377**
(2nd all time)	
RUNS BATTED IN	
Career *(5th all time)*	**1,951**
Season High	**131**
RUNS	
Career *(6th all time)*	**1,949**
Season High	**135**
WORLD SERIES	**1942–1944, 46**
MOST VALUABLE PLAYER	
1943, 1946, 1948	

On April 27, 1968, Baltimore's Tom Phoebus no-hit the Red Sox 6–0. Phoebus was the first, but not the last, major leaguer to pitch a no-hitter in '68. By season's end he was joined by Oakland's Catfish Hunter, George Culver of the Reds, Gaylord Perry of the Giants, and the Cardinals' Ray Washburn.

Pete Rose and the expanded strike zone entered the majors together in 1963. Rose hustled his way to a .273 average and the NL Rookie of the Year Award. Twenty-two years later he broke Ty Cobb's record for most hits in a career.

Pete Rose broke in with the Reds in 1963, the first year of the expanded strike zone, and experienced the defensive improvements firsthand. "The gloves are better today and there are too many fields with artificial turf," he said. "It's difficult to get the ball past the fielders on the artificial turf because they play so deep. I like it better as a defensive player because you can be more aggressive. You get that true bounce."

On balance, infield and outfield defense have probably improved at least as much as either pitching or hitting in the past three decades, and a primary factor has been the change in stadium design, coupled with better ballpark grooming.

Baseball dotes on its past, and many fans and sportswriters scorn the new ballparks as bland "cookie cutter" designs. They praise the distinctive character of the remaining old parks—Yankee Stadium, Fenway Park in Boston, Cleveland Stadium, Wrigley Field and Comiskey Park in Chicago, and Tiger Stadium in Detroit.

Not coincidentally, all of these except Comiskey are home run ballparks, and few pitchers share the fans' fondness for them. At a regional meeting of the Society for American Baseball Research a few years ago, an old pitcher said he couldn't understand why the Red Sox didn't abandon Fenway in favor of Braves Field when the Boston Braves moved to Milwaukee in 1953. His comment drew a gasp from the audience; to proper Bostonians, their beloved Fenway is a virtual shrine. But Braves Field, however homely, may have been a fairer ballpark.

Fenway's "Green Monster" wall in left field is a lovably familiar monument, but it is only 315 feet from home plate. It allows a lot of homers and doubles that would be outs in modern ballparks. If the Red Sox were building

1908 Batting Leaders

American League	Avg.
Ty Cobb, Det	.324
Sam Crawford, Det	.311
Doc Gessler, Bos	.308
Charlie Hemphill, NY	.297
Matty McIntyre, Det	.295
League Average	.239

National League	Avg.
Honus Wagner, Pitt	.354
Mike Donlin, NY	.334
Larry Doyle, NY	.308
Kitty Bransfield, Phil	.304
John Evers, Chi	.300
League Average	.239

In 1968, hitters had their worst year ever. American League batters hit .230 and National League batters hit .243 for a combined .236 average, the lowest in baseball history. You'd have to go back 60 years–to 1908–to find a year when hitters did as poorly.

1968 Batting Leaders

American League	Avg.
Carl Yastrzemski, Bos	.301
Vic Davalillo, Cle	.298
Danny Cater, Oak	.290
Willie Horton, Det	.285
Ted Uhlaender, Minn	.283
League Average	.230

National League	Avg.
Pete Rose, Cin	.335
Matty Alou, Pitt	.332
Felipe Alou, Atl	.317
Alex Johnson, Cin	.312
Curt Flood, StL	.301
League Average	.243

a new stadium today (Heaven forbid!) they not only wouldn't rebuild Fenway, they couldn't. Since 1958, baseball rules have required new ballparks to be at least 325 feet down the lines and 400 feet to center field. Left to right, Fenway measures 315, 390 and 302.

Not every team moved from a hitter's park to a pitcher's park. For example, sluggers were glad to wave good-bye to Braves Field in Boston and Griffith Stadium in Washington, old stadiums where homers were hard to hit, and felt warmly welcome at Fulton County Stadium in Atlanta, the home run paradise to which the Braves moved from Milwaukee in 1966.

New ballparks came on stream one at a time, so the defensive gain was gradual. When the larger strike zone became effective in 1963, the Dodgers and Giants already had moved to modern, more spacious fields. When the Cardinals followed suit in 1966, three of the National League's strongest teams had moved from hitters' parks to pitchers' parks.

To accommodate expansion teams, D.C. Stadium (now called Robert F. Kennedy Memorial Stadium) opened in Washington in 1962, Shea Stadium opened in New York in 1964, the Astrodome opened in Houston in 1965, and San Diego Stadium (now known as Jack Murphy Stadium) opened in 1969.

So the bigger strike zone was installed just as other factors, however accidentally, were making things harder on the hitters and easier on the pitchers. In combination, these factors ushered in a period of defensive dominance. In 1969, after the greatest pitching year in baseball history, the Rules Committee reversed course, tightening the strike zone and lowering the mound from 15 to ten inches.

The leagues had put the bats back into the hands of the hitters. "You can't pitch a shutout anymore," complained the Cardinals' Bob Gibson.

Year of the Pitcher

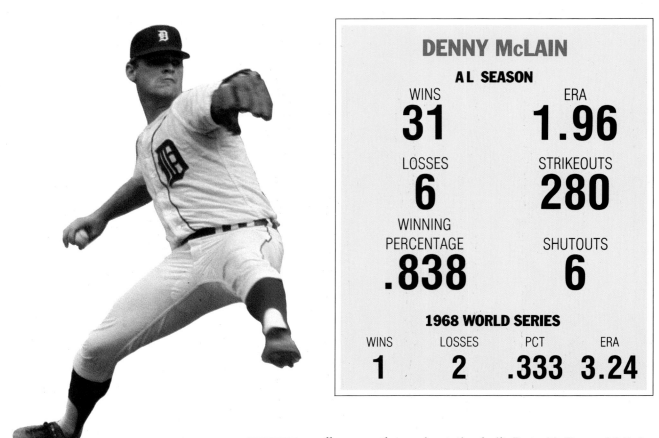

DENNY McLAIN

AL SEASON

WINS	ERA
31	**1.96**
LOSSES	STRIKEOUTS
6	**280**
WINNING PERCENTAGE	SHUTOUTS
.838	**6**

1968 WORLD SERIES

WINS	LOSSES	PCT	ERA
1	**2**	**.333**	**3.24**

In 1968, Don Drysdale (overleaf) set a major league record of 58 consecutive scoreless innings. At the time it seemed unbreakable. But barely 20 years elapsed before it was broken by another Dodger, Orel Hershiser, who completed the 1988 regular season with a string of 59 consecutive scoreless innings.

All season, the confrontation built. Detroit's Denny McLain, a flamboyant right-hander who reveled in the public eye, won 15 games before July 4 and went after the magic number of 30 wins with the news media in hot pursuit. Bob Gibson, the proud, glowering St. Louis Cardinals' fireballer, won 15 straight games, ten of them shutouts.

Both pitched their teams to easy pennants. McLain won 31 and lost only six. He was the first pitcher to win 30 games since Dizzy Dean in 1934, the first to win 31 since Lefty Grove in 1931. The Tigers led the American League all but 15 games of the season and clinched the pennant on September 17.

Gibson won 22, including 13 shutouts, and lost nine. His earned run average of 1.12 was the lowest in baseball history for a pitcher throwing 300 innings or more. The Cardinals led the National League all but 13 games of the season and clinched the pennant on September 15. Both McLain and Gibson were voted the Cy Young and Most Valuable Player awards in their respective leagues.

Baseball fans eagerly awaited the World Series matchup between McLain, he of the Hammond Organ and Hollywood aspirations, and Gibson, a competitor so fierce that he would not speak to opposing players and disliked playing alongside them on National League All-Star teams.

The year was 1968. No one since has matched the exploits of McLain or Gibson, but in that magic—or peculiar—season, they were not alone. Throughout both major leagues, pitchers overwhelmed hitters. Baseball seemed to time-warp back to the early 1900s, when pitchers dominated the game and teams scratched for a run.

In 1968 one game of every five was a shutout, and in the average game

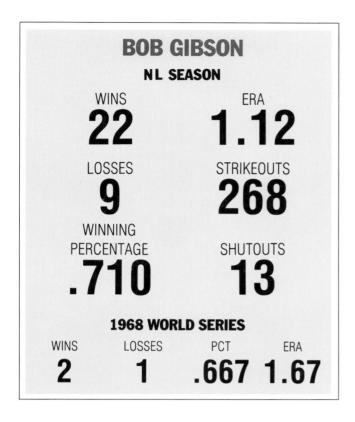

BOB GIBSON
N L SEASON

WINS	ERA
22	**1.12**
LOSSES	STRIKEOUTS
9	**268**
WINNING PERCENTAGE	SHUTOUTS
.710	**13**

1968 WORLD SERIES

WINS	LOSSES	PCT	ERA
2	**1**	**.667**	**1.67**

only 6.84 runs were scored. The only leaner yield in baseball history was the 6.77-run average of 1908, when Ty Cobb was only 21, Babe Ruth a child, and Sam Crawford, Cobb's Detroit teammate, led the American League in home runs with seven.

But 1968 was not a copy of the dead-ball era. For one thing, the ball was far from dead. Home run production was way down—down more than 1,000 from the record level of 3,001 in 1962, down 300 from 1967. But Frank Howard hit 44 homers for the Washington Senators, and Willie McCovey of the San Francisco Giants hit 36. A well-hit ball still traveled.

Trouble was, not many balls were well hit. The overall major league batting average was .237, a record low. Carl Yastrzemski of the Boston Red Sox was the American League's only .300 hitter. He had to put on a late-season surge to lift his average to .301, the lowest ever to lead a major league. The National League managed all of five .300 hitters, led by Cincinnati's Pete Rose at .335.

The pitchers of 1968 worked without a dead ball or, for that matter, without the dirty, scuffed ball that had helped pitchers of 60 years before. Ostensibly, they worked without a spitball or a greaseball, although violators of this rule were legion. In their favor, the pitchers of 1968 worked in big ballparks, threw to a big strike zone, and were backed by skillful fielders with big, modern gloves. Pitchers were better coached, and more of them had mastered the slider. Relief pitching had become more skillful, and managers called on their relievers more readily.

These factors were not peculiar to 1968. Their impact had been building since 1963, when the strike zone was enlarged. As spacious new ballparks came on stream during the 1960s, the pitcher's edge sharpened. And by 1968

Juan Marichal's dominance over opponents was never greater than in 1968 when he posted career highs with 26 wins, 30 complete games, and 325⅔ innings pitched. He struck out 218 and walked 46.

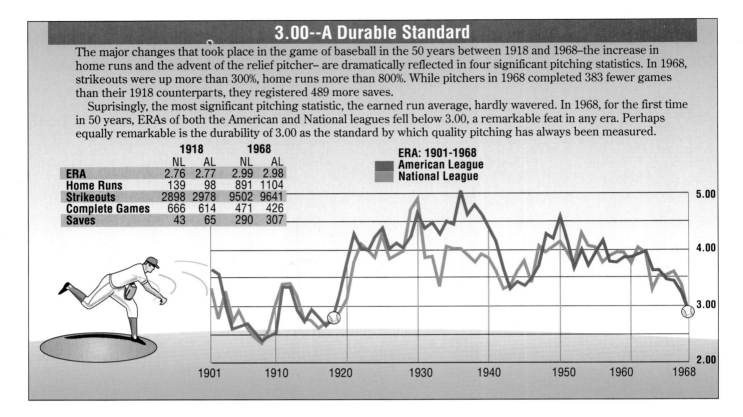

3.00--A Durable Standard

The major changes that took place in the game of baseball in the 50 years between 1918 and 1968–the increase in home runs and the advent of the relief pitcher– are dramatically reflected in four significant pitching statistics. In 1968, strikeouts were up more than 300%, home runs more than 800%. While pitchers in 1968 completed 383 fewer games than their 1918 counterparts, they registered 489 more saves.

Suprisingly, the most significant pitching statistic, the earned run average, hardly wavered. In 1968, for the first time in 50 years, ERAs of both the American and National leagues fell below 3.00, a remarkable feat in any era. Perhaps equally remarkable is the durability of 3.00 as the standard by which quality pitching has always been measured.

	1918 NL	1918 AL	1968 NL	1968 AL
ERA	2.76	2.77	2.99	2.98
Home Runs	139	98	891	1104
Strikeouts	2898	2978	9502	9641
Complete Games	666	614	471	426
Saves	43	65	290	307

ERA: 1901-1968
American League
National League

the pendulum of skill swung toward the mound: the major leagues were rich with superb pitchers, young and old. Some, like Gibson, were hitting the peak of long and distinguished careers. Other bright stars, like McLain, later suffered arm trouble or other disabilities.

In 1968, it seemed, no one had a sore arm, and all the close pitches were strikes. "It seemed," Gibson wrote later of his own 1968 performance, "that every pitch was knee high on the corner." In both leagues, the overall earned run average was under 3.00. In 1987, to take a recent season for comparison, only four *pitchers* had ERAs under 3.00.

Although relief pitching was almost the art it is today, baseball's best pitchers of 1968 were astonishingly durable. In that same 1987 season, for example, Roger Clemens of Boston led the major leagues in complete games with 18. But back in 1968, Juan Marichal of the Giants finished 30 of his 38 starts, Gibson finished 28 of his 34, McLain 28 of his 41, and Ferguson Jenkins of the Cubs 20 of his 40. Jenkins was shut out nine times, yet he finished with a record of 20–15.

Not that the major leagues were devoid of good—even great—hitters. Future Hall of Famers included Al Kaline of Detroit, Frank and Brooks Robinson of Baltimore, an aging Mickey Mantle of the Yankees, Harmon Killebrew of Minnesota, Hank Aaron of Atlanta, Roberto Clemente of Pittsburgh, Willie Mays and Willie McCovey of San Francisco, Ernie Banks and Billy Williams of the Cubs—every one a power hitter. Pitchers also faced such sluggers as Carl Yastrzemski, Willie Stargell and Johnny Bench. The record book shows that for most of them, 1968 just wasn't a particularly good year.

But they were overmatched in 1968 by the coincidental coupling of tech-

Oakland's Bert Campaneris erased Chicago's Glenn Beckert to start a double play in the 1968 All-Star Game in Houston. The game typified pitchers' domination that year, as the National League won the first 1–0 All-Star Game in history.

Born in Ontario, Canada, Ferguson Jenkins was a consistent winner for good—but not great—Chicago Cub teams from 1967 to 1973. In 1968 Jenkins had the second of six consecutive 20-win seasons with the Cubs.

nical factors—a big strike zone, big ballparks—and the explosion of pitching talent. *Sports Illustrated* reported that several baffled hitters actually took their slumps to eye doctors.

Consider the All-Star Game. Fittingly enough for this era of transition, it was played in the Houston Astrodome. Don Drysdale started for the National League, Luis Tiant of the Cleveland Indians for the American. Willie Mays led off the bottom of the first with a single, took second on a wild pick-off throw, third on a wild pitch, and scored on a double play. End of scoring. National League, 1–0. In the first seven innings, 20 straight of the American League's best were retired in order by Drysdale, Marichal, Steve Carlton of the Cardinals, and Tom Seaver of the Mets.

Low-scoring games bored many fans—attendance was down—and the All-Star Game was not the driest example of 1968's hitting drought. On April 15, the Astros scored a run in the bottom of the 24th inning to beat the Mets, 1–0; the game lasted six hours and six minutes. On September 17, Gaylord Perry of the Giants beat the Cardinals with a no-hitter. The next night Ray Washburn of the Cardinals beat the Giants with a no-hitter.

Jim "Catfish" Hunter, 22, of the Oakland Athletics, pitched the American League's first regular-season perfect game in 46 years. Tom Phoebus of the Orioles and George Culver of the Reds also pitched no-hitters.

Don Drysdale, the tall right-hander of the Dodgers, was used to weak support: the 1960s Dodgers had a popgun offense. In May, Drysdale evened his record at 3–3 by pitching two 1–0 shutouts. He pitched two more shutouts and people started talking; the record for consecutive shutouts was five, set by Doc White of the White Sox in 1904.

A crowd of 46,067 turned out to see Drysdale face the Giants in Los Angeles. Drysdale blanked the Giants for eight innings, but walked McCovey to open the ninth. Jim Ray Hart singled and Dave Marshall walked, loading the bases. Drysdale pitched inside to Dick Dietz, and the ball cracked Dietz on the elbow. But McCovey did not score, because umpire Harry Wendelstedt ruled that Dietz didn't try to get out of the ball's way. He called the pitch ball three, and Drysdale retired the Giants without a run.

That pitch illustrated two weapons artfully used by Drysdale and other pitchers of 1968. He brushed hitters back—"headhunting" in dugout parlance—although Drysdale says he never hit a batter on the head. And he doctored the ball. Said one Giant batter, "Somewhere in that routine he gets it—the Vaseline or whatever it is he puts on the ball to make it jump around."

Drysdale pitched a sixth shutout to break White's record. Still ahead was the legendary Walter Johnson's record of $55\frac{2}{3}$ consecutive scoreless innings, set in 1913 when Johnson, "The Big Train," won 36 games for his Washington Senators. Drysdale faced the Philadelphia Phillies on June 8. If he could keep them scoreless through $2\frac{1}{3}$ innings, the record would be his. Gene Mauch, the Phils' manager, put six left-handed hitters in his lineup and posted his best bench jockey—himself—to coach third base.

Drysdale had walked only nine batters during his six shutouts, but he walked Johnny Briggs in the Philadelphia first. The Dodger shortstop, Zoilo Versalles, saved the inning with a spectacular play. Drysdale got through the second inning easily. That tied Johnson's record, and Drysdale beat it by getting Roberto Pena on a ground ball to open the third. He got a big ovation then, and another one when he retired the next two batters.

But Mauch was complaining that Drysdale greased the ball, and as

Willie Mays hit only 23 homers in 1968, but was still enough of a threat to get brushed back often (above). Physically imposing pitchers like Drysdale and Gibson used what Branch Rickey called "the purpose pitch"—a high, tight fastball—to mark their territory, and few umpires or batters challenged it.

Orlando Cepeda, Bob Gibson and Tim McCarver (opposite, left to right) were stalwarts on Cardinal teams that won pennants in 1967 and 1968. Cepeda and Gibson won back-to-back MVP awards in '67 and '68, but by the end of the decade Cardinal dominance was over.

Drysdale walked to the dugout he was intercepted by Augie Donatelli, the plate umpire. Donatelli talked to Drysdale, took off the pitcher's cap, inspected it, and rubbed Drysdale's hair, the partisan Los Angeles crowd booing. The game continued—Drysdale yielded a run in the fifth and was knocked out in the seventh—and no action was taken on the allegedly illegal pitches. But illegal they apparently were. After the game, Donatelli gave reporters this account: "I went to Drysdale and said, 'Don, do you have Vaseline on the back of your head?' He said, 'What do you mean?' I said, 'You know the rule, and if you touch the back of your head again I'm going to have to fine you.' Don said, 'Augie, I'm sweating like hell out here. That isn't Vaseline; that's sweat. Just tell me what the hell I can't do.' "

Now retired, Donatelli gives a more graphic account. "I said, 'Don, you're throwing the greaseball.' He said, 'Oh no, Augie, I'm not throwing a greaseball.' I was standing about three feet from him at least. I said, 'I smell the Vaseline from here.' He said, 'Oh no, you don't mean that.' I said, 'The hell I don't.'

"I got in a discussion where I had to do something. He's a big guy, 6'6" or 6'7". I reached up and grabbed his cap and came down with a handful of Vaseline. And it smelled. He said, 'All right, what do you want me to do?' I said, 'Don't go any higher than your shoulders (with your hands).' He didn't, and the Phillies got him out of there."

The Cardinals were defending world champions. Unlike Drysdale, Bob Gibson had grown accustomed to decent hitting support from a lineup that included Lou Brock, Curt Flood, Roger Maris, Tim McCarver, Mike Shannon and Orlando Cepeda. But in 1968 the Cards weren't

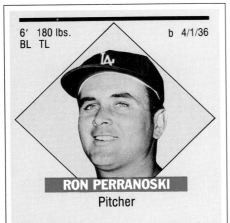

6' 180 lbs.
BL TL

b 4/1/36

RON PERRANOSKI
Pitcher

Ron Perranoski was the premier relief pitcher of the 1960s. Of his 737 appearances with the Dodgers, Twins, Tigers and Angels, 736 were in relief. In 13 seasons he saved 179 games, won 79 while losing only 74, and compiled a 2.79 ERA.

In 1961, his rookie season with the Dodgers, Perranoski began a ten-year streak of 50 or more appearances. Four times during that span he appeared in 70 or more games, including a career-high 75 in 1969; he led the league in 1962, 1963 and 1967. With the Twins in 1969 and 1970, Perranoski led the American League with 31 and 34 saves, respectively.

Perranoski's value is best measured in team performance. In nine of his 13 years his teams never finished lower than second place. He pitched on Dodger pennant winners in 1963, 1965 and 1966 and on the AL West-winning Twins in 1969 and 1970. In addition, Perranoski contributed to five Cy Young Award-winning performances: three by Sandy Koufax and one each by Don Drysdale and Jim Perry. Perranoski himself was a Cy Young Award contender in 1963, when he led the league with 16 relief wins, 69 appearances, and an .842 winning percentage to complement his 1.67 ERA and 21 saves.

Perranoski, whose career was ended by an injury to his pitching arm, joined the Dodgers' coaching staff in 1973, and became the team's pitching coach in 1981.

hitting any better than the rest of the league. In May, Gibson beat the Houston Astros 3–1 in 12 innings and the New York Mets 2–1 in 11 innings. Then things got tougher. He lost 3–2 to the Astros, 1–0 to the Phils in 10 innings, 2–0 to Drysdale, and 3–1 to the Giants. The Cardinals lost 11 of 13 games that month, when Gibson couldn't buy a win, and fell to fourth place.

No one hated to lose more than Gibson. Turning the corner into summer, he pitched five straight shutouts, yielded a run on a wild pitch in another winning effort, pitched another shutout, and ran his string of victories without a loss to 15. In one string of $96^2/_3$ innings he gave up two runs. With their ace winning, the Cards blew the league away with a 54–20 run that put them a dozen games in front.

Of course, Gibson didn't pitch every day. Nelson Briles won 19 games, Ray Washburn 14, and Steve Carlton 13. Reliever Joe Hoerner won eight, saved 17, and posted a 1.47 ERA. The Cardinals hit only 73 home runs—even Whitey Herzog's ping-hitting Cardinal pennant-winners of 1987 hit 94—but the pitching staff posted a 2.49 ERA, lowest in the majors. In 82 games, just over half the season's total, Cardinal opponents scored two runs or fewer. Thirty were shutouts.

The Cardinals played in spacious Busch Stadium, where Flood and Brock could chase down long drives. McCarver was the league's best catcher, and the double play combination of Julian Javier and Dal Maxvill was superb. The Cards had talent.

Most of all, however, the Cards had Gibson. Watching him pitch, said third baseman Mike Shannon, was "like watching Rembrandt paint a picture." Not that Gibson was a finesse pitcher. He threw fastballs about four of every five pitches. Gibson had an unusual fastball that hopped right to left,

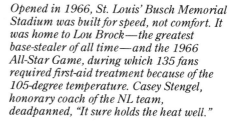

Opened in 1966, St. Louis' Busch Memorial Stadium was built for speed, not comfort. It was home to Lou Brock—the greatest base-stealer of all time—and the 1966 All-Star Game, during which 135 fans required first-aid treatment because of the 105-degree temperature. Casey Stengel, honorary coach of the NL team, deadpanned, "It sure holds the heat well."

A catcher whose career spanned four decades, Tim McCarver was 17 when he joined the Cardinals in 1959. In 1968 McCarver caught two future Hall of Famers—Bob Gibson and left-hander Steve Carlton.

away from a right-handed hitter; it was his strikeout pitch, and it also induced batters to pop up or fly out. For double play situations, he had a dipping fastball that batters tended to hit on the ground. He threw an excellent hard slider, and by 1968 he had perfected a curve as well.

Gibson threw hard, liked to throw inside, and treated hitters as enemies. Batterymate Tim McCarver said, "For my money, the most intimidating, arrogant pitcher ever to kick up dirt on a mound is Bob Gibson. . . . It nearly tore up my hand every time I caught him."

Gibson, Drysdale and Marichal were leading members of the brushback fraternity. Drysdale, who became a baseball broadcaster after his pitching career, recalled in a newspaper interview an opening day game when Jim Ray Hart of the Giants faced Gibson and "got it right on the coconut."

Drysdale explained that Gibson was teaching Hart not to crowd the inside part of the plate. "Welcome to Bob Gibson's school of what you better do and what you better not do," Drysdale said. "You have to move them off the plate; you have to get them out of there. This was part of the game and everybody accepted it as part of the game."

Gibson had excellent control—in 1968, 268 strikeouts and only 62 walks in 304 innings—but he was a power pitcher and rarely fooled with a change-up. Dizzy Dean, who seemed to adopt the pitching stars of 1968 as his legitimate offspring, explained it this way: "Great pitchers like Gibson and me never fool around with the hitters. We both like to throw the ball with something on it. And we don't pitch to spots. When you pitch to spots and go for the corners, you take something away from your power pitch."

"I never pace myself," Gibson said. "I just go out there and give all I've got as long as I can." Many pitchers with that philosophy look for help from

Continued on page 50

Dodger Stadium

Located in Chavez Ravine, on a 166-acre hillside overlooking downtown Los Angeles, Dodger Stadium became the Dodgers' permanent home in 1962, but not without commotion. In 1959 irate taxpayers carried a lawsuit all the way to the U.S. Supreme Court, claiming that team owner Walter O'Malley had received favoritism from the city council. In addition, O'Malley had to contend with "squatters' rights."

For years Chavez Ravine had been home to jackrabbits, gophers, possums and squatters. Among the last, the family of Manuel Arechigas raised the greatest fuss, winning considerable support nationwide in their refusal to vacate the land. On May 8, 1959, members of the family inflicted bites and bruises on sheriff's deputies who led the kicking and screaming Arechigas family from the site. But when an investigation revealed that Mr. Arechigas owned 11 properties in the city of Los Angeles, sympathy for the squatters quickly dissipated and the last occupants stole quietly away. Not a very auspicious beginning for what was to become baseball's finest stadium.

After the Brooklyn Bums vacated their beloved Ebbets Field and moved west in 1957, the Dodgers found a temporary home in the Los Angeles Coliseum—originally built for the 1932 Olympics and converted from its football configuration—through 1961. At last, on April 10, 1962, Dodger Stadium officially opened. But even then, all was not quite right: drinking fountains had not been installed, the foul poles were actually in foul territory, and by the end of the day, Cincinnati's Wally Post had hit a three-run homer and the home team had dropped its opener to the Reds, 6–3. The Dodgers drew a major league record 2,755,184 fans in 1962; 20 years later they established a new attendance record of 3,608,881.

Owned by O'Malley and the Dodgers, Dodger Stadium was the first privately financed ballpark since the completion of Yankee Stadium in 1923. Designed by architect Emil Prager to accommodate future expansion to 85,000 seats, the park was built specifically for baseball. Known as the Taj Mahal—and occasionally Taj O'Malley—of baseball, Dodger Stadium is a six-tiered park that retains the classic, although expanded, layout of baseball's urban, steel-and-concrete stadiums. Special features of the facility include field-level box seats and four scoreboards, including two giant ones in left center and right center fields. The field itself is one of the most visually appealing in all of baseball. The dirt portion of the field—infield, baselines, pitcher's mound, batter's box and warning track—consists of red brick dust and clay, offering a sharp contrast to the lush natural turf. The rolling hills beyond the outfield fences provide a peaceful backdrop to the action on the field.

The site of the 1980 All-Star Game and the National League home field of the 1963, '65, '66, '74, '77, '78, and '81 World Series, Dodger Stadium has been home to some of baseball's greatest pitching feats, including Sandy Koufax's perfect game against the Cubs in 1965, and Don Drysdale's sixth consecutive shutout, on June 4, 1968. But the sweetest moment in Los Angeles Dodger history was provided by a batter, as Frank Howard's home run helped the Dodgers sweep their old nemesis, the New York Yankees, in the World Series on October 6, 1963.

Dodger Stadium

1000 Elysian Park Avenue
Los Angeles, California

Built 1962

Los Angeles Dodgers, NL
 1962–present
Los Angeles (California)
 Angels, AL 1962–1965

Seating Capacity 56,000

Style
Grass surface, symmetrical,
 permanent baseball

Height of outfield fences
Left center to right center,
 8 feet
Foul poles to bullpens,
 4 feet

Dugouts
Home, 3rd base
Visitors, 1st base

Bullpens
Outfield, recessed
Home, left center
Visitors, right center

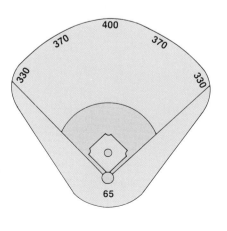

Bullpen benches were more crowded than usual in 1968, as starting pitchers dominated the game. The New York Yankee bullpen (above) was the AL's least productive that season, earning just 27 saves.

the bullpen in the seventh or eighth inning, but not Gibson. From September 12, 1967, until July 4, 1969, he was never—not once—knocked out of a game, leaving only for an occasional pinch-hitter. That's 53 straight games, including the entire 1968 season. And it doesn't count six straight complete games in two World Series.

"I've never come out on my own," Gibson told *Sport* magazine. "Never have I asked a manager to take me out. Never." Pitching the seventh game of the 1964 World Series on two days' rest, Gibson yielded a three-run homer to Mickey Mantle in the sixth inning, cutting the Cardinal lead to three runs. Johnny Keane, then the Cardinal manager, visited the mound but left Gibson in. "I wasn't going to take him out," Keane explained to reporters after Gibson had wrapped up the victory and the world championship. "I had a commitment to his heart."

On July 15, 1967, Roberto Clemente hit a sharp drive that cracked Gibson's right leg between the knee and the ankle. He fell in pain. The Cardinal trainer sprayed the leg with a pain-killer, and Gibson refused to come out. He walked Willie Stargell and got Bill Mazeroski on a pop fly. Pitching to Donn Clendenon with his usual follow-through—an extravagantly graceful motion that seemed to bring him a third of the way to the plate, facing the first-base line—he came down on the right leg. The bone, already cracked, snapped. In mid-season of 1973, he did much the same thing. He was on first base, and as he dived back to avoid being doubled up on a line drive out, his right knee gave way. He sent the trainer back to the dugout, walked to the mound, began warming up, and fell. His right knee had buckled. Both knees were bad, and though Gibson came back late that season and pitched through 1975, he was handicapped by his ailing knees and an aching arm.

Gibson grew up in the black ghetto of Omaha, Nebraska. His father died before he was born, and his mother raised seven children on her wages as a laundress. "He was born sick," his mother told *The New York Times* of her youngest son, "and he got sicker. He had rickets, hay fever, asthma, pneumonia and a rheumatic heart. I hardly let him out of the house until he was 4 years old. I never thought he'd make it. Neither did he. When he was 3½ he got pneumonia. He was so weak we had to carry him into a hospital, bundled in a blanket.

"I'll never forget that moment. His oldest brother, Josh, was holding him. Bob looked up at Josh and asked, 'Am I going to die?' Josh looked down and said, 'You'll make it. And when you come home I'll get you a baseball glove and bat.'"

Gibson was too skinny for high school football, but he starred in baseball and basketball and earned a basketball scholarship to Creighton University, where he was the team's star and its first black player.

As a sophomore, Gibson traveled with the team for a game at Tulsa and was told he would not be allowed to eat or sleep with his white teammates there. When he reported to his first spring training with the Cardinals in 1958, he walked into the team hotel at St. Petersburg, Florida, and was ushered out a side door and into a taxi, which took him to lodgings with a black family.

Gibson carried a big racial chip on his shoulder—he says so in his autobiography—and was by nature not much for small talk. He was rarely friendly to writers, although he usually answered their questions. His demeanor was somewhat frightening. Sometimes he would sign autographs for fans and sometimes he would not. "I owe the public just one thing," he said. "A good performance."

Mel Stottlemyre (above, left) went 21-12 for the offense-poor 1968 Yankees: New York averaged just 3.3 runs per game that year, but Stottlemyre's ERA was 2.45. Jim Kaat (center) won 14 games with a 2.94 ERA for the Twins in 1968, the tenth of his 25 major league seasons. Proving that you didn't have to be svelte to be successful in 1968, Mickey Lolich (right) won 17 games in Denny McLain's shadow, then stepped into the limelight, winning three World Series games.

Tony Cloninger (above, left) won 24 games for the Milwaukee Braves in 1965 but is perhaps best remembered for one big day at the plate. On July 3, 1966, Cloninger hit two grand slams and drove in nine runs against the Giants. The Cleveland Indians' Luis Tiant (center), an ageless Cuban, was 21–9 in 1968 with a league-leading 1.60 ERA. Tiant did not allow one sacrifice fly in his 258 innings. The most notorious spitball pitcher of his era, San Francisco's Gaylord Perry (right) never pitched in a World Series. In 1968 he won 16 games—and completed 19—with a 2.45 ERA.

"Do you want to know why I get surly and bitter sometimes?" Gibson asked Bob Addie of *The Washington Post.* "Take a look at some of the mail I get." He showed Addie some racial hate letters with passages like "Why don't you and the other blackbirds on the Cardinals move to Africa where you belong?"

Gibson did not join in the trappings of black self-expression, but his racial anger fit the times. Black consciousness was sweeping America. This was the era of dashikis, clenched fists, student demands for more black admissions to colleges, and more courses in black history. On April 4, 1968, Martin Luther King was assassinated in Memphis, sparking riots that scarred a number of cities, including Washington, DC. Baseball's season opener was postponed in King's honor.

On the field, Gibson was fiercely competitive. He played purely to win, once stunning writers by telling them matter-of-factly that in several hundred games of tic-tac-toe with his young daughter he had never lost to her. After college, he had played a season of basketball with the Harlem Globetrotters. "I hated that clowning around," Gibson told Roger Angell of *The New Yorker.* "I wanted to play to win."

But Gibson was a clubhouse jokester and made close friends among his white teammates. The Cardinals, he said, won three pennants in the 1960s partly because the black, white and Hispanic players were able to get along together.

McCarver and Gibson were close, but the Cardinal catcher got no privileges when Gibson was pitching. Gibson worked quickly and had no patience for visits from his catcher. "Get back where you belong," he told McCarver once. "The only thing you know about pitching is that it's hard to hit."

Gibson, who pitched his entire career with the Cardinals, was 32 in 1968. He won another Cy Young Award in 1970, and pitched through the 1975 season. He was elected to the Baseball Hall of Fame in 1981, when he first became eligible. Following his playing days, he worked as a pitching coach for the Atlanta Braves. His old teammate, Joe Torre, was the manager and hired Gibson to teach his pitchers not how to throw, but how to *win.*

Like Gibson, Denny McLain was a spectacular fastball pitcher with good control and a durable constitution. But McLain was a cocky, garrulous playboy. If Gibson exemplified black pride, McLain, who was only 24, exemplified the youthful spirit that was also part of the late 1960s.

"When you can do it out there between the white lines," he said, using the ballplayers' term for the field of play, "then you can live any way you want. Me? I like to travel fast—and always first class."

McLain's tongue, said his detractors, sometimes traveled faster than his brain. In 1966 McLain was quoted as calling the Tigers a "country-club team where everybody does what they want." He denied saying any such thing. "May God strike me dead if I said those things," he said. His roommate, pitcher Joe Sparma, asked for a room change, explaining that "God might make a mistake and get the wrong guy."

Detroit fans were deprived of many of McLain's comments during the 1968 season, because the city's two newspapers were on strike. Maybe it was just as well. McLain told an out-of-town writer, "The Detroit fans are the worst I've ever seen anyplace."

McLain was a talented organist who knew how to capitalize on his fame. Between starts, he traveled to concerts and recording sessions. He kept win-

Baltimore southpaw Dave McNally (above, left) had a stellar 1968—22 wins, a 1.95 ERA, and 202 strikeouts. It was his first of four straight 20-win seasons. "Sudden" Sam McDowell (center) won just 15 games for the Indians in 1968, but led the league with 283 strikeouts and had a career-best 1.81 ERA. McDowell led the league five times each in strikeouts and walks. In 1967 Boston's Jim Lonborg (right) was 22–9, led the league with 246 strikeouts, and pitched a one-hitter in the World Series. In 1968 he slumped to 6–10.

ning, and as his wins approached 30 he eagerly accepted invitations to appear on the Smothers Brothers, Steve Allen, and Ed Sullivan television variety shows. "I have agents for everything," McLain told a *Sports Illustrated* writer, "but when it comes down to it, nobody can make the decisions but the personality himself." *Personality?*

He dreamed of being a millionaire; he spent money as if he were. His Tiger salary in 1968 was good for the times, but it was less than $50,000. Even with additional earnings, McLain was spending himself into a hole.

McLain followed his brilliant 1968 season with a 24–9 record in 1969, good enough for a second consecutive Cy Young Award, this time sharing it with Mike Cuellar of Baltimore. But in 1970 he got into trouble. Commissioner Bowie Kuhn suspended him twice—for consorting with gamblers and for carrying a gun—and the Tigers suspended him for dumping ice water on two sportswriters. He declared bankruptcy. His wife, Sharyn, daughter of Hall of Fame shortstop Lou Boudreau, filed for divorce. His arm went bad. He won three, lost five, and, after the season, was traded to the woebegone Washington Senators, for whom he lost 22 games in 1971.

McLain washed out of baseball a year later, at 28, but that was not the bottom. He and his wife got back together, but his life went from bad to worse. He failed at several business enterprises; perhaps his most successful after-baseball occupation was as a free-lance golf hustler.

He got mixed up with a shady brokerage operation, and in 1985 was convicted of racketeering, conspiracy to commit racketeering, extortion, and possession of cocaine with intent to distribute. McLain denied the charges, although he acknowledged making book. He was sentenced to 23 years in federal prison and served almost $2^{1}/_{2}$ years.

6'5" 205 lbs.
BR TR

b 12/13/43

FERGUSON JENKINS
Pitcher

Ferguson Jenkins pitched 19 years in the major leagues and won 284 games, with a winning percentage of .557 and an ERA of 3.34. Yet he never played on a pennant winner.

Brought up by the Phils in 1965, Jenkins was traded to the Cubs after one appearance in 1966. He then won 20 or more games for six consecutive years. In 1971, his Cy Young Award season, Jenkins led the league with 24 wins, 39 starts, 30 complete games, and 325 innings pitched, in addition to hitting six home runs. In 1973, his first year with the Texas Rangers, Jenkins led all American League pitchers with 25 wins.

Throughout his career, Jenkins was a model of durability and control. For 15 consecutive seasons he pitched 184 or more innings, including five years of 300 or more and seven of 200 or more. Four times he led his league in complete games and three times in starts. Jenkins' 3,192 strikeouts ranks ninth on the all-time list. He is the only pitcher with 3,000 strikeouts and less than 1,000 walks.

Jenkins' numbers would be even more impressive had he received more support. In 45 of his 223 career losses, his team was shut out, including nine of his 15 losses in 1968.

After pitching for Boston in 1976 and 1977, Jenkins was traded back to Texas in 1978 and went 18–8 with a 3.04 ERA. He returned to the Cubs in 1982, winning 14 games and posting a 3.15 ERA. He retired following the 1983 season.

After leading the National League with 111 RBI in 1967, Cardinal first baseman Orlando Cepeda—like most hitters—slumped in 1968 to a .248 average and 73 RBI. Knee injuries hampered Cepeda throughout his career.

In September 1987 his conviction was overturned on appeal; the court ruled that the judge in McLain's trial had run such a disorderly court that the trial was not fair. McLain was released and seemed to turn over a new leaf, taking a job as promotions manager for a minor league hockey team in Fort Wayne, Indiana. He lost that job, wrote a new autobiography with a ghostwriter and, with his lawyers, arranged a plea-bargain agreement on the racketeering charges, allowing him to remain free.

But in 1968 McLain was on top of the baseball world. Dizzy Dean, who won his 30 for the Cardinal Gashouse Gang of 1934, was on hand to congratulate McLain when he notched Number 30 in Detroit against the Oakland Athletics, despite two home runs by a brash young outfielder named Reggie Jackson.

There was nothing shallow about McLain's achievement. Dean himself had predicted that no modern pitcher would win 30, because starters no longer were used in relief. "I pitched 15 or so times in relief," Dean said. "I won a lot of games in September."

Indeed, McLain did not relieve once during the 1968 season, but he led the league in innings pitched and yielded only 1.96 earned runs a game. That's a startlingly low ERA for a Detroit pitcher, because Tiger Stadium, one of the surviving old-style fields, has short fences and is considered a home run ballpark.

The 1968 Tigers were a home run ballclub. They led the major leagues in homers with 185 and led the American League in runs with 671, although their most memorable hitter, Al Kaline, missed nearly half the season because of injury. Willie Horton hit 36 homers, Bill Freehan and Norm Cash

Bob Gibson lost his bid for a second consecutive three-win performance in World Series play when the Tigers defeated St. Louis in Game 7 of the 1968 Series, but he remains one of the fall classic's all-time greats: nine starts, eight complete games, a 7–2 record, and 92 strikeouts in 81 innings.

Willie Horton homered in Detroit's 8–1 win over the Cardinals in Game 2 of the 1968 World Series. Horton, a feared power hitter, was extremely superstitious; he used the same batting helmet for 17 years, repainting it each time he got traded.

hit 25 each, and Jim Northrup hit 21, including three grand slams in early July as the Tigers pulled 8½ games ahead at mid-season.

McLain won his 31st game in late September, after the pennant had already been clinched. He had the game won, and when Mickey Mantle came up, needing one home run to climb to third place on the career homer list, McLain grooved him an easy fastball. Mick hit it out for Number 535. It was his second-to-last home run; Mantle retired after the 1968 season.

So it came down to Detroit versus St. Louis, McLain versus Gibson, baseball's best pitchers squaring off in the World Series in a season that already was being called The Year of the Pitcher. Before the first game, played in St. Louis, McLain said he wanted to humiliate the Cardinals. Gibson said he just wanted to win. Reflecting years later, Mike Shannon, the Cardinal third baseman, said, "Most of them had never seen Gibby before, and they had no *idea* what they were up against."

After the game, McLain said it best: "I was awed." Not that McLain pitched badly: he yielded three runs in the fourth inning, two of them on a single by Julian Javier, and was pulled for a pinch-hitter in the sixth.

Gibson gave up five hits, one walk, no runs. He struck out Kaline in the first inning, Cash, Horton and Northrup in the second, Freehan and McLain in the third, Kaline again in the fourth.

Sandy Koufax had set the record for strikeouts in a World Series game with 15 against the Yankees in 1963. When the Tigers came up in the ninth, Gibson had 14 strikeouts. He claimed he didn't know he was approaching the record, which is the kind of thing players often say, but in this case one that McCarver, the catcher, confirms.

Lou Brock showed little respect for 31-game winner McLain in Game 4 of the 1968 World Series, hitting the second pitch of the game into the upper deck at Tiger Stadium. Brock hit .464 and tied his own Series record for stolen bases with seven.

Mickey Stanley led off with a single. Gibson struck out Kaline for the third time. That tied the record, and the scoreboard flashed a message saying so. McCarver stepped in front of the plate and pointed, trying to call Gibson's attention to the message, but Gibson was not interested. "Throw the goddamn ball back, will you!" he shouted.

McCarver pointed again. Gibson turned around, read the message, and doffed his cap. Then he fanned Cash for the third time to break the record, and Horton to bring his total to 17. Gibson had been hired by the New York *Daily News* to write daily accounts of the World Series games, and he wrote this: "When I got Willie Horton for my 17th strikeout, I was happy because the game was over."

Detroit pounded back in the second game behind Mickey Lolich, who hit his first major league homer in beating the Cardinals 8–1. In front of a Detroit crowd two days later, the Tigers jumped to an early lead. McCarver changed that with a three-run homer in the fifth, and Orlando Cepeda did the same in the seventh, giving the Cards a 7–3 victory.

Gibson faced McLain again in the fourth game, with similarly lopsided results. The Cardinals knocked McLain out in the third inning. Gibson pitched another five-hitter, struck out ten, and hit a home run himself as the Cardinals coasted, 10–1. It was Gibson's seventh straight World Series victory, another record.

The Cardinals were up three games to one, and in the fifth game they scored three times in the first inning off Mickey Lolich, who had beaten them in Game 2. But Lolich settled down. The Tigers won, and in Game 6 McLain finally made his contribution, striking out seven in a 13–1 Detroit victory. The Series was tied.

HALL OF FAME

6' 185 lbs.
BR TR

b 10/20/38

JUAN MARICHAL
Pitcher

With a leg kick that appeared to come out of the heavens and a seemingly infinite variety of pitches and deliveries, Juan Marichal blazed his way through 16 major league seasons as one of the greatest right-handers of all time.

A native of the Dominican Republic, Marichal broke in with the San Francisco Giants in 1960. He averaged 18 wins and 259 innings pitched in 13 full seasons in San Francisco. From 1963–69 Marichal averaged 22 wins a year. He won 20 or more games six times, leading the league with 25 wins in 1963 and 26 in 1968. His 243 wins and 142 losses equal a .631 career winning percentage, 11th best among 200-game winners.

Marichal was arguably the most durable, as well as the most dominant, pitcher of his era. Over the course of his career, he registered 244 complete games, 52 shutouts, 2,303 strikeouts, and a 2.89 earned run average. His 7.8 runners-allowed-on-base per game in 1966 is the lowest since Walter Johnson's record 7.0 for the Washington Senators in 1913.

The winner of a 1–0 no-hitter against the Houston Colt .45s in 1963, he was also phenomenal in All-Star Game competition. In eight All-Star games and 18 innings, he allowed just seven hits and one earned run. Following the 1974 season with the Red Sox and two games in 1975 with the Dodgers, Juan Marichal retired without ever having won the Cy Young Award.

Mickey Lolich carried the pitching load for the Tigers in the 1968 World Series, and when it was over, catcher Bill Freehan returned the favor. Freehan was probably as relieved as he was happy, hitting just .083 in the Series after a solid, 25-homer regular season.

Confetti, computer cards and toilet paper showered Detroit after the Tigers' 4–1 win over St. Louis in Game 7. After waiting 23 years for this 1968 world championship, Tiger fans began an 18-year wait for the next one.

A man of extremes, McLain lost 22 games in his first and only season, 1971, with the Washington Senators. In a truly dismal deal, the Senators gave up shortstop Eddie Brinkman, third baseman Aurelio Rodriguez, and pitcher Joe Coleman, who that year went 20–9 for the Tigers.

For the third time in the decade, Bob Gibson was pitching the seventh game of a World Series on short rest. But the script had a new star in Lolich, the portly Detroit southpaw who had won most of his 17 games during the latter portion of the season and now, like Gibson, was 2–0 in the World Series.

The game was scoreless through six innings. With two out in the Tiger seventh, Cash and Horton singled. Northrop drove the ball deep to center field, a can-of-corn for Curt Flood, the best center fielder in baseball. But Flood misjudged the ball, came in, slipped as he reversed course, and was unable to catch up. It fell for a triple, and Freehan doubled Cash home.

Gibson struck out eight, bringing his total for the Series to 35, and breaking his own record of 31 set in 1964. But Lolich held the Cardinals to five hits and the Tigers won, 4–1. It was Lolich's third Series win, and it made the Tigers world champions.

Of course, there was more than pitching to this World Series. Veteran Al Kaline, finally playing in a Series, hit two homers and drove in eight runs. Lou Brock, like Gibson playing in his third and last World Series, stole seven bases to tie his own Series record, got 13 hits to tie another Series record, and brought his career World Series batting average to .391, second only to Pepper Martin, who hit .418 for the Cardinals back in the 1930s.

But the year was 1968, and that World Series is remembered for the pitching of Bob Gibson, Mickey Lolich, and, to a lesser extent, Denny McLain. It was a pitcher's year, and there hasn't been one like it since. ◑

Early Wynn's Long Season

Early Wynn's 300th victory was not a Hall of Fame performance. In fact, it was nearly the win that wasn't.

In a career that spanned four decades, Wynn had won 20 or more games in a season five times. In 1959, at the age of 39, he won a league-leading 23 games and the Cy Young Award in pitching the White Sox to the American League pennant. Yet when the 1963 season began, Early Wynn was home in Venice, Florida, with 299 career wins . . . and without a contract.

Wynn had pitched impressively throughout the spring. "On our last day in spring training," he recalls, "I pitched three innings against Cincinnati and struck out the side in the final inning. I was feeling good, but I knew the White Sox wanted to take a look at Gary Peters. I knew they were going to release me." That afternoon, they did.

Back in Venice, he continued to work out. "I threw and I ran, and there were offers from the Athletics and the Cardinals. But they wanted me to come down there, try out, and pitch batting practice, and I wasn't ready for that stuff yet."

Early Wynn did not *need* another victory. In 22 seasons, he'd all but earned election to Cooperstown. He'd also earned a reputation as a relentless pitcher. The joke was that he'd brush back his mother if she crowded the plate. His reputation, however, was no joke. He did not want to be remembered as a reclamation project or a public relations gimmick to keep the turnstiles turning.

Then, in June, Cleveland called with an offer to pitch and coach. Going to the Indians was a homecoming. Wynn had spent his finest years in Cleveland, 1949–1957. Four of his 20-win seasons were with the Tribe, and in 1954 he had been one of three Hall of Fame pitchers—along with Bob Feller and Bob Lemon—to pitch the Indians into the World Series. Three months into the 1963 season and manager Birdie Tebbetts was telling Wynn, "Take your time. Work out as you see fit and tell me when you're ready."

Wynn had no idea how ready he had to be. As a team, the Indians hit .239 in '63, second lowest in the American League, and Wynn was not spared his teammates' ineptitude. In his second start of the season, he was masterful against the White Sox. For seven innings he pitched hitless ball. "Then, in the eighth, that shortstop Ron Hansen hit a curve—no, a slider—off me for a two-run homer. We lost it 2–1."

The Indians arrived in Kansas City on a sweltering weekend in mid-season. On July 13, Wynn took the mound in the second game of a Saturday doubleheader. His gout, a disease he'd suffered from for years, was acting up, and he struggled through the first four innings.

In the top of the fifth, with the score tied 1–1, Wynn drove in the go-ahead run as Cleveland scored four times. But in the bottom of the inning Ken Harrelson and Gino Cimoli singled, and Jose Tartabull beat out a bunt to load the bases. Then Jerry Lumpe doubled everyone home. But that was all the scoring for the day. Lumpe was thrown out trying to stretch his double into a triple, and Wynn retired the next two batters. In the sixth Tebbetts called on Jerry Walker, Wynn's roommate, in relief. Walker went the rest of the way for the save.

Wynn watched the remainder of the game alongside Cleveland broadcaster Jimmy Dudley in the radio booth. It was a rare perspective—to watch his 300th win, one he'd earned.

Wynn made 15 more appearances over the rest of the '63 season, starting twice. He finished the season with a 2.28 ERA in $55\frac{1}{3}$ innings. His record was 1–2.

EARLY WYNN

Right-Handed Pitcher
Washington Senators 1939–1948
Cleveland Indians 1949–1957
Chicago White Sox 1958–1962
Cleveland Indians 1963
Hall of Fame 1972

GAMES	**691**
INNINGS	
Career	**4,564**
Season High	**285⅔**
WINS	
Career	**300**
Season High	**23**
LOSSES	
Career	**244**
Season High	**19**
WINNING PERCENTAGE	
Career	**.551**
Season High	**.692**
ERA	
Career	**3.54**
Season Low	**2.72**
GAMES STARTED	
Career	**612**
Season High	**37**
COMPLETE GAMES	
Career	**290**
Season High	**22**
SHUTOUTS	
Career	**49**
Season High	**6**
STRIKEOUTS	
Career	**2,334**
Season High	**184**
WALKS	
Career *(4th all time)*	**1,775**
Season High	**132**
WORLD SERIES	**1954, 1959**
CY YOUNG AWARD	**1959**

Early Wynn went from the Washington Senators to World War II and back again before being traded to the Indians in 1949 (right). Fourteen years later, after a Cy Young year with the White Sox in 1959, he closed out his 23-year, 300-win career with Cleveland (above).

Expansion Theater

Expansion did not come easy to baseball. For 49 years, from 1903 until 1953, no team moved and no franchises were added. On the major league map, the United States extended south to Washington, DC, west to St. Louis, and no farther. Then the Braves franchise moved from Boston to Milwaukee, the Athletics from Philadelphia to Kansas City, and the old St. Louis Browns became the new Baltimore Orioles. Big stuff, but in 1958 came the shock of Gotham, or Hollywood, proportions. The Brooklyn Dodgers moved to Los Angeles, and the New York Giants to San Francisco.

New York was outraged, but baseball owners were delighted. They had moved west—not quite on the heels of Lewis and Clark, to be sure, but they had passed over the Rockies and found life on the other side. They still had the same 16 teams, now spread from the original ten cities to 15. Only Chicago still had two teams. Quiet, America, and play ball.

But the ice was broken. Repercussions from the franchise moves forced the majors to expand and prompted further franchise shifts. To avoid competition, as well as to counter lawsuits and to soothe senators who were threatening baseball's antitrust exemption, jilted cities were given new teams. Far from planning its expansion, major league baseball was pushed, prodded and sued every step of the way.

The most innovative prodders were in New York, which was determined to regain a place in the National League. Mayor Robert Wagner appointed William A. Shea, an energetic lawyer, to head the effort. Shea got nowhere

President John F. Kennedy got the second incarnation of the Washington Senators started in 1961. The "Nats" went on to lose at least 100 games in each of their first four years.

Onward, Outward and Inward

For nearly 60 years, both major leagues had eight teams and an eastern bias. By the end of the 1960s, the symmetry had changed.

National League

1903-1952
Boston Braves
Brooklyn Dodgers
Chicago Cubs
Cincinnati Reds
New York Giants
Philadelphia Phillies
Pittsburgh Pirates
St. Louis Cardinals

1953
Braves to
Milwaukee

1958
Giants to San
Francisco
Dodgers to Los
Angeles

1962
New franchises:
New York Mets
Houston Colt .45s

1965
Houston Colt .45s
become Astros

1966
Braves to
Atlanta

1969
New franchises
San Diego Padres
Montreal Expos

Divisional Play 1969

NL East	NL West
Chicago Cubs	Atlanta Braves
Montreal Expos	Cincinnati Reds
New York Mets	Houston Astros
Philadelphia Phillies	Los Angeles Dodgers
Pittsburgh Pirates	San Diego Padres
St. Louis Cardinals	San Francisco Giants

American League

1903-1953
Boston Red Sox
Chicago White Sox
Cleveland Indians
Detroit Tigers
New York Yankees
Philadelphia Athletics
St. Louis Browns
Washington Senators

1954
Browns to
Baltimore
become
Orioles

1955
Athletics to
Kansas City

1961
Senators to
Minneapolis,
become
Minnesota Twins
New franchises:
Washington
Senators
Los Angeles Angels

1965
Angels to
Anaheim

1968
Athletics
to Oakland

1969
New franchises:
Kansas City Royals
Seattle Pilots

Divisional Play 1969

AL East	AL West
Baltimore Orioles	California Angels
Boston Red Sox	Chicago White Sox
Cleveland Indians	Kansas City Royals
Detroit Tigers	Minnesota Twins
New York Yankees	Oakland Athletics
Washington Senators	Seattle Pilots

through negotiation, so he turned to creative pressure. He hired Branch Rickey, and together they announced formation of a third major league.

They called their new league the Continental League and said they hoped it would be accepted "under the umbrella of organized baseball." They awarded franchises to New York, Houston, Denver, Minneapolis-St. Paul, Toronto, Dallas, Atlanta and Buffalo. Shea said, "There are enough good players around right now to staff a new league. You can't tell me that a nation of 160 million can't produce 200 more big-league ballplayers."

Baseball could not afford to risk competition with a league headed by Rickey. As general manager of the St. Louis Cardinals, Rickey had invented the baseball farm system while turning a moribund franchise into a consistent contender. He then moved on to the Brooklyn Dodgers, where he produced another winning team and broke baseball's color line.

The Continental League existed only on paper and probably never intended to sell a ticket. Aghast at the prospect of competition, the American and National League club owners quickly voted to take in the proposed Continental League franchises by expanding, first to ten teams each and then to 12. Rickey and Shea said "thank you," and disbanded their league.

The National League picked New York and Houston. In exchange for allowing a rival to the Yankees in New York, the American League insisted on a new franchise in Los Angeles. The American League wanted Minneapolis-St.Paul, too, but Calvin Griffith grabbed that location as the new home of his weak Washington Senators, renaming the team in honor of the Twin Cities. Politicians growled fiercely at baseball for abandoning the nation's capital, so the American League hastened to put its second expansion team in Washington, recycling the name Senators as if nothing had changed.

Three key figures in 1950s and 1960s baseball—from left, Commissioner Ford Frick, Dodger general manager Buzzy Bavasi, and Dodger owner Walter O'Malley—put their heads together at a 1959 All-Star Game. Frick's pro-owner posture helped galvanize player support for unionization in the 1960s, while Bavasi was O'Malley's hatchet man on player salaries.

BRANCH RICKEY

The Continental League—conceived in 1959 and disbanded before it signed any players—lasted long enough for The Fleer Company to issue a baseball card of Branch Rickey, the proposed league's founder and one of baseball's most influential front-office men.

The American League went to ten teams in 1961, the National League in 1962. The new franchises were forced to pay for their entry and to buy second-string players and minor leaguers from the established teams. All four teams talked hopefully of resurgent veterans and promising youngsters, but none of the four newcomers wound up with much in the way of talent.

On a cold April day in Washington, John F. Kennedy, the new president, inaugurated expansion baseball by throwing out the first ball of the 1961 season. He threw wildly, over the heads of the players who were waiting to catch the ball. A Washington fan who had been out of touch for the winter might have wandered into old Griffith Stadium that day and found a whole new team—almost as unsettling as coming home from work and finding a new spouse. The new Senators, like the old, lost with regularity.

Other cities began courting teams, sometimes offering new stadiums as bait. The script became familiar: club owner pledges undying loyalty to home city; media reveals that he is secretly bargaining with another city; club owner pleads poverty and asks home city for a new stadium or a better deal on the existing one; politicians threaten legal action in case of a move; club owner grabs the best deal he can get, at home or elsewhere.

The bidding and bartering, not to mention the lying, cheapened the image of baseball just at a time when the public seemed to be tiring of the old game. Professional football was the darling of television, and media prophets said that busy, urban Americans would no longer sit still for a slow and pastoral game like baseball.

After a surge in gate receipts in the years following World War II, radio and television revenue was becoming an increasingly bigger factor in team finances. Teams in smaller media markets began to feel the pinch. The Kan-

Continued on page 70

North of the Border

The year was 1969, the end of a decade. An American walked on the moon, Ho Chi Minh died, the Mets won the World Series. It was the summer of a weekend of music and more on a farm near Woodstock, New York. It was the spring when major league baseball went international in the city of Montreal, Canada.

Opening day, April 14, 1969, at Montreal's Parc Jarry was everything doomsayers in Buffalo, Milwaukee and Dallas—the cities Montreal beat out for the 12th National League franchise in 1968—had predicted. Despite the sun and the 60° weather, there were five-foot snowbanks beyond the outfield fence. Melting frost in the subsoil raised huge lumps in the outfield turf, caused the pitcher's mound to sink five inches, and turned the basepaths, according to Ted Blackman of the Montreal *Gazette,* into "a hunk of Gouda cheese." Home plate was cockeyed, skewed toward left field, and the scoreboard was not equipped to display the game's line score. "I've played on some bad diamonds," said Curt Flood of the visiting St. Louis Cardinals, "but this is the worst." Actually, the worst was yet to come: the Expos won the opener 8–7, and an overflow crowd of 29,184 momentarily forgot the Stanley Cup Playoffs. Three days later, in Philadelphia, Montreal's Bill Stoneman no-hit the Phillies, 7–0.

There was joy in Quebec that April, but back in 1968, when National League owners were considering expansion proposals, the principals from contending cities laughed at the thought of a major league team in Montreal. They pointed to language, weather and hockey as three reasons why baseball would not succeed there. Besides, patriotism dictated that major league baseball be restricted to U.S. boundaries. Montreal's mayor Jean Drapeau, who had attracted Expo '67 to Montreal the year before, was a model of ambition and full of promises: a $10 million league entry fee, a temporary stadium that would hold 45,000 spectators, a 55,000-seat domed stadium by 1971. In addition to baseball, Drapeau was actively recruiting the 1976 Winter Olympics, all the while reminding team owners that with a population of 2.5 million, Montreal was larger than 13 major league cities. And he had the gall to invoke tradition, reminding skeptics that Babe Ruth hit his first professional home run on September 5, 1914, in Toronto's Hanlan's Point Park.

The Dodgers had established a dynasty as the outright owners of the AAA Montreal Royals in the 1940s and 1950s. In 1946, when his life was threatened in American ballparks, Jackie Robinson was a hero in Montreal. Roy Campanella, Duke Snider, Don Newcombe, Junior Gilliam, Joe Black and Carl Furillo were showcased there. Walter Alston and Tom Lasorda managed there. Buzzy Bavasi was the team's general manager. In 1949 the Royals drew 600,000 fans and earned a $332,000 profit. When Drapeau talked about baseball in Canada, he had a lot to say, and Los Angeles Dodgers' owner Walter O'Malley, the prime force behind the 1968 expansion, liked what he heard.

There was no Casey Stengel in Montreal in 1969 to ask, "Can't anyone here play this game?" Manager Gene Mauch, a Royals' infielder in 1943–44, fielded a team that, at worst, had the potential to be reasonably competitive. Red-headed Rusty Staub, "Le Grand Orange," was an immediate hero, hitting .302 with 29 homers. Jose "Coco" Laboy, a 28-year-old rookie third baseman, led the league in hitting for the first month of the season and was a strong contender for Rookie of the Year honors. Mack Jones had 22 homers and 79 RBI. Bill Stoneman could pitch.

Parc Jarry was situated in a recreational area in northeast Montreal, and home runs to right field often landed in a public swimming pool. Although the park was inadequate at best, the Expos drew over one million fans in each of their first six seasons.

But as with most first-year expansion teams, Expo frustration took many forms. Montreal pitchers gave up a league-record 702 walks as the team finished 52–110, last in the National League East. Montreal's longest winning streak of the season was four games, and at one stretch the team lost 20 straight. In June, shortstop Maury Wills, unhappy with the club since the beginning of the season, announced his retirement, only to return two days later; by the end of the month he was traded to the Dodgers, and on August 16, he hit the only grand slam of his career against his old mates.

Still, it was big-league ball all the way. And even in Parc Jarry, with its international flavor, a fan took his seat in *l'estrade populaire*—the bleachers—ate his *chien chaud*—hot dog—kept one eye on the field and one on *le tableau indicateur*—the scoreboard—counted the *points, coups surs* and *erreurs*, and prayed for next year.

Baseball moved around a lot in the 1960s, and was welcomed wherever it landed. After moving 799 miles southeast from Milwaukee in 1966, the Braves paraded into Atlanta and in 1969 won the first National League West Division crown.

sas City Athletics said they were getting only one-fifth as much broadcast revenue as the New York Yankees. The Milwaukee Braves predicted their broadcast revenue would triple if they moved to Atlanta.

To soothe local fans, the Athletics and Braves kept insisting that they had no intention of moving. Their talks with other cities kept getting exposed in the press. Other club owners were uncomfortable, because previous franchise moves had been from cities that had two teams—three in the case of New York. Those cities—New York, Philadelphia, Boston and St. Louis—still fielded major league teams.

In contrast, Milwaukee and Kansas City would become baseball orphans if their teams moved. Baseball's antitrust exemption was founded on the fiction that the enterprise was primarily a game, not a business. It wouldn't look good for a team to cold-shoulder its home city just for more dollars elsewhere.

After moving from Boston in 1953, the Milwaukee Braves became the first National League team to draw 2 million fans in a season, and did it four years in a row. But in 1962 attendance dipped below 800,000. To pay their debts, the Braves offered $1 million in stock to Wisconsin residents. Only $120,000 worth was sold. Atlanta, San Diego and Indianapolis wooed the Braves; Dallas, Fort Worth and Seattle also expressed interest.

Charles Finley, an eccentric millionaire, bought the Kansas City A's in 1960 and started looking for a more profitable home. In 1962 he asked AL owners for permission to move to Dallas. They turned him down. He signed a deal with Louisville in 1964; they turned him down again. He started talking to interested parties in Atlanta and Oakland. American League owners told Finley to sign a new stadium lease in Kansas City or get out of baseball.

Poor attendance throughout the 1960s caused the Senators to leave Washington, DC, twice in ten years. On September 30, 1971, when fans couldn't wait to rip up the turf at R.F.K. Stadium, the Senators' last home game went into the books as a forfeit.

Atlanta also made a strong pitch to the Cleveland Indians, who had drawn only 563,000 fans in 1962. The Indians looked fondly at Seattle and Dallas, too, and got an offer from interests in Oakland. The Pirates threatened to leave Pittsburgh unless the city pushed forward with construction of a new stadium. The messages came across: the cities of Cleveland and Pittsburgh offered better stadium deals, so the Indians and Pirates stayed put.

The Braves, however, struck a deal with Atlanta, and asked the National League for permission to move south in 1965. The Milwaukee County Board of Supervisors filed suit to block the move, and the league told the Braves they had to play the 1965 season in Milwaukee to fulfill their stadium lease obligation. The Braves offered Milwaukee County a half-million dollars to let them leave quickly, but the county turned them down.

Exposed as turncoats, the 1965 Braves played before sparse crowds. The Schlitz Brewing Company said it would no longer underwrite Braves games on radio or television, and no other sponsor came forward. The Braves gave away broadcast rights in Wisconsin and sold rights to broadcast their games to Atlanta.

The 1965 Braves were a good team, in contention for the pennant until September. Hank Aaron and Eddie Mathews, heroes of previous Milwaukee champions, played well as lame ducks. There was talk that the Braves, if they won, might seek to play their World Series games in Atlanta. Commissioner Ford Frick said he wouldn't allow it; anyway, the Braves sagged to fifth place.

The Braves opened in Atlanta in the spring of 1966. The franchise had been the first to move, and now it became the first to move *twice*.

The Athletics were not far behind. In October 1967 the American League approved Finley's request to move his team to Oakland. With a nerv-

5'10" 160 lbs.　　　　b 12/25/27
BL TR　　　　　　　　d 12/1/75

NELLIE FOX
Second Base

The opening of the Astrodome in 1965 appropriately signaled the end of the 19-year career of Nellie Fox, one of the greatest second basemen of all time. After 21 games of indoor baseball, Fox called it quits. He'd lasted three decades in the majors, but when baseball went indoors, Fox didn't belong.

In an era of power hitters, Fox was feared for his singles; he didn't just swing, he "handled" the bat. In 19 years in the majors, Fox collected 2,663 career hits, 2,161 of which were singles. Only Hall of Famers Joe Sewell, Willie Keeler and Lloyd Waner were more difficult to strike out than Fox, who once went a record 98 consecutive games without striking out.

Fox broke in with the Philadelphia Athletics in 1947 and was traded to the White Sox in 1950. For the next 14 seasons he was Chicago's regular second baseman, averaging 140 games a year and teaming with shortstop Luis Aparicio for seven seasons as one of the game's best double play combinations.

A .288 hitter, Fox led the American League in hits four times, and hit .300 or better six times, including a career-high .319 in 1954. Fox received the ultimate tribute when he was named the American League Most Valuable Player in 1959, the White Sox last pennant-winning season. In that World Series, against the Dodgers, Fox hit .375 with nine hits in six games.

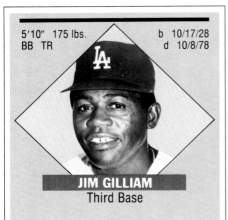

5'10" 175 lbs.   b 10/17/28
BB TR   d 10/8/78

JIM GILLIAM
Third Base

In 1953, a 25-year-old rookie named James William "Junior" Gilliam unseated Jackie Robinson as the starting second baseman of the Brooklyn Dodgers. Fourteen years later, the Dodgers were in Los Angeles, Robinson was retired, and Gilliam was still playing.

Gilliam hit .278 that first season, in addition to leading the National League with 17 triples and winning Rookie of the Year honors as Brooklyn ran away with the pennant. In the 1953 World Series against the Yankees, he hit .296 with three doubles and two home runs.

In his 14-year career, all with the Dodgers, Gilliam was as versatile as he was durable. He played second base, third base and the outfield equally well, and even filled in at first for manager Walter Alston. Gilliam averaged 140 games a year during his career. From 1958 to 1966, the Dodgers tried 29 players at third, but no one played it better than Gilliam.

Most of all, Gilliam was dependable. He rarely struck out and regularly led the Dodgers in bases on balls. A .265 lifetime hitter who had the power to hit an occasional homer, Gilliam scored 100 or more runs in each of his first four seasons. Gilliam is the only Dodger—Los Angeles or Brooklyn—ever to play on four world championship Dodger teams. His uniform number—19—is one of eight numbers to have been retired by the Dodgers.

A's owner Charlie Finley (right) and his wife Shirley (left) were welcomed to Oakland in 1968 by Oakland Coliseum president Robert Nahas (center). That year, the A's had their first .500 season since 1952, when they were still in Philadelphia.

ous eye on Kansas City officials and Missouri politicians, the league simultaneously voted to expand by two teams—one in Kansas City, the other in Seattle. They wanted to delay the expansion until 1971, but Senator Stuart Symington of Missouri threatened Congressional punishment unless Kansas City got another team pronto.

So another round of expansion was scheduled for 1969, but only in the American League. On the Senate floor, Symington described Finley as "one of the most disreputable characters ever to enter the American sports scene." He said a year without baseball in Kansas City would be too bad, but "is more than recompensed for by the pleasure resulting from our getting rid of Mr. Finley." Many who knew Finley agreed, but in Oakland he was greeted with "We Luv You Charlie" banners.

The National League was jarred. President Warren Giles accused the American League of "premature expansion." Actually, the National League had hoped to cop Seattle for itself. But the senior league bowed to reality and chose San Diego and Montreal as its new expansion cities. San Diego had a new ballpark. Montreal didn't, and almost lost its franchise; Parc Jarry—capacity 3,000—was hurriedly expanded for the 1969 season. Construction that spring was interrupted only by the occasional ballgame.

Baseball attendance hadn't grown much during the 1960s, partly because both leagues had been saddled with ten-team pennant races since the first round of expansion. Not many fans go to see an also-ran, and a ten-team league has too many also-rans. Always alert to novelty, the American League had the bright idea of splitting itself into two divisions of six teams each.

The National League refused. "We just do not subscribe to divisional play," Giles said. "Baseball is built on history and tradition, and we do not

believe the public will accept a World Series contender that might have had the third- or fourth-ranked record in its league."

Joe Cronin, president of the American League, was more realistic. "You can't sell a 12th-place team," he said. The National League held out for a month, then capitulated under pressure from the new baseball commissioner, William Eckert. Both leagues began divisional play in 1969, but not before the National League went through convulsions in deciding which teams would play in its Eastern Division and which in the West.

The Cardinals, obvious candidates for the Western Division, insisted on playing in the same division as the Cubs, because their long-standing Midwestern rivalry helped attendance in both cities. The Mets wanted to be in the same division as the Dodgers and Giants, but that proved too much of a map-stretching exercise.

As a compromise, St. Louis and Chicago were put in the Eastern Division with New York, Philadelphia, Pittsburgh and Montreal. Cincinnati and Atlanta found themselves in the Western Division—never mind their location on the map—along with Los Angeles, San Francisco, San Diego and Houston. The result: all the old NL cities except Cincinnati became the NL East; the NL West got the gold, glitter and sunshine of California and Texas.

For all its recalcitrance, the National League fared better. All its expansion cities—New York, Houston, San Diego and Montreal—were good choices, and all four clubs prospered, although the Padres suffered several lean years.

The American League was saddled with weak ownership in Washington and finally approved the franchise's move to Dallas-Fort Worth in 1972, leaving the national capital bereft of the national pastime. The Angels

Sick's Stadium in Seattle, home of the 1969 expansion Pilots, was a disaster from the start. It opened with a capacity of just 18,000, and if attendance climbed above 14,000, water pressure all but disappeared. The team fared no better, finishing last in the AL West and moving to Milwaukee in 1970.

Cubs' College of Coaches

To Philip K. Wrigley, firing a manager was an onerous job that didn't make good baseball sense. So in December 1960, the Cubs' owner announced that his team would play the 1961 season *without* a manager. Instead, they would have a corporate-like management team consisting of four coaches who would alternate as head coach—Wrigley had dictatorially eliminated the word *manager* from the Cubs' lexicon—for up to two months at a time. He called his brainstorm the Cubs' College of Coaches. Innovative to a fault, Wrigley saw his team finish seventh in 1961 and ninth the following year, but no one could blame the manager.

Wrigley's plan was to rotate coaches throughout the Cubs' minor league system. After a month or two in the bushes, the coach would return to the Cubs. The idea was to encourage and develop minor league talent as quickly as possible. In a fit of prescience, the man who refused to install lights at his home field boldly stated, "It's an age of specialists." Wrigley welcomed the skeptics good-naturedly. At a press conference called to announce his idea, he carried a sign that read: Anyone who remains calm in the midst of all this confusion simply does not understand the situation.

Wrigley's faculty convened in Mesa, Arizona, the Cubs' spring training site: eight coaches were indoctrinated with the party line. "This is the best thing that's happened to baseball since the spitball," said Elvin Tappe, a catchers' coach.

Along with Tappe, Wrigley signed pitching coaches Vedie Himsl and Goldie Holt, Verlon Walker to help with the catchers, infield coach Bobby Adams, outfield coach Harry Craft, hitting instructor Rip Collins, and Charley Grimm as rover.

With youngsters Billy Williams, Ron Santo and Dick Ellsworth and veterans Ernie Banks, Ri-chie Ashburn and Don Zimmer, the Cubs roared through spring training, winning the Cactus League with an 11–8 record. But by opening day it was clear that Mr. Wrigley's brainchild was predestined to self-destruct.

The team opened the season with Vedie Himsl, normally a pitching coach, as head coach and Goldie Holt assigned to San Antonio as a pitching instructor, leaving the Cubs without a pitching coach. Thus Holt was called back from the Texas League and Rip Collins was assigned to take his place. Which meant that San Antonio would have to make do without a pitching instructor while Cubs' hitters had to tutor each other in batting.

And that's just about how it went all year. By October, the head coaches' records were: Himsl, 10–21; Craft, 7–9; Lou Klein (he was hired in mid-season), 5–7; Tappe, 42–53. Home attendance at Wrigley Field fell off by 136,713 from 1960 to an embarrassing 673,057. Still, the team's 64–90 record was four games above its 1960 mark. P. K. Wrigley remained a believer.

Wrigley carried his college banner into 1962, convinced that the kinks could be worked out. But when Chicago finished with a 59–103 mark, Wrigley fired head coach Charlie Metro. In January, he announced the hiring of Robert Whitlow as "athletic director." Whitlow, a retired Air Force colonel, had no baseball experience. His job: to oversee all baseball operations. When questioned as to how the College of Coaches would function, Whitlow replied, "We'll play it by ear." Whitlow's first appointment was that of Bob Kennedy as head coach. Kennedy held tight to the reins for 162 games in 1963, and the Cubs finished with an 82–80 record, good enough for seventh place. The system worked. Kennedy was named *manager* in 1964. Midway through 1965 he was—right—fired.

Each new franchise and team move in the 1960s brought new decals and logos. Those of the Pilots and Angels quickly became collector's items: the Pilots moved to Milwaukee after just one year; the Angels moved to Anaheim in 1966 and have been known as the California Angels ever since.

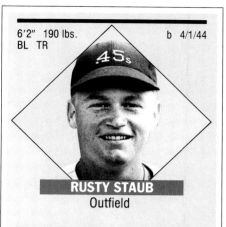

6'2" 190 lbs.
BL TR   b 4/1/44

RUSTY STAUB
Outfield

"Le Grand Orange" in Montreal, "Big Red" everywhere else, Rusty Staub had a major league career that was born of the expansion era. After breaking in with the Houston Colt .45s in 1963, the team's second year, Staub spent 19 of his 23 major league seasons with Houston, the Montreal Expos, and the New York Mets—all 1960s expansion teams—setting team or major league records with all three clubs.

Staub's .333 average with Houston in 1967 is still a team record. In 1970, his second year with Montreal, he established a team-record 30 home runs. The following year he set Expo season highs with 97 runs batted in and a .311 average. With the New York Mets in 1983, Staub set a major league record with 81 pinch-hit appearances. Among his league-leading 24 pinch hits that season were three home runs.

Despite playing on losing teams for 16 seasons, including stints with the Detroit Tigers and the Texas Rangers, Staub hit .300 or better five times, drove in 100 or more runs three times, and batted .279 lifetime with 292 home runs. His 2,716 career base hits and 2,951 games played rank 38th and seventh, respectively, on the all-time list.

In 1973, with the Mets, Staub was finally a member of a pennant winner. In the World Series against the Oakland Athletics, Staub's .423 average, 11 hits, and six RBI led both clubs.

couldn't compete with the Dodgers in Los Angeles but waxed fat after moving to nearby Anaheim in 1965. The Oakland A's had to compete for fans with the neighboring San Francisco Giants, weakening both franchises. Seattle had looked promising, but the Pilots didn't draw well, were poorly financed, and went on the bankruptcy block after one season. Milwaukee interests bought the club, restoring major league baseball to the jilted bratwurst city less than a week before the 1970 season began.

In a now-familiar scenario, Senator Warren G. Magnuson of Washington, chairman of the Senate Commerce Committee, brought up the subject of baseball's antitrust exemption. "When you move these franchises around like pawns, just because you think you'll do better in some other town, then you're running a business, not a sport," Magnuson said. Mindful of Congressional displeasure, the American League admitted another new franchise in Seattle in 1977, adding Toronto at the same time and saddling the American League with cumbersome seven-team divisions.

The National League wound up with two balanced divisions; the American League East, with the traditional bulwarks of New York, Boston, Detroit and Cleveland, outplayed and outdrew the AL West from the start. The AL West had only Chicago from the ten cities that had manned the baseball fort since the new century began. ◗▮

The Incredibly Common Park

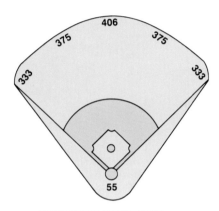

ANAHEIM STADIUM
California Angels, AL
Built 1966
Natural grass

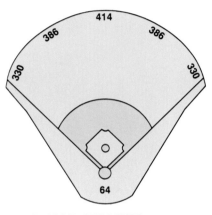

BUSCH STADIUM
St. Louis Cardinals, NL
Built 1966
Natural grass
Artificial turf, 1970

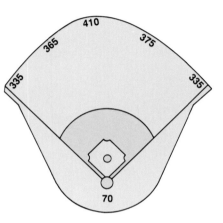

CANDLESTICK PARK
San Francisco Giants, NL
Built 1960
Natural grass

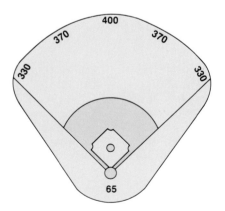

DODGER STADIUM
Los Angeles Dodgers, NL
Built 1962
Natural grass

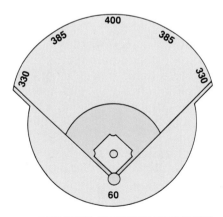

FULTON COUNTY STADIUM
Atlanta Braves, NL
Built 1966
Natural grass

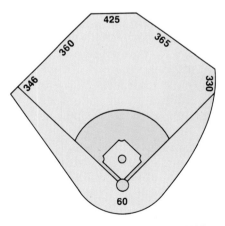

METROPOLITAN STADIUM
Minnesota Twins, AL
Built 1961
Natural grass

I n 1958, when they moved to the West Coast, the Dodgers and Giants left behind two of the quirkiest parks in baseball history, Ebbets Field and the Polo Grounds. But ballparks of irregular dimensions were the norm prior to the 1960s. By the end of the decade 12 new ballparks were in use in the major leagues, and their dimensions were uncommonly similar. In the diagrams below, field surface and dimensions to foul poles, power alleys, center field fence, and back stop—all from home plate—are as of 1969.

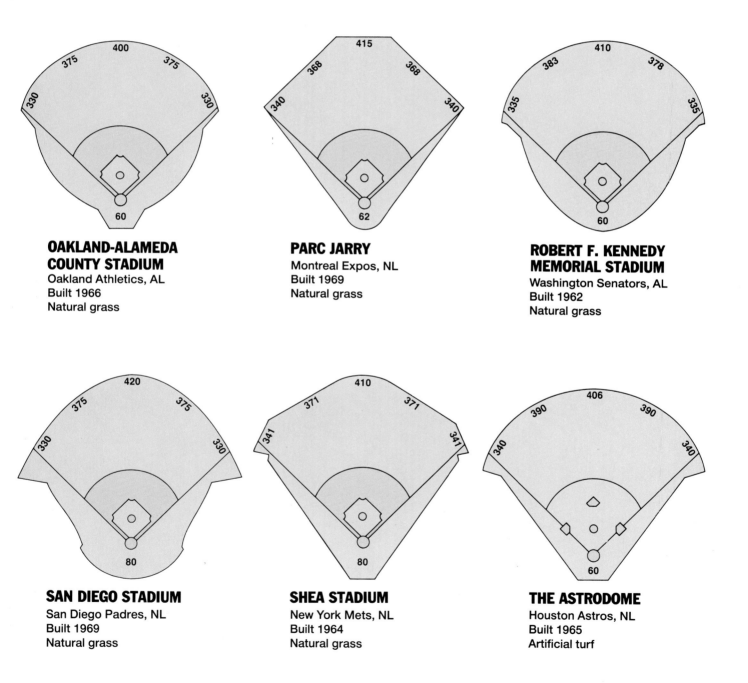

OAKLAND-ALAMEDA COUNTY STADIUM
Oakland Athletics, AL
Built 1966
Natural grass

PARC JARRY
Montreal Expos, NL
Built 1969
Natural grass

ROBERT F. KENNEDY MEMORIAL STADIUM
Washington Senators, AL
Built 1962
Natural grass

SAN DIEGO STADIUM
San Diego Padres, NL
Built 1969
Natural grass

SHEA STADIUM
New York Mets, NL
Built 1964
Natural grass

THE ASTRODOME
Houston Astros, NL
Built 1965
Artificial turf

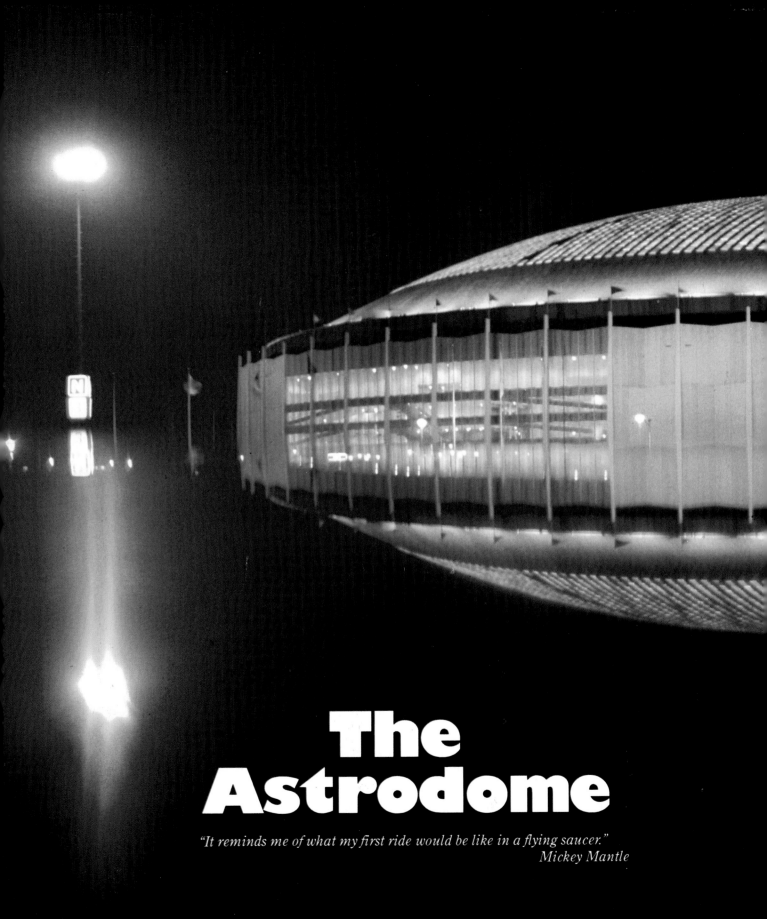

The Astrodome

"It reminds me of what my first ride would be like in a flying saucer."
Mickey Mantle

Only in the Astrodome would you expect to find extraterrestrials working as groundskeepers. But in 1965, despite the best efforts of these Astrognomes, the stadium's grass and dirt surface got so little sun that it was like playing baseball on the moon. In 1966 technology came to the rescue again in the form of Astroturf, ushering in the new age of carpeted baseball.

Roy Hofheinz, born dirt-poor but now Texas-rich, stood looking at the Colosseum in Rome. It was round, and he liked that. Why not a round stadium for Houston's new baseball team? He looked into the history of the Colosseum and learned that slaves used to pull a papyrus roof into place on hot days. Good idea. Emperors and other top dogs, he read with fascination, sat in the top seats—what's Latin for skybox?—not down at field level, where the lions might get uncomfortably close.

Those Romans knew what they were doing, and so did Hofheinz. He was elected a judge at age 24, ran two congressional campaigns for Lyndon Johnson, left politics to get rich in oil and other businesses, served two terms as mayor of Houston, got bounced in a special election, and in 1960 was hired to run the Houston organization that was campaigning to get one of the National League's two expansion franchises. Let's wow them with a stadium plan that will bust their eyeballs, Hofheinz said, and he did.

Houston was awash in oil money and optimism back then, and the citizens approved a bond issue to pay for the structure. It cost $31.6 million, an enormous amount by the standards of the early 1960s. It was called the Harris County Domed Stadium, and it was *big*. How big? A snazzy Hilton hotel stood nearby and would have fit under the dome. The hotel is gone, but the Astrodome itself covers $9\frac{1}{2}$ acres, and the entire Astrodome complex covers 260 acres. A Texas-sized spread.

The Mercury astronauts were Houston's hottest celebrities of 1965. The baseball team changed its name from Colt .45s to Astros, and everyone called the new ballpark the Astrodome. People still do.

Judge Hofheinz, as everybody called him, was not bound by convention.

Astrodome-mania (left) took Houston by storm in 1965.

The ol' bleacher seat may sound romantic, but why stick some poor slob on a hard bench in the Texas sun? Give him an upholstered seat, a roof over his head, and air conditioning. Mmmmmm.

That's for bleacher slobs, who could get in for $1.50 back in 1965, when the stadium opened. Way up top on the ninth level—or rather, the Blue Level—boxes of two dozen or more seats cost $15,000 to $34,000 a year. The players were so far away they "look like Texas-size mosquitoes," Red Smith wrote in the *New York Times,* but a butler served drinks and hors d'oeuvres, and the lighting was carefully chosen to flatter the ladies.

Between innings—heck, any old time—a boxholder could step back into his private room, equipped with bath, bar, icemaker, Dow-Jones ticker and a closed-circuit TV on which he could watch the game while, say, shaving. The skybox rooms were lavishly decorated in motifs ranging from Oriental to parasol-Southern.

With a blue-level box, you got to eat in the Skydome, with stylish Japanese cuisine. A few levels down, at the yellow and red levels, the players looked bigger and you could use the Astrodome Club—not Skydome fancy, but fancy. Heck, even bleacher slobs could eat hot dogs under plastic trees in the Domeskeller.

It is easy to make fun of the Astrodome, but it is probably the most innovative sports stadium ever built. It was and is a smashing success. The Astros, born of expansion in 1962, played their first three seasons in a temporary ballpark, since hauled to Mexico and put back together for use by a Mexican League team. The Astrodome opened in 1965, and although the team was lousy—ninth place—attendance tripled to 2,151,470.

Judge Roy Hofheinz—the man behind the dome—was indeed a saviour to Houston baseball fans. He rescued them from Colt Stadium's devastating heat, humidity, and mosquito clouds and delivered them into a stadium in which the comfort and entertainment of fans was given top priority.

The shell of the unfinished
Astrodome provided an intricate
filter for a 1963 Houston sunset.

In the heat of the 1965 pennant race and the cool of the Astrodome, San Francisco's Willie Mays launched his 500th home run. The real heat in Houston was on the groundskeepers, who fought a losing battle to keep the dome's natural grass alive. It was eventually replaced by Astroturf.

After 21 games of indoor baseball, Astros' second baseman Nellie Fox saw the handwriting on the ceiling, and ended a 19-year career.

Another 400,000 paid a dollar each to take guided tours, offered when no game or other attraction was on.

Hofheinz's lavish skyboxes were ridiculed—and imitated. So were the private clubs. The massive electronic scoreboard, 474 feet long, entertained the fans and startled opposing players. It was the first to incite fans to yell "CHARGE!" and the first to use cartoons to boost the home team and make fun of the visiting team. When an Astros' pitcher was yanked, a cartoon showed the reliever as a heroic astronaut. When the visiting pitcher was yanked, the cartoon showed a sad fellow dolefully showering. Other teams complained—and copied.

Cities throughout the torrid South and frozen North talked of building their own domed stadiums. Some were daunted by cost, but the Seattle Mariners, Minnesota Twins, Montreal Expos, and, most recently, the Toronto Blue Jays now play in domed facilities. In addition, domed stadiums house professional football teams in New Orleans; Indianapolis; Pontiac, Michigan; and Vancouver, British Columbia.

The Astrodome's other lasting innovation was artificial turf, and it was an accident. The Astrodome started out with regular dirt and real grass, which got plenty of light through the 4,596 transparent Lucite panels that made up the roof. But the grass started dying even before the first season got under way. "You can't use the same amount of water as on the outside," said George Myers, the grounds superintendent, "because you don't have the sun, wind and air to dry it out. If I tried over-watering I'd wind up with a bunch of mud puddles."

Hofheinz had thought of most everything—water pressure, for example, was strong enough so 40,000 people could wash their hands at the same

On April 28, 1965, New York Mets'
announcer Lindsey Nelson made
broadcasting history when he called a game
from a gondola suspended from the apex of
the Astrodome—208 feet above second base.

An All-Star Game was no place to be
embarrassed by misjudging a fly ball, so
Washington outfielder Frank Howard tested
the Astrodome's glare to make sure his first
exposure to indoor baseball would be
error-free. But in 1968 the hitters had more
trouble than the fielders as the NL won, 1–0,
its sixth straight.

time, given enough sinks—but it had not occurred to him that sunlight, diffused through the roof panels, might make fly balls invisible to the players.

On Thursday, April 8, 1965, the Astros trotted out for the first indoor baseball game. A coach began hitting fungoes. As the fly balls rose past the multicolored seats and silver girders into the glare of sunlight through Lucite, the outfielders cringed. Some covered their heads with their gloves. Baseballs fell around them "like so many Texas hailstones," observed sportswriter Wells Twombly. Ron Davis, a Houston outfielder, said, "I was able to catch two of the 12 balls hit in my direction, and one was by accident. I never saw the ball. It just landed in my glove."

The game was an exhibition against the Astros' Oklahoma City farm team. Fly balls rained all day. "Balls that could have been caught by a drizzle-nosed Little Leaguer plopped on the turf while runners walked home," Twombly wrote.

What to do? The New York Yankees and Baltimore Orioles were coming in to christen the Dome with five gala pre-season games, and it wouldn't do to have Mickey Mantle blinded and brained. Hofheinz went for a rainbow approach, equipping outfielders with sunglasses of various hues and dying ten dozen baseballs yellow, orange, cerise and other colors. "We'll hit some fungoes to find out which color works best," the Astros decided, "and use balls of that color in the game." Warren Giles, president of the National League, solemnly approved the use of colored baseballs in Houston.

They weren't immediately needed, because the exhibition opener was played at night, and the Astrodome gleamed with half again as much lighting as a normal stadium. A sellout crowd of 47,876 turned out. President and Mrs. Johnson joined Hofheinz in his box—on the Blue Level, of course. John

Connally, governor of Texas, threw out the first ball. Mantle hit the first Astrodome home run in the sixth inning.

The game was tied 1–1 after eight innings. The President had to leave—he and Lady Bird were headed for the ranch at Johnson City—so Hofheinz touched off the scoreboard's "ecstasy" display, which was supposed to be used only for Astro homers and Astro victories. As LBJ watched, the light show began with a ball bursting through the Dome's ceiling, then soaring across the scoreboard amid explosions. Cowboys on each side of the scoreboard fired ricocheting bullets. Steers popped up with U.S. and Texas flags on their horns. Rockets and fireworks exploded all over. It was quite a show.

In the 12th inning, Nellie Fox, the former Chicago White Sox star, pinch-hit for Houston pitcher Hal Woodeshick and singled Jim Wynn home with the winning run: 2–1, Houston.

Day and night doubleheaders were held Saturday and Sunday, the Astros playing the Yankees and Orioles twice each, and nature saved both days by providing a cloud cover that cut the glare, though the outfielders still had a hard time. The Astros opened the season on the road, and Hofheinz had the plastic roof panels spray-painted.

The glare was gone, but the lack of sunshine was the final KO for the grass. The Astros watered it, installed fresh turf, and finally sprayed green dye on the dead, brown grass blades. Line drives kicked up dust, and balls hopped off the dry, hard ground as if it were—well—Astroturf.

By the next season, it was. Hofheinz turned to the green thumb of Monsanto Chemical Company. Artificial turf had been used at harness racing tracks, but that variety wouldn't do. Moreover, Astroturf had to be movable

At $2 per square foot and with little or no maintenance costs, Astroturf was cheaper than grass and had more bounce, as Houston catcher Ron Brand found out in a 1965 pre-season game.

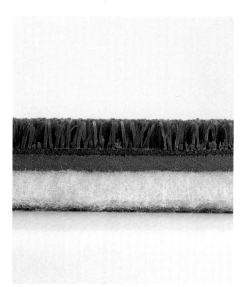

Baseball's first synthetic surface featured about as many layers as a baseball itself. On top were blades of green nylon, backed by a thin layer of acrylic fiber, then a spongy layer of porous foam made from polyvinyl chloride, and anchored by a thick layer of acrylic fiber.

and removable so the field could be converted for football, tennis, revivals, business conventions and other sports. Circuses were important, because Hofheinz owned half of the Barnum and Bailey circus and couldn't wait to stage it under the dome.

Monsanto came up with a nice green nylon grass on thin backing, and Hofheinz first laid it out in the huge Astrodome parking lot. There he had it tested. He got horses to run on it, football players to scrimmage on it, elephants to trample it and even to do on it what they do everywhere else. It held up fine.

Monsanto made the stuff in sections 221 feet long and 14 feet wide, zippered together on the bottom. Each section was fitted, or tailored, to cover the infield just so. The Astros opened the 1966 season on an infield of Astroturf and installed it in the outfield in July.

Reviews were mixed. Astroturf was better than dead grass, and infielders appreciated the true bounce. Ground balls scooted through more quickly, and infielders adapted by playing a little deeper. But some people were offended, including Leo Durocher, who was managing the Chicago Cubs after 11 years out of baseball. "They spent $20 million to build a ballpark," said Durocher, underestimating the figure, "and then they put in a ten-cent infield."

Artificial turf has become common, but many people still find it offensive. "The World of Perspiring Arts has fostered some remarkable scientific improvements, but synthetic turf isn't one of them," columnist Blackie Sherrod wrote in the Dallas *Morning News.*

The Dome was also the first air-conditioned ballpark, and visiting managers initially complained that the Astros turned the dial to make balls

blow out while the Astros were at bat and to make them blow in when the visitors were up. The commissioner's office dispatched an engineer, who reported that it wasn't so. In fact, the Astrodome is a pitcher's park. Batted balls just don't carry, no matter who hits them. No one is sure why.

The Astrodome was the first true multi-purpose stadium, and in that way was a model of practicality. It brought football indoors, and more than doubled the potential gate receipts for basketball.

The Astrodome was Judge Hofheinz's baby, and he lived in it, occupying a sumptuous suite up at the Blue Level. Late at night, hours after a game, cleanup workmen would look up and see a cigar glowing in the Judge's box; he would sit there alone, looking out upon his creation. He lost the Astros and the Astrodome in a financial squeeze in 1975, and the creditors who took it over let the Dome get a little worn. John J. McMullen, a naval architect and business mogul, bought the Astros in 1979, and got Harris County to restore the Astrodome's splendor with $42 million in renovations.

Another $60 million was pumped in beginning in 1987. Some of Hofheinz's more lavish touches are gone, and the magnificent scoreboard is giving way to 10,000 new seats, but the Astrodome still looks ahead of its time.

When Billie Jean King beat Bobby Riggs in the "Battle of the Sexes" tennis match in 1973, she did it in the Astrodome. When Elvin Hayes and the University of Houston ended UCLA's 47-game basketball winning streak in 1968, they did it in the Dome. When Muhammad Ali unveiled the Ali Shuffle—"so fast it can't be seen by the human eye"—he did it in the Dome.

For rain-out fans, here's an Astrofact: on June 15, 1976, a game at the Astrodome was rained out. The field was dry, but the streets of Houston were flooded. It's quite a ballpark. As Astros' pitcher Jim Owens once told author/pitcher Jim Bouton, "It isn't much, but we call it home." ◑

The Astrodome

The first of nine domed stadiums that have revolutionized both the playing and viewing of baseball and football over the past 25 years, the Astrodome continues to astonish fans with its facts and figures.

The dome itself consists of 4,596 Lucite panels. It spans 642 feet, $9^1/_2$ acres of floor space, and six levels of color-coded seating, with each seat facing a spot 20 feet behind second base. Eighty percent of all seats can be reached by walking down from the stadium's entrance level. To convert the stadium from a baseball configuration to a football field, the stands are rotated on steel rails so that they parallel the football sidelines. The Astrodome is air-conditioned at 72 degrees year-round. Its sound system is housed in a 27,000-pound gondola, 64 feet in diameter and eight feet high. The gondola can be raised from floor to roof in six minutes.

The Astrodome has undergone a number of renovations over the years, the most obvious being the replacement of Tifway 419 Bermuda grass with Chemgrass, later called Astroturf, in 1966. Until they were changed in 1985, the 390-foot power alleys were the longest in the major leagues except for those in Yankee Stadium. In 1987 a $60 million renovation was begun with the pouring of a concrete floor to replace the original dirt floor. Additional improvements will include installation of two separate turfs for baseball and football, both of which can be stored in pits in center field and rolled onto the field on a cushion of air. The scoreboard, with its explosive graphics, will also be replaced.

Indoor baseball provided National League umpires with a whole new set of interesting ground rule possibilities. In Houston, a ball that hits a speaker or the roof in fair territory is playable; it is judged fair or foul according to where it hits the ground or is touched by a fielder. The batter is out if a fielder catches the ball. Any ball that hits a speaker or the roof in foul territory is a foul ball and the ball is dead. The potential for confusion is an umpire's nightmare.

Although the *idea* of indoor baseball probably will always seem novel, the game itself has flourished under the dome in Texas and elsewhere. In its relatively brief history, the Astrodome has provided some of baseball's most exciting, memorable and historic moments.

On September 13, 1965, Willie Mays hit the 500th home run of his career, becoming the second National Leaguer to reach that plateau. Three seasons later, on July 9, 1968, Mays scored the only run as the National League shut out the American League 1–0 in baseball's first indoor All-Star Game. Of the eight division and league championship playoff games held in the Astrodome in 1980, 1981 and 1986, five have gone into extra innings, including the Mets' 16-inning, pennant-clincher over the Astros in 1986.

Pitcher Nolan Ryan has flourished in the Dome. In 1981 Ryan pitched his major league record fifth no-hitter, defeating the Dodgers, 5–0. Four years later Ryan became the first pitcher in history to strike out 4,000 batters. But the most memorable moment for Houston fans came on September 25, 1986, when Mike Scott clinched the NL West championship for Houston with a 2–0 no-hitter against the Giants.

The Astrodome

Kirby Drive
Houston, Texas

Built 1965

Houston Astros, NL
  1965–present

Seating Capacity 45,000
(expansion to 55,000
  September 1989)

Style
Multipurpose, symmetrical
  dome with artificial turf

Height of outfield fence
10 feet

Apex of dome 208 feet

Dugouts
Home, 1st base
Visitors, 3rd base

Bullpens
Home, right field foul line
Visitors, left field foul line

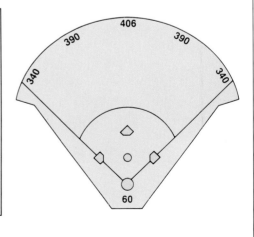

Pennant Race Parity

Equal opportunity swept through baseball in the 1960s like an April breeze on opening day. Teams rushed in to fill the void left by the collapsing New York Yankees, and cities new to the major leagues enthusiastically boosted surprise contenders. Seven of the decade's 20 pennant-winners were teams new to their cities; an eighth was an expansion team—until that year, a *bad* expansion team.

The Washington Senators had won their last pennant in 1933, and the team that packed up and moved to Minnesota in 1961 didn't look like much. But the Minnesota Twins had a great slugger in Harmon Killebrew, a superb pitcher in Camilo Pascual, and a host of promising youngsters—southpaw pitcher Jim Kaat, shortstop Zoilo Versalles, and power hitters Bob Allison and Don Mincher.

The Twins crowded the Yankees in 1962. In 1964 they brought up young Tony Oliva, who walked away with Rookie of the Year honors and proceeded to lead the American League in batting his first two seasons. Minnesota's pitching jelled as Mudcat Grant and Jim Perry became solid winners. When the Yankees sank in 1965, the Twins beat out the Chicago White Sox and Baltimore Orioles for the pennant. In 1969, the first season of divisional play, the Twins won the American League West—Killebrew hit 49 homers and drove in 140 runs—but lost in the American League Championship Series to Baltimore, another relative newcomer.

The Orioles carried a heavy burden. They had been the St. Louis Browns, a team so dreadful that it won only one pennant in a half-century of

Minnesota's Tony Oliva (opposite) was among the best of the Hispanic players of the 1960s. The 1965 Twins won the pennant with help from Cuba—the birthplace of Oliva, shortstop Zoilo Versalles, and pitcher Camilo Pascual.

existence, that in the talent-short wartime year of 1944. But in Baltimore, the team edged its way up. An alert scout signed a young third baseman from Arkansas named Brooks Robinson. Manager and general manager Paul Richards, who brought the Orioles along with determination and consistency, told him, "Look, we got no talent! And if you got something on the ball, kid, you're going to be here in a hurry and you're going to get a chance to play." Robinson played his first big-league game in 1955, at the age of 18, and by 1960 he was hitting with power and performing defensive heroics. "He is the greatest third baseman of all time, and that includes Pie Traynor," said Bill Veeck, who had been a baseball executive since Traynor's era. Richards also signed a big, jovial first baseman named Boog Powell who excited Oriole fans with his home run punch.

Baltimore was blessed with a wise front office. Lee MacPhail, whose mercurial father, Larry, brought night baseball to the major leagues, ran the team from 1958 until 1965, when Frank Cashen and Harry Dalton took over. All three emphasized the development of young players, particularly young pitchers like Wally Bunker, who won 19 games at age 19. Milt Pappas, Dave McNally and Steve Barber were steady winners, and a tall, handsome and tanned pitcher named Jim Palmer won 15 games in 1966; he was 20.

The Orioles won the pennant that season, whereupon Palmer suffered a sore arm that took him out of action for most of two seasons. He could have been drafted by either of the new expansion teams after the 1968 season, but neither took a chance on the fragile Palmer. They should have; his arm got better, and Palmer went 16–4 as the Orioles won another pennant in 1969. He blossomed into a steady 20-game winner thereafter.

New franchises and new ownership were the keystones of major league

Jim Palmer kicked off his remarkable career in 1965, and went on to earn three Cy Young awards. He compiled eight seasons as a 20-game winner, an 8–3 record in postseason play and one no-hitter. But perhaps the Oriole right-hander's most astounding statistic is that in almost 4,000 innings pitched he never gave up a grand-slam home run.

baseball's dramatic new age, but perhaps more important, the majors abandoned unbridled competition in the signing and development of young talent. They agreed on a uniform method of support for their farm systems, and on an organized draft of amateur talent, with the last-place teams getting first pick. Teams began pooling scouts, or sharing scouting reports, and the expansion draft contributed to competitive parity by stripping the better teams of bench strength.

Minor league teams used to be largely self-supporting, so ambitious, well-organized clubs like the Yankees, Cardinals and Dodgers could afford to build extensive farm systems and hire lots of scouts to find young players. The minors peaked in 1949. Nearly 9,000 players in 59 minor leagues scattered over 464 cities were competing for a shot at the majors, which at the time employed only 400 players.

Minor league pay and playing conditions were awful. The booming postwar economy lured many young men into more promising occupations, including such growing professional sports as football and basketball. At the same time, television brought major league sports and other entertainment into small towns that had nurtured their minor league teams for decades.

So players and fans alike began deserting the minor leagues. The teams lost money. Needing the minors to develop young talent, the major leagues began an organized system of subsidies in 1956. Nevertheless, the number of minor leagues dwindled to 22 by 1960. Wealthy teams like the Yankees and Dodgers supported solid farm systems and scouting staffs, but poorer teams could not.

The Yankees and Dodgers, not coincidentally, kept winning pennants. "It's good to see some good, young players coming into the league," said

In the 1967 World Series, the pitching of St. Louis' Bob Gibson and Nelson Briles gave Cardinal fans reason to stand up and cheer. Fans had to move quickly, as the average length of each of the three games played in St. Louis was a brisk two hours and 13 minutes.

Cleveland manager Jimmy Dykes, "but why do they always have to be wearing that Yankee uniform?" Dykes had suffered more than his share of talent shortages, managing five American League teams for a total of 20 seasons without ever winning a pennant.

In 1962, major league teams agreed to support at least five farm teams each. The minor leagues were reorganized and streamlined. Payments and subsidy formulas were standardized. The changes went a long way toward evening out farm systems, so weaker big-league clubs could hope to develop as many good, young players as their wealthier competitors.

But they did not go far enough for the club owners. Owners wanted parity, and they also wanted to reduce the costs of player development. Wealthier teams were bidding up bonuses paid to the most promising college and high school baseball stars. In 1964 the Los Angeles Angels paid $200,000 to sign Rick Reichardt, fresh out of the University of Wisconsin.

To restrain bonuses, the majors in 1965 started an annual draft of amateur players modeled after those used by professional football and basketball. A team could no longer go out and sign a prospect; it had to wait its turn in the draft. The incentive to scout youngsters was reduced; after all, why pay a lot of scouts when the players they recommend are likely to be drafted by your competitors?

The Yankee farm system had started to decline well before 1965, but the amateur draft coincided with the Yankees' fall into the second division—and helped keep the Yankees from building another dynasty. Ford Frick, then the commissioner of baseball, made no bones about it: baseball wanted no more dynasties.

Frick got his wish. The 1960s set the major leagues on a course that led

Baltimore shortstop Mark Belanger slid in past Minnesota catcher Earl Battey in this 1965 game, but it was the Twins who took the league lead in July and never looked back. One year later the Orioles had Frank Robinson, and not only dusted their AL competition but swept the Dodgers in the World Series.

When 21-year-old outfielder Reggie Jackson joined the Kansas City Athletics in 1967, he was reunited with Arizona State University teammates Sal Bando and Rick Monday. The trio moved with the A's to Oakland in 1968, where Jackson's 29 home runs helped the team jump from tenth to sixth place.

to increasingly close and unpredictable pennant races, with championships passing from one city to another. To be sure, well-run teams like the Orioles and Dodgers continued to win more than their share of pennants. But by the late 1960s, the Oakland A's had young Reggie Jackson, Sal Bando, Bert Campaneris, Catfish Hunter and Blue Moon Odom; that team won three straight world championships in the early 1970s. Cincinnati was installing key parts of the Big Red Machine—Johnny Bench, Pete Rose, Tony Perez. But these were mini-dynasties, teams strong enough to win or contend for several years—not decades.

The National League had never lacked for fierce, competitive races. The NL had a new winner every year from 1958 through 1962—five seasons, five different champions—and again from 1968 through 1971. The Pittsburgh Pirates, who hadn't won a pennant since 1927, came through in 1960 behind the hitting of young Roberto Clemente and former college basketball star Dick Groat, the National League MVP. Bill Mazeroski was one of baseball's best at second base, and reliever Roy Face, who had an astounding record of 18–1 the season before, won ten games and saved 24.

The Pirates collapsed to sixth place in 1961—remember, this is the National League—and the Cincinnati Reds won their first pennant since 1940. Frank Robinson hit 37 homers, drove in 124 runs and batted .323; centerfielder Vada Pinson hit .343.

I n 1962 the Dodgers and Giants reenacted their old New York head-to-head rivalry on the West Coast. The Giants had the muscle—49 homers by Willie Mays, 35 by Orlando Cepeda, 20 by a young part-timer named Willie McCovey, and 25 by Felipe Alou, whose teammate and little brother,

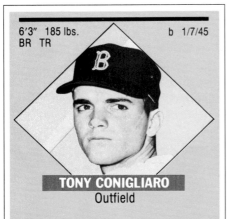

6'3" 185 lbs. b 1/7/45
BR TR

TONY CONIGLIARO
Outfield

"Tony C" was a natural in a Boston Red Sox uniform. He was handsome and local, with a home run swing tailor-made for Fenway Park. He was the right-handed power hitter Red Sox fans had been longing to cheer. Then, in the thick of the 1967 pennant race, Conigliaro was struck in the face by a Jack Hamilton fastball. The pitch crushed Conigliaro's left eye, disabling him for the remainder of the season and all of 1968, ultimately ending his career.

Conigliaro's talent and potential are evident in his numbers. He broke into the majors in 1964 and set a major league record for home runs by a teenager, hitting 24 for the Red Sox at age 19. In 1965 his 32 home runs made him the youngest player ever to lead the American League in that category. During his first four seasons he averaged .276 with 26 homers, 74 RBI, and a .510 slugging percentage. In 1970, with his younger brother Billy in his first full season with Boston, Conigliaro set career marks with 36 homers and 116 RBI. That season, at age 25, he became the youngest ballplayer ever to be named Comeback Player of the Year.

But Conigliaro's vision problems were chronic. Traded to California following the 1970 season, he retired after only 74 games with the Angels in 1971, including one game in which he struck out five times. Four years later, a final comeback with Boston lasted only 21 games.

The 1962 Giants had a lot to smile about, thanks in large part to Willie Mays' hitting and Juan Marichal's pitching. Marichal (above, right) went 18–11 and Mays (above, left) hit a league-leading 49 home runs as San Francisco won the NL pennant.

Matty, batted .292. Juan Marichal, a young pitcher, joined veterans Jack Sanford, Billy O'Dell and Billy Pierce to form a strong pitching rotation, and old junk-baller Stu Miller won five and saved 19 in relief.

San Francisco had quite a team, but it couldn't keep up with the Dodgers. Shortstop Maury Wills stole 104 bases to break Ty Cobb's record of 96, set in 1915. Tommy Davis, only 23, led both leagues in batting with .346 and RBI with 153. "Every time Tommy Davis came up with a man on second, he drove him in with a single," said Sandy Koufax. "When he came up with a man on first, he drove him in with a double."

Koufax won 14 games by mid-season but then was sidelined by a circulatory ailment that numbed a finger. Don Drysdale came through with the best season of his career, 25–9; relievers Ron Perranoski and Larry Sherry combined for 13 wins and 31 saves. The Dodgers had first place to themselves from July 8 until September 30. In mid-September they led the Giants by four games with only 13 to play. The Giants, far from heroic, won only seven of their last 13.

But one of them was on the final day of the season—September 30—on a homer by Mays. The Dodgers dropped ten of their final 13, and the race ended in a tie. A two-of-three playoff was set, and Pierce shut out the Dodgers in the opener while Mays hit two homers. The Dodgers trailed 5–0 in the second game but exploded for seven runs in the sixth inning. Duke Snider, an old Brooklyn hero, started the rally with a pinch-hit double. The Giants tied it, but Wills dashed home on a short fly ball to win for Los Angeles in the ninth.

Snider started two Dodger rallies in the decisive third game, and Wills widened the Dodger lead to two runs in the seventh by singling, stealing

Dodger shortstop Maury Wills avoided Minnesota's Tony Oliva (6) to complete a double play as Dick Tracewski looked on in Game 3 of the 1965 World Series. The Twins beat Dodger aces Sandy Koufax and Don Drysdale in the first two games, but Claude Osteen threw a shutout in Game 3, and the Dodgers won the Series in seven games.

Cincinnati's Johnny Bench was perhaps the most complete catcher of all time. In 1968—his rookie season—Bench led all National League catchers in putouts and assists. Two years later he led the league in home runs and RBI.

second and third, and scoring on a wild throw. Los Angeles took a 4–2 lead into the bottom of the ninth. Matty Alou singled. McCovey and Felipe Alou walked. Mays singled off the bare hand of pitcher Ed Roebuck. Cepeda tied the score with a sacrifice fly off reliever Stan Williams. Ed Bailey drew an intentional walk. Jim Davenport came up with a chance to repeat Bobby Thomson's heroic Giant homer of 1951. Davenport walked, and the pennant-winning run trotted home.

This marked the fourth time the National League race had wound up in a tie, forcing a playoff. The Dodgers had played in all four, and lost three of them. The team's late-season collapse in 1962 was the worst in history. But the Dodgers came back to win in 1963, repelling a late-season drive by the Cardinals, and in 1964 the dubious honor for worst collapse passed to the Philadelphia Phillies.

Through most of that season Philadelphia manager Gene Mauch appeared to have a sure winner. Jim Bunning and Chris Short were among the league's best pitchers. Rookie third baseman Dick Allen hit 29 homers and batted .318, but he outraged management with his egotistical and independent behavior. With 12 games to play, the Phils led the Cardinals and Reds by 6½ games.

Then the Phils lost three straight to the Reds, four to the Milwaukee Braves, and three to the Cardinals. In their part of the debacle, the Braves displayed classic form as spoilers. They were led by catcher Joe Torre, who hit .579 with 11 hits, including pairs of triples and homers, and seven RBI. Philadelphia entered those dark four days 3½ games up and left them one-half game in the hole. The Reds won nine in a row, the Cards eight. The Reds took the lead on September 27 by sweeping two from the Mets behind

There was too much pennant-race parity in the 1960s to suit Chicago Cubs' slugger Ernie Banks. In 19 years with the Cubs Banks never played on a pennant-winner, despite 512 career home runs, two MVP awards and a berth in the Hall of Fame.

Jim Bunning was a consistent winner for Detroit from 1957 to 1963, but he got even better after being traded to the Phillies in 1964. He averaged 19 wins and had a 2.48 ERA from 1964 to 1968, including a perfect game in 1964 against the Mets.

pitchers Jim O'Toole and Joey Jay. The Cardinals edged ahead on the pitching of Bob Gibson, Ray Sadecki and veteran Curt Simmons, who had starred for the Phils when they last won a pennant in 1950.

With one game to go, the Cardinals and Reds were tied, with Philadelphia one game back. If the Phillies beat the Reds and the Cardinals lost to the Mets, the three teams would wind up tied. The Phillies finally won a big one, beating the Reds 10–0 behind Bunning's pitching and Allen's hitting. But the Cardinals pasted the poor Mets 11–5 and won their first pennant since 1946.

In his autobiography, Koufax wrote, "The 1965 season came to an end for us on May 1 in the fourth inning of a Saturday night game against San Francisco, when Tommy Davis broke his ankle." To replace their best hitter, the Dodgers brought up Lou Johnson, 30 years old and the epitome of a journeyman—18 clubs in 13 years, mostly in the minor leagues. Johnson hit, hustled, got hit by pitches, and won games. Don Drysdale cracked two ribs but kept pitching. Jim Gilliam, a coach, was reborn as a player. Wills stole 94 bases and sparked the team. Koufax, Drysdale, Claude Osteen and Ron Perranoski pitched superbly.

But the Dodgers had no punch. Big Frank Howard was traded to Washington for Osteen. No Dodger hit more than 12 homers. For the Giants, Willie Mays hit 17 in August alone. He wound up with 52; McCovey hit 39.

The race may have turned in San Francisco on August 22 in a game pitting the two pitching aces, Koufax and Marichal. In the Dodger first, Wills beat out a bunt and Ron Fairly doubled him home. Marichal, following his usual custom, knocked Wills and Fairly down next time up. So Koufax

Giant pitcher Juan Marichal (27) sparked one of baseball's ugliest incidents when he hit Dodger catcher Johnny Roseboro (center) on the head with his bat, August 22, 1965. Marichal and Dodger Sandy Koufax (32) had been trading brushback pitches before the incident, and as a result Marichal was suspended for nine days and given a $1,750 fine—then the stiffest in NL history.

knocked down Mays. "If I'm going to throw at somebody, I'm going to throw at their best," he later wrote.

Marichal led off the Giant third. He took two pitches, then whacked Johnny Roseboro, the Dodger catcher, on the head with his bat. The dugouts emptied, Roseboro left the game with his head a bloody mess, and Mays hit a three-run homer to win the game.

In September, the Giants won 14 games in a row, 17 of 18. They led the Dodgers by four games with 12 to play. But the Dodgers then won 13 in a row, 15 of their final 16, to win by two games. The beaning had cost Marichal a nine-day suspension, and may have cost the Giants a pennant.

Knockdowns continued. On opening day 1966 Bill Faul of the Cubs knocked Mays down. Baseball courtesy required Marichal, the Giant pitcher, to knock down Ernie Banks, the Cubs' slugger, but he didn't do it. In the dugout, Mays asked him why.

Marichal: "Banks is a nice guy."

Mays: "Well, so am I!"

Drysdale had an off year in 1966, and Wills was slowed by injuries, but the Dodgers kept in the race behind the pitching of Koufax, Osteen, rookie Don Sutton, and reliever Phil (The Vulture) Regan, a Detroit castoff who won 14 games and saved 21 more with a 1.62 ERA. Regan credited his slider, which some batters called a spitball. The Vietnam War was hot, and Regan, taking off on a jingoistic song of the day, wrote a Dodger fight song called "The Ballad of the Blue Berets."

Marichal and Gaylord Perry each won more than 20 games for the 1966 Giants; Mays, McCovey, Jim Ray Hart and Tom Haller pounded homers.

Walt "No-Neck" Williams' first year with the Chicago White Sox—1967—was a strange one. Williams' .240 average was one point away from being the team's best, and despite a team ERA of 2.45 and a record for least runs allowed in a 162-game season, the White Sox finished fourth.

Mays broke Mel Ott's National League home run record by hitting his 512th on May 4, and wound up the season with 542, second only to Ruth's 714 on the all-time list. But Mays was 35, and his best years were behind him. Playing in Atlanta for the first time, Hank Aaron led the league with 44 homers. He was three years younger than Mays, and more durable.

The Pirates slugged their way into the 1966 race. Matty Alou, now in Pittsburgh, led the league at .342. Roberto Clemente and Willie Stargell drove in more than 100 runs each, and Donn Clendenon drove in 98.

The Dodgers, however, had pitching—20 shutouts and a team ERA of 2.62, the league's lowest in 23 years. Baseball was becoming more and more a pitcher's game, and pitching was the game the Dodgers played best. They won 21 of their final 31 games and edged the Giants by $1^1/_2$ games, the Pirates by three. It was the third and final Dodger pennant of the decade. The Giants, after winning in 1962, became the decade's bridesmaid, finishing second in 1965, 1966, 1967, 1968 and 1969.

The National League itself had been something of a bridesmaid. Through 1959, the American League had won 35 World Series to 21 for the National League and 16 All-Star games to 11 for the National League. The American League seemed to come up with more than its share of the game's brightest stars—Ty Cobb, Tris Speaker, Walter Johnson, Babe Ruth, Lou Gehrig, Lefty Grove, Ted Williams, Joe DiMaggio, Bob Feller, Mickey Mantle.

But much of the AL's edge resulted from the consistently superior play of the Yankees, who spent a lot of Octobers playing World Series. National League teams finally began to shake the dynasty; the Dodgers swept New

Cincinnati's Frank Robinson slides in smothered—by Yankee catcher Elston Howard—but safe in Game 2 of the 1961 World Series. Joey Jay threw a four-hitter to even the Series for the Reds, but the Yankees took the Series in five games.

York four straight in the 1963 Series, and the Cardinals edged the Yanks four games to three in 1964. National League teams won six of ten World Series in the 1960s, and 11 of 12 All-Star games. (From 1959 through 1962, two All-Star games were played each year. One game in 1961 wound up a tie when rain curtailed play.)

Although the American League was not short on outstanding players, more of the most glittering names of the decade—Aaron, Mays, Clemente, Koufax, Drysdale, Gibson—played in the NL. Contributing to the National League's rise was its corner on black and Hispanic stars. In 1963, Elston Howard of the Yankees became the first black named Most Valuable Player of the American League. Seven black players—Jackie Robinson, Roy Campanella, Mays, Aaron, Ernie Banks, Frank Robinson and Maury Wills—already had been named National League MVP.

Neither league, and no team, could really claim superior status for more than a few years at a time. Fans argued, and still do, as to which player was better, which team stronger, and which league superior. The downtrodden could no longer be counted on to stay down, as the expansion New York Mets proved with their surprising—*amazin'*!—world championship in 1969. Parity had arrived in major league baseball. ⚫

5'11" 187 lbs.
BR TR
b 3/8/42

DICK ALLEN
First Base

In a career that lasted 15 years, Richard Anthony Allen symbolized the emerging independence of major league players of the 1960s. He broke in as Richie and retired as Dick, played six different positions on five ballclubs, and always spoke his mind. "Baseball," he once said, "is a form of slavery. Once you step out of bounds they'll do everything possible to destroy your soul."

With a career batting average of .292, a slugging average of .534, and 351 homers, Dick Allen was most feared for his bat. The 1964 NL Rookie of the Year with Philadelphia, Allen hit .318 with 29 homers and 91 RBI. Through 1969 with the Phils, Allen hit .300, averaging 30 homers and 90 RBI a season. But for management, Allen's personality fell short of those numbers.

In a move that ultimately challenged baseball's reserve clause, Allen was traded to St. Louis in October 1969. Despite his 34 homers and 101 RBI in 1970, the Cardinals traded Allen to Los Angeles. Again he lasted only one year.

In 1972 he joined longtime friend Chuck Tanner, manager of the Chicago White Sox, and was named MVP, hitting .308, with a league-leading 37 homers, 113 RBI and a .603 slugging average.

After three seasons with the Sox, Allen returned to the Phils in 1975. In 1976 he contributed 15 homers as the Phils won the NL East Division.

The Impossible Dream

Never has a pennant race been closer than the American League's of 1967, and never has there been a more improbable winner or a more heroic star. On August 22 the White Sox led the Red Sox by one percentage point, and the Twins and Tigers by a game. On September 6 all four teams were tied for the lead, and on September 18 the Red Sox, Twins and Tigers were tied, with the White Sox one-half game back.

When the season opened, Minnesota and Detroit were expected to contend; Chicago and Boston were dark horses at best. Both had tough, feisty managers. "We're better from the neck up than any other team in contention," said White Sox manager Eddie Stanky, who got so mad after a loss in Minnesota that he ordered a guard to bar all visitors from the clubhouse. Among those sternly sent on their way was Vice President Hubert Humphrey.

The Red Sox had finished ninth the year before, only one-half game out of last place. They were known for their casual, country club acceptance of losing, like a golfer whose favorite hole is the 19th. Dick Williams, Boston's rookie manager, knew the team well, having played on it in 1963 and 1964. Williams clamped down, imposing a curfew and briefly benching slugger George Scott and third baseman Joe Foy for being too fat.

Boston pitching was still thin. Right-hander Jim Lonborg won 22 games but also led the league in hit batsmen with 19. The team leaned on Carl Yastrzemski, who was having his finest season, and young Tony Conigliaro, a handsome slugger and singer who belted 104 homers before his 23rd birthday.

Conigliaro was notorious for his inability to get out of the way of inside pitches, and on August 18 a fastball caught him just beside the left eye, ending his season—he already had 20 homers—and threatening his career. The Red Sox responded by winning 12 of their next 15 games, and took advantage of a coincidental burst of foolishness by Charlie Finley, owner of the last-place Kansas City A's.

Overreacting to player hijinks during an airplane trip, Finley started a disciplinary feud with his team. He fired manager Al Dark and slugger Ken Harrelson, who had called Finley "a menace to baseball." A fired ballplayer is a free agent, and the Red Sox embraced Harrelson with a $75,000 bonus, sizeable for that era. "The first thing I'm going to do is send Charlie Finley some money I owe him, a thank-you note and a dozen roses," said Harrelson, who homered in his first at-bat with the Sox.

Boston also picked up Elston Howard, the veteran Yankee catcher, and Gary Bell, a strong starting pitcher from Cleveland. *Man of La Mancha* was playing on Broadway, and Red Sox fans adopted its hit song, "The Impossible Dream"—sung, fittingly enough, by an actor playing Don Quixote, who tilted at windmills the way the Red Sox tilted at pennants. Boston briefly took the lead in late August; not for 18 years had the team been on top so late in the season.

The testy Stanky said Yastrzemski was an all-star "only from the neck down." In a doubleheader against the White Sox, Yaz went 6 for 9, tipping his cap to Stanky as he passed the Chicago dugout on a home run trot. Stanky aggravated everybody, the more so because his superb pitchers—Joe Horlen, Gary Peters, Bob Locker, Tommy John (then 24) and Hoyt Wilhelm (then 43)—kept the White Sox in the race although the team scored fewer runs than any contender. A saying had it that "losing to the White Sox is like drowning in three inches of water."

The summer of '67 continued tense and tight. The Tigers lost their ballpark in late July when it

One of the Red Sox brightest stars—and best hopes for a pennant in 1967—went out on August 18 when Tony Conigliaro (left, center) couldn't get out of the way of a Jack Hamilton fastball. The 1967 pennant hopes of the Chicago White Sox rested on pitchers like Tommy John (below), who, at age 24, tied teammate Joe Horlen for the league lead in shutouts with six.

was shut down by inner city riots and surrounded by National Guardsmen—including Tiger pitching ace Mickey Lolich—called out to subdue the disorder. In late August, the Twins' Dean Chance pitched two no-hitters in 19 days, the first a five-inning job against Boston. Horlen no-hit the Tigers in September. Earl Wilson, a Detroit right-hander known for his sartorial elegance, homered to win his 20th game of the season.

With a week to go, the White Sox faced the delicious prospect of five games against lowly Kansas City and Washington. They lost all five. Now there were only three contenders, and the Twins had the edge. They came to Boston for the final weekend of the season, leading the Red Sox and Tigers by one game. The Twins and Red Sox were scheduled for single games on Saturday and Sunday. The Tigers faced back-to-back doubleheaders, at home, against California.

The Tigers won their opener and led in the nightcap, but lost it. The Twins had to win just one, and jumped ahead Saturday behind the strong pitching of tall Jim Kaat. Kaat hurt his elbow, but re-

Boston's Carl Yastrzemski (8) accepts congratulations from teammates Jose Tartabull (left) and George Scott (right) after his three-run homer in the seventh inning of Game 2 of the 1967 World Series. Yaz homered three times and hit .400 in the Series on the heels of his Triple Crown season, but the Red Sox lost in seven.

liever Jim Perry clung to a one-run lead until the fifth, when a bad-hop ground ball struck the Twins' superb rookie Rod Carew in the face and Boston scored twice. Minnesota tied it, but George Scott homered for the Red Sox, and Yastrzemski put it away with a three-run blast. Harmon Killebrew homered for Minnesota in the ninth, tying Yaz for the league lead at 44, but the game went to Boston, 6–4. When he homered, Yaz said, "I knew the dream was no longer impossible."

It was Chance against Lonborg Sunday. The Twins scored in the first on a double by Tony Oliva and an error by Scott, and in the third on a single by Killebrew and an error by Yastrzemski. In the seventh, Yaz singled with the bases loaded to tie the score, and the Red Sox scored three more on Minnesota fielding lapses. The Twins threatened in the eighth, but Yastrzemski cut down Bob Allison at second base with a superb throw. Boston won, 5–3.

In the two games, Yastrzemski hit five singles, a double and a home run; he was retired once. In the season's final two weeks, he was 23 for 44 with five homers and 16 runs batted in. He won the Triple Crown, leading the league with 121 RBI and a .326 average, and tying Killebrew for the home

run title with 44.

The Red Sox victory ended with the Tigers and Angels still playing in Detroit. Detroit won the opener and now needed a sweep to tie Boston and force a playoff, but the Angels knocked out Denny McLain in the nightcap and won. Boston—and New England—had their champions for the first time since 1946. It was the first time in history a team had climbed from next-to-last to a pennant in just one year.

In the World Series, the St. Louis Cardinals were too much for Boston. Yastrzemski hit .400 with three home runs, while Boston pitchers stifled Orlando Cepeda, who managed only three hits in 29 at-bats. But the Cards' Roger Maris batted .385, and Lou Brock hit .414 and stole a record seven bases. Down three games to one, the Red Sox fought back and extended the Series to a seventh game. Gibson and Lonborg had won two games each and squared off in the finale, but only Gibson survived. St. Louis won, 7–2. It marked the sixth time the Cardinals had played in a seven-game World Series, and the sixth they won. The Boston dream had run its course.

Jim Lonborg's dream season turned into a nightmare in Game 7 of the World Series against St. Louis. His winning ways—22 regular-season wins and two more in the Series—ended when he had to come back for Game 7 on two days' rest and gave up two homers in a 7–2 loss.

Carl Yastrzemski left a part of himself in Fenway Park's left field, but then he took something with him, too. When left field was resodded after the 1967 season, Yastrzemski used the old turf for the lawn of his suburban Boston home.

Sandy Koufax

For five consecutive seasons, from 1962 through 1966, Sandy Koufax pitched as well as any pitcher in baseball history. His pitching won three pennants for the Los Angeles Dodgers, and only an injury to the index finger of his pitching hand cost the Dodgers a fourth. He pitched the team to two world championships. No other player of the decade had such an overwhelming effect on the outcome of pennant-race and World Series action.

Koufax's statistics and awards are impressive enough, but more significant was his ability to win important games, tough games, games in which the Dodgers gave him very few runs to work with. His five years of excellence began in 1962, the year the Dodgers moved into Dodger Stadium. It was—and is—a pitcher's ballpark, and it surely helped Koufax.

But it helped opposing pitchers, too. The slugging Dodgers of Ebbets Field became the pitch-and-run Dodgers of Chavez Ravine. In his *Historical Baseball Abstract,* Bill James surveyed two of Koufax's big seasons, 1963 and 1964. In games when the Dodgers scored only one, two or three runs for him, Koufax was 18–4. James called it "an unbelievable accomplishment." That includes four games in which the Dodgers scored just one run—Koufax won three of them. The Dodgers scored so few runs that after one of Koufax's no-hitters, his sidekick, Don Drysdale, asked, "Who won?"

When Koufax retired after the 1966 season, a victim of injury to his arthritic pitching elbow, the Dodgers dropped from first place to eighth. They stayed in the second division for three years. Although a starting pitcher sits

Even in a city of stars, Koufax (opposite) shone: "I became a good pitcher when I stopped trying to make them miss the ball and started trying to make them hit it."

After Koufax's 18 wins in 1961, the Dodgers set an all-time attendance mark the following season, drawing 2,755,184 fans to Dodger Stadium.

The arthritic elbow that cut short Koufax's brilliant career became puffy and painful after each game he pitched. Even combing his hair became "a very gritty" experience.

out three games of every four, Koufax was clearly the difference between a winning team—a champion—and a losing one.

Much was made of Koufax's arthritis and the pain he suffered when pitching, but in fact he was a hardy, durable pitcher. He soaked his ailing left elbow in ice water for one-half hour after each start, yet he led the National League in complete games and innings pitched in 1965 and 1966, his final two seasons. When he retired at age 30, after a 27–9 season and an ERA of 1.73, it was not because of the pain but the prognosis: if he kept pitching, his arm would be crippled.

Koufax won big games, and he won them on little rest. Three days after pitching a two-hit shutout, he clinched the 1965 pennant for Los Angeles by beating the Milwaukee Braves 3–1 on the second-to-last day of the season.

He declined the starting assignment in the World Series opener against the Minnesota Twins because it fell on Yom Kippur; Koufax is Jewish. Drysdale got shelled, and a wag suggested that the Dodgers would have been better off if Drysdale had been Jewish, too. The Twins beat Koufax in the second game, but Claude Osteen, the Dodgers' third starter, pitched a shutout in Game 3.

Drysdale then beat the Twins 7–2, and Koufax shut out Minnesota 7–0 in the fifth game. Jim Grant, pitching on two days' rest, beat the Dodgers 5–1 to tie the Series. Koufax came back to pitch the seventh game on two days' rest and shut out the Twins 2–0—two straight shutouts against a lineup with Tony Oliva, Harmon Killebrew and Don Mincher.

In 1966 the Dodgers needed to win the season's finale to clinch the pennant. Los Angeles Manager Walter Alston called on Koufax, again on two days' rest; again he won, beating the Philadelphia Phillies, 6–3. He lost his

only start of the 1966 World Series, and the Dodgers fell to Baltimore in four straight games.

Koufax was modest, but he was never awed. He faced Whitey Ford in the opening game of the 1963 World Series in Yankee Stadium. Ford had won more World Series games than any other pitcher in history, and was fresh from pitching 33 consecutive scoreless innings—a record—in the World Series of 1960, 1961 and 1962. The Yankees had a stronger lineup, and the Dodgers had a dreadful record in World Series competition against the Yankees.

Koufax quickly burst the Yankee bubble, striking out the first five batters he faced: Tony Kubek, Bobby Richardson, Tom Tresh, Mickey Mantle and Roger Maris. He went on to strike out 15, then a record, while beating the Yankees, 5–2. He beat Ford and the Yankees again, 2–1, in the final game, as Los Angeles swept four straight.

Koufax was consistent. He led the league in earned run average five years in a row—a feat that has never been matched in either league. He led the league in winning percentage twice and in wins three times—the Dodgers' pennant years of 1963, 1965 and 1966. The same three years he won the Cy Young Award, which then was given to only one pitcher, not one in each league as it is today. He was named the Most Valuable Player of the 1963 and 1965 World Series. His career ERA was 2.76. In World Series play—eight games—it was 0.95.

Koufax pitched four no-hitters; only Nolan Ryan has pitched more. His final no-hitter was a perfect game in the September heat of the 1965 pennant race. The opposing pitcher, Bob Hendley of the Cubs, pitched a one-hitter, and the Dodgers scored the game's only run on a walk, a bunt, a stolen base,

Koufax and catcher Johnny Roseboro celebrated as the Dodgers' 2–1 win in Game 4 of the 1963 World Series against the Yankees completed one of the most awesome displays of pitching in postseason history. Koufax pitched two complete games, allowing just 12 hits and three walks while striking out 23. The Dodgers used just four pitchers in the Series, and gave up just four runs. Koufax and Roseboro were a battery from 1957 to 1966.

Five Great Seasons

From 1962 through 1966, Sandy Koufax was baseball's dominant pitcher. On the basis of these five years, Koufax was elected to the Hall of Fame in 1972, the youngest player ever to be so honored. (*Red denotes league leader.*)

	W	L	Pct.	ERA	IP	CG	
'62	14	7	.667	2.54	184.1	11	Out with finger injury from mid-July to end of season.
'63	25	5	.833	1.88	311	20	11 shutouts, including one that helped stop Cards' late-season challenge. Two World Series wins over NY. Cy Young Award, MVP, World Series MVP.
'64	19	5	.792	1.74	223	15	Led league with 7 shutouts.
'65	26	8	.765	2.04	335.2	27	Won pennant clincher 2nd-to-last day of season on 2 days' rest. Two World Series shutouts over Twins. Cy Young Award, World Series MVP. NL season record 382 strikeouts.
'66	27	9	.750	1.73	323	27	Won pennant clincher last day of season on 2 days' rest. Cy Young Award.

Koufax was just a promising rookie pitcher with the Brooklyn Dodgers in 1955, so he decided to make sure he had something to fall back on by enrolling at Columbia University in the off-season.

and a wild throw. Clinging to that 1-0 lead, Koufax struck out the side in the eighth and ninth innings. "He threw it right past us," said slugger Ernie Banks.

That 1–0 game was typical of the Dodger offense, yet Koufax never seemed to run out of patience. "We win because we stay in the game," he told newsmen during the 1966 race. "We get one or two runs behind, but never more than that. It's tough on a pitcher, waiting for our runs to come, but you learn to live with it. We have to keep it close so the other guys can win it."

Koufax overpowered hitters with his fastball. "No ball can get up to the plate that quick," claimed Ken Boyer, one of the era's best sluggers. He also threw a superb curve and change-up. He led the league in strikeouts four times, striking out 382 batters—a 20th century National League record—in 1965. Over his career he averaged more than one strikeout an inning.

He pitched with graceful, classic form, and his control was excellent. He struck out nearly three batters for every one he walked, and he rarely hit a batter, although he would brush one back when the occasion arose. In 1966 he pitched 323 innings without hitting a single batter. In contrast, his teammate Drysdale led the league in hit batsmen five times.

As a boy, Koufax considered himself more of a basketball player than a baseball player. He played first base on his high school baseball team, starred on the basketball team, and was recruited by the University of Cincinnati as a basketball player. But he pitched for the college baseball team and for sandlot teams in Brooklyn, where he grew up. He was signed by Al Campanis, then the Dodgers' head scout.

Koufax was wild and untutored, but he had what scouts look for in a pitcher—a helluva fastball. The Giants, Pirates and Braves also courted him.

Though he was wild early in his career, rarely has a pitcher combined power and control as well as Koufax did in his prime (opposite). He struck out three batters for every one he walked, and hit batters less frequently than any pitcher in history —averaging one every 128 innings.

Despite the youthful promise, Koufax was never much of a hitter—his lifetime average was .097. But the hitters who faced Koufax didn't fare much better, as his .209 lifetime pitching average (hits allowed divided by batters faced) and 9.28 strikeouts per nine innings are second only to Nolan Ryan's.

Koufax was represented by a good lawyer—his father. In 1954 they struck a deal with the Dodgers for a $14,000 bonus plus the major league minimum salary of $6,000.

Koufax needed minor league training, but he didn't get it. Because the major leagues had bound themselves with a foolish rule intended to discourage bonuses—and thus save money—any player who got a bonus of more than $4,000 had to stay with the major league club for at least two seasons.

So Sandy Koufax, 19-year-old "bonus baby," joined the Brooklyn Dodgers, where he sat and sat and sat. He pitched in 12 games in 1955 and 16 in 1956. A lesser team might have given him more work, but the Dodgers won pennants both years. Manager Walter Alston used ten pitchers in the 1955 World Series and eight in the 1956 Series, but Koufax sat.

He threw hard, but his wildness was legendary. One story has it that in spring training a coach would warm him up behind a building, where he couldn't be seen and wouldn't be embarrassed. Koufax got better, but he was used only as a spot starter through 1960—six years of second-class status, enough to make Koufax think of leaving baseball. He was caught in a classic Catch-22: too inexperienced to pitch, yet denied the experience that would qualify him.

Then Dodger catcher Norm Sherry casually told him, "Sandy, I think your troubles would be solved if you would just throw easier, throw more change-ups, just try to get the ball over."

It worked. Koufax finally cracked the Dodger rotation in 1961 and won 18 games. "I used to try to throw each pitch harder than the previous one," Koufax told *Sport* magazine. "There was no need for it. I found out that if I take it easy and throw naturally, the ball goes just as fast. I found that my

Thirty Years After: A New Brand of Southpaw

In the 1930s Lefty Gomez, Lefty Grove and Carl Hubbell set the standard by which left–handers of all time would be judged. Thirty years later a new generation of southpaws–Whitey Ford, Sandy Koufax and Warren Spahn—were equally exceptional.

The 1930s

	Best Season	20–Win Seasons
Gomez	26–5 ('34) 2.33 ERA	1931,'32, '34, '37
Grove	31–4 ('31) 2.06 ERA	1930,–'33, '35
Hubbell	23–12 ('33) 1.66 ERA	1933–'37

The 1960s

	Best Season	20–Win Seasons
Ford	25–4 ('61) 3.21 ERA	1961, '63
Koufax	25–5 ('63) 1.88 ERA	1963, '65, '66
Spahn	23–7 ('63) 2.60 ERA	1960, '61, '63

control improved and the strikeouts would take care of themselves." His strikeouts took care of a good many batters, too. In 1961 he struck out 269 batters, setting a National League record. He broke that record in 1963 and again in 1965 with 382, the best in the National League this century.

Now the Dodgers had two aces: Koufax, the southpaw, and Drysdale, the right-hander. Both were power pitchers; no team in baseball had a pair to match them.

In 1962 Koufax and Drysdale pitched the Dodgers into first place. Koufax was 14–5 when, in mid-July, a circulatory ailment caused the index finger of his pitching hand to go numb. Skin scaled off, and doctors—Koufax learned later—thought of amputation. He was out of action until late September. Without Koufax to fill the stopper's role, the Dodgers collapsed, fell into a tie with the San Francisco Giants on the final day of the season, and lost a best-of-three playoff for the pennant.

Koufax got a lot of help in 1963 from reliever Ron Perranoski, who won 16 games and saved 21 more. Drysdale won 23 games in 1965, and reliever Phil Regan had a big year in 1966, winning 14 games, saving 21, and posting a 1.62 ERA. Maury Wills was a great baserunner, a fine shortstop, and a team leader. Tommy and Willie Davis starred for those Dodger teams. John Roseboro, Jim Gilliam, Ron Fairly and Jim Lefebvre made strong contributions.

But the Dodgers rode to those pennants on Sandy Koufax's pitching. Rarely has one player achieved so much for both himself and his team. ◑

The Great Holdout

fter pitching the Los Angeles Dodgers to the pennant and world championship in 1965, Sandy Koufax and Don Drysdale asked for contracts that were considered outrageous on at least four fronts. They wanted to negotiate together rather than separately. They wanted the Dodgers to deal with their lawyer, J. William Hayes. They wanted three-year contracts. And the figure they proposed was $1 million, divided evenly between the two players and payable over the three seasons.

The Dodger front office was aghast, and so was most of the sporting press. Dodger owner Walter O'Malley said he had feared that the team's move to Los Angeles might bring about just such Hollywood foolishness. "I never have discussed a player contract with an agent and I like to think I never will," O'Malley said. Hayes, it was noted with horror, also represented an actor or two.

"At first," reported *Sports Illustrated,* "the K-D entry demanded three-year contracts, full ownership of California and Nevada and the Strategic Air Command, plus options on the Mississippi River and Philadelphia, all of which was well above the presidential guidelines."

As for a three-year contract, Dodger general manager Buzzy Bavasi said no Dodger would ever get signed for more than one year at a time. "You're both athletes," Bavasi recalled telling the two pitchers, "and what you're selling is your physical ability, and how can you guarantee your physical ability three years in advance?"

In 1966, the joint holdout tactics of Sandy Koufax (opposite, left) and Don Drysdale (opposite, right) terrorized the Dodgers' front office.

Koufax and Drysdale showed the Dodgers they meant business—show business—when they signed to play featured roles in Warning Shot, *to be directed by Buzz Kulik (above, center). In a bit of prescient casting, Drysdale was to play a TV commentator.*

Koufax and Drysdale were asking for big money. Salary figures weren't made public back then, but Willie Mays was believed to be baseball's highest-paid player, earning $105,000 annually. Inflation has more than tripled wages and prices since the mid 1960s; the $1 million that Koufax and Drysdale wanted would amount to about $3.25 million today. In modern dollars, they were requesting less than $550,000 each, per year. In 1988 the average annual big-league baseball salary was $447,291, and top stars were getting more than $2 million a year.

In 1965 Koufax and Drysdale won 49 games between them, plus three in the World Series. The Dodgers were known to be an immensely profitable operation. They were drawing about 2.5 million fans a year. Crowds swelled by several thousand whenever Koufax or Drysdale pitched.

O'Malley and Bavasi acknowledged that the Dodgers could not contend without the two pitchers. Still, they said, they could not meet such demands. Principle was at stake. How could baseball survive if players were represented by *agents*? If salaries reached such heights? If players were signed for two or three years at a time? Bavasi said that if he let Koufax and Drysdale negotiate together, next the whole Dodger infield would come in as a bargaining team. Babe Ruth and Lou Gehrig had once considered bargaining together, but Gehrig, the gentleman, had declined (and, critics noted, was underpaid throughout his career).

Principle aside, what the Dodgers had working for them was the reserve clause, a provision in the standard player's contract that prevented a player from switching teams. Koufax and Drysdale would eventually sign with the Dodgers, and both sides knew it; their only option was to leave baseball.

Still, it was a darn good holdout. Koufax and Drysdale sat out spring

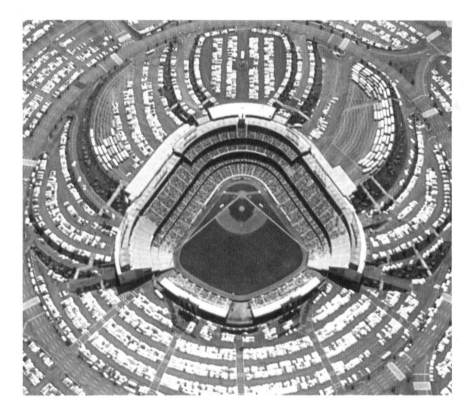

In 1965 the Dodgers drew 2,553,577 fans, then the third largest total in baseball history, to Dodger Stadium, and Koufax and Drysdale were their star attractions. The Dodgers have since drawn over 3 million fans eight times.

One on one, Dodger general manager Buzzy Bavasi was nearly unbeatable as a negotiator. But following the 1965 season, Koufax and Drysdale—who combined to win 49 games, more than half of the team's pennant-winning total of 97—double-teamed Bavasi and got more than anyone thought possible.

training. They played golf and told writers they had other careers in mind. They signed to star in a movie, to be called *Warning Shot*. Eventually, Bavasi sat down with Drysdale, who was dealing on behalf of both pitchers; the despised agent, Hayes, was barred.

According to Bavasi, the Dodgers signed Koufax for $125,000 and Drysdale for $110,000. That made them the highest-paid players in baseball; their raises—$40,000 for Koufax, $30,000 for Drysdale—were believed to be the biggest in baseball history. The contracts were for one year—Koufax's final season, as things turned out.

Holdouts were big news back then, but more important than the absence of two pitchers from spring training in 1966 was the presence of a quiet, well-groomed man whom players were considering as the first full-time director of the moribund Major League Baseball Players Association. His name was Marvin J. Miller, and he was touring the spring training camps to talk to the players and win their approval.

The Players Association had been around since 1953, mostly to bargain for better pension coverage. Bob Feller was its first president and, he said later, was fed lots of lunches but given little in the way of improved player benefits.

The players hired a lawyer, a step that outraged the owners; Commissioner Ford Frick refused to meet with the player representatives of each team unless they left their counsel behind. The players turned to a prominent fan, Judge Robert C. Cannon of Wisconsin, whose father had represented "Shoeless Joe" Jackson in a suit demanding back salary.

Cannon donated what time he could spare to the players—he was, after

DON
DRYSDALE

Right-Handed Pitcher
Brooklyn Dodgers 1956–1957
Los Angeles Dodgers 1958–1969
Hall of Fame 1984

GAMES	**518**
INNINGS	
Career	**3,432⅓**
Season High	**321⅓**
WINS	
Career	**209**
Season High	**25**
LOSSES	
Career	**166**
Season High	**17**
WINNING PERCENTAGE	
Career	**.557**
Season High	**.735**
ERA	
Career	**2.95**
Season Low	**2.15**
GAMES STARTED	
Career	**465**
Season High	**42**
COMPLETE GAMES	
Career	**167**
Season High	**21**
SHUTOUTS	
Career	**49**
Season High	**8**
STRIKEOUTS	
Career	**2,486**
Season High	**251**
WALKS	
Career	**855**
Season High	**93**
WORLD SERIES	**1956, 1959**
	1963, 1965, 1966
CY YOUNG AWARD	**1962**

SANDY KOUFAX

Left-Handed Pitcher
Brooklyn Dodgers 1955–1957
Los Angeles Dodgers 1958–1966
Hall of Fame 1971

GAMES	397
INNINGS	
Career	2,324⅓
Season High	335⅔
WINS	
Career	165
Season High	27
LOSSES	
Career	87
Season High	13
WINNING PERCENTAGE	
Career	.655
Season High	.833
ERA	
Career	2.76
Season Low	1.73
GAMES STARTED	
Career	314
Season High	41
COMPLETE GAMES	
Career	137
Season High	27
SHUTOUTS	
Career	40
Season High *(6th all time)*	11
STRIKEOUTS	
Career	2,396
Season High *(2nd all time)*	382
WALKS	
Career	817
Season High	105
WORLD SERIES	1959, 1963
	1965, 1966
CY YOUNG AWARD	1963
	1965, 1966
MOST VALUABLE PLAYER	1963
NO HITTERS	1962, 1963, 1964
	1965 **(perfect game)**

Big Money

The numbers look almost quaint today, but in the late 1960s baseball salaries seemed to be growing by leaps and bounds. With wonder, *Sports Illustrated* reported that the St. Louis Cardinal payroll for 1968 totaled $565,000. It was the highest in baseball, and when the Cardinals foundered in 1969 after winning back-to-back pennants, many observers said the players had grown soft from too much money. Remembering what inflation has done to wages and prices since 1968, here are those would-you-believe-it salaries for the Cardinal starters:

LOU BROCK, lf	$70,000
CURT FLOOD, cf	$72,500
ROGER MARIS, rf	$75,000
ORLANDO CEPEDA, 1b	$80,000
TIM McCARVER, c	$60,000
MIKE SHANNON, 3b	$40,000
JULIAN JAVIER, 2b	$45,000
DAL MAXVILL, ss	$37,500
BOB GIBSON, p	$85,000
RED SCHOENDIENST, mgr.	$42,000

all, a working judge. But he was loath to offend club owners, partly because he hoped they would hire him as commissioner when Ford Frick retired in 1965. Although owners were getting more money from television and from other innovations of the 1960s—expansion, the 162-game schedule, and the draft of amateur players, which reduced the costs of scouting and signing young prospects—players' salaries and pensions increased very little.

In 1965 the Players Association was down to $5,400 in its treasury. It had one file cabinet, no office, no employees. The players decided they needed a full-time director. Three players were selected to find the right person. One of the three was Robin Roberts, the great Philadelphia Phillies' pitcher who was then pitching for Baltimore and nearing the end of his career.

The committee got some friendly advice from Richard Nixon, a lawyer and fan with past—and future—familiarity in Washington. Seeking recommendations for a full-time director, Roberts phoned George Taylor, a University of Pennsylvania business professor known for his success in settling labor disputes. Taylor recommended Miller, then special assistant to the president of the United Steelworkers Union and a 16-year veteran of that organization.

Far from militant, the players were skittish about hiring a union man. Roberts and his colleagues approached two company men and were blessed when neither expressed interest in the job. One was Chub Feeney, vice-president of the San Francisco Giants and later president of the National League. The second was Judge Cannon, who may have turned his back on a baseball connection because baseball had shunned him for the commissionership, turning instead to a retired general, William D. Eckert.

Roberts' committee put together a list of six candidates, including

In 1966 Marvin Miller (left) was just getting started as executive director of the Players Association. Player representatives like Clete Boyer (center) and Roy McMillan (right) could not have imagined the salaries Miller would help players earn in the next 17 years.

Miller, and gave it to Eckert for clearance, promising to cross off anyone to whom the commissioner objected. Eckert said any of the six would be fine.

Blessed again, this time by the commissioner himself, the committee next turned to Miller. He accepted, agreeing to meet with the players on each team during spring training. They would vote him in or out.

Miller knew the players tended to be conservative, did not consider themselves laborers, and did not want to think of the Players Association as a union. Jimmy Hoffa, president of the Teamsters Union, had talked of organizing professional athletes, and his proposal had aroused antipathy from all sides. "I'm not a union organizer," Miller told *The Sporting News*. "I'm a professional economist with background in pension plans and mediation."

Miller toured the spring training camps in 1966. He impressed the players, and they hired him. He set up offices in New York and quickly negotiated a new funding formula for the pension plan and a dues check-off to fund the Association—you know, like the check-off plans used by unions.

He got the players to stop signing releases for use of their pictures on baseball cards sold by the Topps Chewing Gum Company and negotiated a lucrative contract for them with Topps. In 1968 he negotiated the first basic agreement between the Players Association and the owners. The minimum salary, stuck for years at $6,000 and then $7,000, climbed to $10,000.

In 1969 Miller was bargaining for improved pensions, health insurance and life insurance; he advised the players not to sign their contracts until an agreement was reached. "The players have a right to know what is in their 1969 benefit plan before they sign their contracts," he said. "The two go hand in hand."

Management had never experienced such opposition, and some owners

CURT FLOOD
Outfield

5'9" 165 lbs.
BR TR
b 1/18/38

In a letter to Commissioner Bowie Kuhn in December 1969, Curt Flood wrote: "I do not feel I am a piece of property to be bought and sold irrespective of my wishes." Two months earlier Flood refused a trade; he was now prepared to sit out the entire 1970 season. By doing so, he challenged baseball's reserve clause. He lost his case, but in 1975 an arbitration ruling granted players the right to free agency that Flood sought.

In 1956 Flood went from high school in an Oakland ghetto to the Cincinnati Reds. After just eight at-bats in two years with the Reds, Flood was traded to St. Louis, where he immediately became the starting center fielder for the Cardinals.

Flood came into his own in 1961, hitting .322, one of six times he topped .300 with the Cards. From 1961 to 1969 he averaged .302, hitting a career-high .335 in 1967 and twice making 200 or more hits, including a league-leading 211 in 1964. The winner of consecutive Gold Gloves from 1963 to 1968, Flood set a NL record in 1966 by playing 159 games without an error. A longtime Cardinal co-captain, he played on St. Louis pennant winners in 1964, 1967 and 1968.

After sitting out the 1970 season, Flood attempted a comeback with the 1971 Washington Senators but retired after only 13 games. In 15 seasons Curt Flood hit .293, made 1,861 hits, and knowingly jeopardized a Hall-of-Fame career by saying "no."

When Kansas City A's owner Charlie Finley released first baseman Ken Harrelson (above) in a 1967 fit of pique, little did he realize the bidding war Harrelson's moderate talent would start. Boston won, and was amply rewarded as Harrelson hit 35 homers and drove in a league-leading 109 runs in 1968.

While their Dodger teammates were sweating off their winter weight at the team's spring training camp in Vero Beach, Florida, Koufax and Drysdale stayed cool and played golf until March 30, when the pitchers agreed to terms.

spoiled for a fight, especially as it became clear that the vast majority of the players were ready to boycott spring training. Paul Richards, a former player and manager who was then general manager of the Atlanta Braves, said, "Let 'em strike. Maybe if they do, it will get the guys who don't want to play out of the game and let the fellows who appreciate the major leagues play." Frank Lane, a veteran front-office man then with the Orioles, called Richards and said, "Paul, for God's sake, stop talking. All you're doing is aiding the enemy."

Charles O. Finley, owner of the Oakland Athletics, said he would open the season with minor leaguers. But the owners had just signed a lucrative television contract, and network executives told the owners that they weren't about to pay full price unless real major leaguers were playing.

The owners meanwhile had fired Eckert—"the unknown soldier," as one sportswriter dubbed him. His replacement, Bowie Kuhn, who for years had been a lawyer for the National League, counseled compromise, and an agreement was reached.

By then Miller was in solid with the players and could speak with candor. "Labor relations-wise," he told writer Stan Fischler, "the owners have not yet reached the 19th century. This business of owning people is the worst form of slavery I've seen."

Players were "owned," of course, through the reserve clause. By hiring Miller, the players had set in motion the series of events that eventually would lead to salary arbitration, free agency, and million-dollar salaries.

Koufax and Drysdale had given players an inkling of a star's worth. In 1967 they got another piece of evidence when Finley fired Ken "Hawk" Harrelson in a fit of temper. Major league baseball was learning that players were

America's love affair with outer space was amply reflected by baseball in 1965, with examples including the Astrodome and this World Series program. Koufax and Drysdale accounted for three of four Dodger victories in the Series.

not as compliant as they used to be. Mike Epstein, the Minor League Player of the Year in 1966, was farmed out again in 1967 by the Orioles, who were rich with talent. Epstein refused to report to the minors. That kind of defiance traditionally had earned a player nothing, but this time the Orioles traded Epstein to the Washington Senators, who made him their regular first baseman.

Two years later Harrelson did much the same thing. The Hawk represented a lot that traditionalists didn't like. He was a splashy symbol of the exotic '60s, wearing Nehru jackets, jewelry and styled hair. He also made an accidental contribution to the game when he arrived for a night game fresh from 36 holes of golf. Harrelson hadn't expected to play, but his name was in the lineup. With a hand sore from the links, Harrelson wore a golf glove as protection and hit two homers; the batting glove was born.

Harrelson blossomed into a star in Boston, driving in 109 runs in 1968 to lead the American League. When the Red Sox traded him to Cleveland in 1969 he refused to report unless the Indians gave him a raise. Cleveland capitulated.

The dike was leaking, and baseball executives correctly identified Miller as their principal antagonist. He was striking tough deals and putting funny ideas in the heads of players. "Either Miller or baseball has to go," said Paul Richards in 1969. "We need to make it the way it was when Judge Landis was commissioner."

But Landis had been dead for 25 years. And even as Richards spoke, Dave McNally of the Orioles and Andy Messersmith of the Angels were establishing themselves as star pitchers. Six years later, their grievance cases led to the advent of free agency. ◗

Trading Up

Bill DeWitt learned his baseball as an assistant to Branch Rickey, who believed in trading players at peak value, just before their skills began declining. DeWitt was no fool. He put together the makeshift wartime St. Louis Browns team that won the 1944 pennant and, after taking over the Reds in late 1960, he engineered a series of trades that carried the team from sixth place in 1960 to a pennant in 1961.

DeWitt got rid of Billy Martin (yes, *that* Billy Martin), age 32 and a .246 hitter; Roy McMillan, 30, a fine shortstop without punch; Cal McLish, 35, a pitcher who had won 19 games in 1959 but only four in 1960; and Ed Bailey, 30, a good catcher and decent hitter whose arm was all but shot. In exchange, the Reds got pitcher Joey Jay, 25; third baseman Gene Freese, 26; second baseman Don Blasingame, 28; and catcher Bob Schmidt, 27.

Ho-hum. But the Reds won the pennant in 1961. Jay won 21 games and Freese hit 26 homers. Frank Robinson was then only 25, but he delivered 37 homers, 124 RBI, and a .323 average. He was named the league's MVP.

In 1965 DeWitt's Reds led the National League in hitting, runs scored and fielding, yet finished fourth. DeWitt went shopping for a pitcher and dangled his team's brightest star, outfielder Frank Robinson. In ten years with the Reds, Robinson had averaged 32 homers, 101 RBI, and batted over .303. He led the league in slugging average three times, twice in runs scored.

But Robinson was 30—"an old 30," DeWitt later said. "We had Robinson here 10 years," he said. "We won one pennant with him." Over the winter, DeWitt struck a deal with the Baltimore Orioles: Robinson for Milt Pappas, a solid starting pitcher; reliever Jack Baldschun, whom Baltimore had just acquired from the Phillies; and rookie outfielder

Dick Simpson, who was young, fast and promising. The trade was one of history's legitimate blockbusters. Pappas won 16 games for the Reds in 1967, but neither Baldschun nor Simpson came through.

Robinson seethed. He came to Baltimore with a mission. He homered opening day, and the next two days as well. He had always been an aggressive player, an intimidating batter and baserunner. His slugging and his confident, bear-down style inspired the talented Orioles.

Baltimore opened a wide lead, but Detroit pulled to within six games in mid-July. The Tigers came to Baltimore for three games. Robinson hit four homers as the Orioles won all three, scoring 29 runs on 47 hits. By the end of July the Orioles led by 13 games. "If we don't win they ought to line us up and shoot us," said first baseman Boog Powell. He weighed in at 240 pounds; Robinson called him "Crisco."

Powell hit 34 homers and drove in 109 runs, and the other Robinson, Brooks, hit 23, drove in 100, and anchored a tight infield defense that also featured shortstop Luis Aparicio. The Orioles were good, and their best was Frank Robinson, who won the Triple Crown—49 homers, 122 RBI, a .316 average. Baltimore coasted to its first pennant, and a gag among ballplayers went this way: "You know how little boys say their prayers in Baltimore? They get down on their knees every night and say, 'God bless Mommy, God bless Daddy and God bless Bill DeWitt.' "

Robinson was a unanimous choice as the league's Most Valuable Player, and the trade was credited with turning a good Oriole team into a great one. It continued to pay dividends. Robinson wracked himself up in a ferocious collision while sliding into second base in 1967. He suffered from double vision and did not regain his sharpest edge

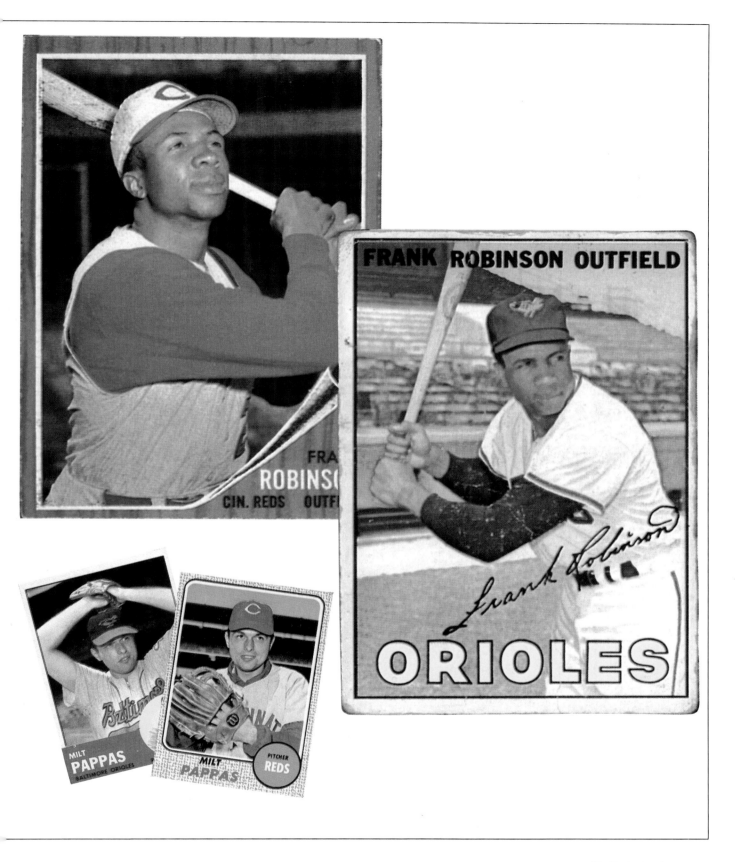

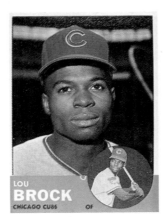

until 1969. Neither did the Orioles. With Robinson slugging again, they won pennants in 1969, 1970 and 1971.

It's rare for a general manager to get fired during a pennant-winning season, rarer still when the GM has pulled off a memorable trade. But it happened to Bing Devine of the Cardinals on August 17, 1964. Two months earlier, Devine had traded pitcher Ernie Broglio, who had won 18 games the season before, to the Cubs for a young outfielder who had shown a lot of speed and power, but little consistency. His name was Lou Brock, and his assignment was to fill the shoes of Stan Musial, the Cardinal hero who had retired after the 1963 season.

Brock joined an eighth-place team that had lost 17 of its last 23 games. He electrified the Cardinals, batting .348 for the remainder of the season, hitting 12 homers, and stealing 33 bases. He and center fielder Curt Flood cut off drives with their speed, and Brock led off a lineup that included Flood, Bill White, Dick Groat, Tim McCarver and Ken Boyer, who led the league with 119 RBI.

The Cardinals climbed, but the Phillies seemed to have the pennant won. August A. Busch, Jr., the Cardinals' owner, thought his team should be on top. So he fired Devine, who had been with the Cards for 25 years. Two other Cardinal executives resigned in protest on the spot, and the team's manager, Johnny Keane, secretly agreed to manage the Yankees the next season. The Yankees, just as secretly, had already decided to fire their manager, Yogi Berra.

Then the Phillies collapsed, losing ten straight games. St. Louis won the pennant on the season's final day. In the World Series, Keane was in the uncomfortable position of managing against the team he would be managing the next spring. Brock hit .300 and drove in five runs as the Cards won the Series, four games to three. Like Frank Robinson, he was on his way to the Hall of Fame.

The soap opera began unfolding the next day. Keane resigned, humiliating Busch. The Yankees announced the replacement of Berra with Keane. Keane was voted Manager of the Year, and Devine was voted Major League Executive of the Year. Devine went to work for the New York Mets, but he and his wife kept their roots in St. Louis. Meantime, the Cardinals had pulled off another important trade—pitcher Ray Sadecki to the Giants for first baseman Orlando Cepeda, a slugger whom the Giants distrusted because of a bad knee.

The Cardinals jelled behind Cepeda's jovial leadership. He introduced a red-and-white ball for infield practice, and after a Cardinal win led this clubhouse cheer:

Cepeda: "El Birdos!"
Team: "Yeah!"
That three times, and then:
Cepeda: "_____ Herman Franks!"

El Birdos? A Hispanic nickname in conservative St. Louis? On a team that 20 years before threatened to strike rather than play against Jackie Robinson? Indeed, and those changes reflected an evolution throughout baseball, where black and Hispanic stars were growing in number and prominence.

Cepeda's slugging helped the Cards to pennants in 1967 and 1968. In 1967 Busch needed a new general manager for the Cardinals. He rehired Bing Devine.

GIANTS
1st BASE
ORLANDO CEPEDA

1st BASE
CARDS
ORLANDO
CEPEDA

CARDS
RAY SADECKI pitcher

RAY SADECKI • PITCHER
GIANTS

Return of the Running Game

"When I make a move on the bases, I think I'm going to be safe every time. It takes a perfect throw to get me."
Maury Wills

Dodger speedster Willie Davis (3) slid into first base but couldn't elude the tag by Milwaukee first baseman Gene Oliver at County Stadium on July 20, 1963. Davis stole at least 20 bases in 11 straight seasons for the Dodgers, and along with teammate Maury Wills gave Los Angeles the best one-two baserunning duo in baseball.

he Yankees weren't used to this kind of treatment. The day before, in the opening game of the 1963 World Series, New York had been humiliated by Sandy Koufax. Now Los Angeles shortstop Maury Wills had opened the second game of the Series with a single to center field, and he was taking an outrageously long lead off first base.

They knew he would steal, and it wasn't the way baseball was supposed to be played. The Yankees had won the American League pennant by hitting home runs—188 of them. That was how Yankee teams had won pennants and World Series for 40 years, and this pipsqueak Dodger team had no business challenging them.

Al Downing, a left hander, was pitching for the Yankees. A southpaw is supposed to make it hard on baserunners because he faces first base in his stretch. But Wills liked to steal on lefties, and he took off even before Downing committed himself to come to the plate.

Downing threw to first baseman Joe Pepitone, who made a hurried—and bad—throw to second. Wills was safe. Jim Gilliam then singled to right. Wills didn't have a chance to score, but he rounded third far enough to draw a throw, allowing Gilliam take second base.

Wills was a threat to steal home, so Downing was reluctant to risk any kind of off-speed pitch, like a curve. He threw a fastball, and Willie Davis lined it to the right field fence for a double, scoring Wills and Gilliam. The Dodgers scored twice more, but those two runs were enough, because Johnny Podres allowed the Yankees only one. Some days, no one hits a homer. The Yankees, in fact, hit only two in that whole World Series—and lost four straight games.

Pittsburgh's Roberto Clemente showed that speed isn't only for stealing bases. He stole just 83 bases in 18 years, but speed elevated all phases of his game, and his aggressive style typified the National League in the 1960s.

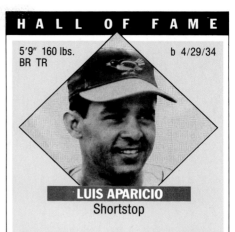
From 1956 to 1973, Luis Aparicio played 2,581 games at shortstop. No other major league shortstop has ever played so many; few have played so well.

Aparicio's father was the first Venezuelan ever offered a major league contract, although he never made it to the majors. The successor to fellow Venezuelan Chico Carrasquel at shortstop, Aparicio, a native of Maracaibo, Venezuela, was named Rookie of the Year in 1956 for the Chicago White Sox. He won nine Gold Gloves, establishing major league records by leading the AL in fielding percentage and assists for eight and six consecutive seasons, respectively.

With 21 stolen bases in 1956, Aparicio began a record-setting string of nine years during which he led the league in steals. During that span he averaged 41 steals a year, stealing 50 or more bases four times. In 1964, the final year of his streak and his second season with the Orioles, Aparicio stole a career-high 57 bases.

A .262 lifetime hitter with 2,677 hits, "Little Looie" hit a career-high .313 with White Sox in 1970. His 182 hits in 1966 tied Frank Robinson's as the most on Baltimore's 1966 world champion Orioles. By the time he ended his career with the Red Sox in 1973, Aparicio had played on infields with Boston's Carl Yastrzemski at first base, Chicago's Nellie Fox at second, and Baltimore's Brooks Robinson at third.

A year later, it happened again. This time the Yankee bats weren't silent—Mickey Mantle hit three homers, and Phil Linz and Tom Tresh hit two each. After that, you don't expect to lose a World Series on a stolen base by a guy like St. Louis' Tim McCarver. He's a catcher, for heaven's sake.

Seventh game, scoreless tie, last of the fourth. The Cardinals scored one run, and with one out McCarver was on third, Mike Shannon on first. Shannon headed for second, and when Elston Howard threw to second, McCarver dashed for home. It was the double steal, a play from the Ty Cobb era, against the best catcher in the American League, and with two guys running who, between them, stole six bases all season. Suicide!

But surprise is another weapon of the running game, and the Yankees were surprised. Shannon was safe at second and McCarver beat the throw back to Howard. Dal Maxvill singled Shannon home, and Bob Gibson held on to win, 7–5. A two-run margin—and that double steal netted the Cards those two precious runs.

The Minnesota Twins learned the same lesson in the 1965 World Series, and again Maury Wills was the teacher. The Twins were up two games to one when Wills beat out a grounder to open the fourth game. He stole second, and went to third as his running partner, Willie Davis, beat out a roller. Ron Fairly grounded to second and Wills scored.

In the Dodger second, Wes Parker beat out a bunt, stole second, took third on a wild pitch, and scored as Twins' second baseman Frank Quilici, worried about stopping the run, fumbled a grounder. In the Dodger sixth, a bunt single by Lou Johnson contributed to a three-run rally. The Dodgers won 7–2 to even the Series. In seven games that fall, the Twins got a home run each from Harmon Killebrew, Tony Oliva, Don Mincher and Bob Allison.

Baserunning and Offensive Strategy

Runs were precious during the first two decades of this century, and the best offensive players were good hitters and good runners, too. By the 1930s, the home run had consigned the stolen base to novelty status, and sluggers rarely ran. The 1960s brought on versatile offenses, with running specialists. Three stars from each era illustrate the evolution of the running game.

	BATTING AVERAGE		STEALS		HOME RUNS	
	Career	Best Season	Career	Best Season	Career	Best Season
Dead-Ball Era—Playing for One Run						
Honus Wagner, 1897–1917	.329	.381—1900	722	61—1907	101	10—'98,'08
Ty Cobb, 1905–1928	.367	.420—1911	892	96—1915	118	12—'21,'25
George Sisler, 1915–1930	.340	.420—1922	375	51—1922	99	19—1920
Home-Run Era—Offensive Specialists						
Joe DiMaggio, 1936–1951	.325	.381—1939	30	6—1938	361	46—1937
Ted Williams, 1939–1960	.344	.406—1941	24	4—'40,'48	521	43—1949
Stan Musial, 1941–1963	.331	.376—1948	78	9—1943	475	39—1948
1960s & Beyond—Versatile Offenses with Running Specialists						
Luis Aparicio, 1956–1973	.262	.313—1970	506	57—1964	83	10—1964
Maury Wills, 1959–1972	.281	.302—'63,'67	586	104—1962	20	6—1962
Lou Brock, 1961–1979	.293	.315—1964	938	118—1974	149	21—1967

Even Zoilo Versalles and pitcher Jim "Mudcat" Grant homered. But the Dodgers won four games to three.

The running game was back, and it gave baseball a dimension that had been lacking for decades. In the dead-ball era, running was an essential part of every team's strategy. Homers were rare, and it was worth the risk to try a steal so that a single could bring the runner home. Some of the best hitters were great runners, too. Among them, Ty Cobb, Honus Wagner and George Sisler—great hitters, men who never had to skin their thighs to hold a job—won 15 base stealing titles.

But by the 1920s, as home runs began proliferating, stolen bases and other risky base running strategies became less desirable. If a runner was thrown out and the next guy homered, that steal attempt cost the team a run. In the 1930s, 1940s and much of the 1950s, a stolen base was a novelty. Why take risks to score one run when the other team might score three or four with one swing of the bat?

Joe DiMaggio and Stan Musial were fast, intelligent baserunners, and Ted Williams wasn't bad, but real hitters of their generation just did not steal. Musial's season high was nine stolen bases, DiMaggio's six, and Williams' four. Stan Hack of the Cubs led the National League in stolen bases with 16 in 1938 and 17 in 1939. Dom DiMaggio of the Red Sox, Joe's brother, led the American League with 15 in 1950.

The running game began to return when baseball lowered its color bars. Black and Hispanic players in both leagues set new standards for speed and base running skill. In 1947, his rookie year, Jackie Robinson led the National League in stolen bases with 29. Luis Aparicio, playing most of his career for

Continued on page 136

Shortstop Luis Aparicio's ability as a base-stealer (opposite) is magnified when you consider that he was a pretty mediocre hitter—.262 lifetime—who didn't walk much. Aparicio's speed and intelligence netted 506 career steals and a success rate of 79 percent.

The Latin American Impact

The 1960s was a decade of unprecedented Latin American influence in American baseball. Roberto Clemente won four National League batting titles. Tony Oliva led the American League in hits four times. Luis Aparicio and Bert Campaneris combined for 13 straight AL base-stealing crowns. From 1961–69 Juan Marichal *averaged* nearly 21 wins a year. And a team from Monterrey, Mexico, even won the Little League World Series in Williamsport, Pennsylvania.

Hispanics had been in the majors since 1911 when Armando Marsans, a Cuban, broke in with the Reds. But until 1947 the color barrier that prohibited black players in the majors also restricted Hispanics, with one exception: light-skinned Hispanic players were permitted in the majors so long as "racial purity" could be verified. Such was the case with Marsans, as well as Dolf Luque. Called "The Pride of Havana," Luque broke in with the Braves in 1914, pitched 20 years, and won 193 major league games, including a league-leading 27 wins for the 1923 Reds.

But Marsans and Luque were exceptions. Not that anyone ever doubted the abilities of Hispanic players. In 1908 the Cincinnati Reds toured Cuba and lost seven of 11 games against Cuban nationals. John McGraw, recognizing the quality of the competition on the island, regularly took his great Giants' teams to Havana. Still, major league baseball was adamant about maintaining the color line. In 1948, one year after Jackie Robinson and Larry Doby became the first black players in the National and American leagues, respectively, Mike Guerra of the Athletics was the only Hispanic in the majors.

Then in 1954, Cleveland's Bobby Avila, a Mexican, hit .341 to become the first Latin American player to win a major league batting title. Along with Minnie Minoso, Chico Carrasquel, Vic Power, Hector Lopez and Ruben Gomez, Avila was among a handful of Hispanics who established impressive careers in the 1950s. Less visible, but infinitely more influential, was what was taking place on the ballfields of Cuba, Venezuela, the Dominican Republic, Panama, Mexico and Puerto Rico, where a vast network of major league scouts feverishly recruited talent. In the first ten years after World War II, Washington Senators' scout Joe Cambria, stationed in Havana, signed 400 Cuban players, including Pedro Ramos, Camilo Pascual and Zoilo Versalles. Cambria, who eventually had a cigar named after him, twice rejected a Cuban pitcher named Fidel Castro.

By the 1960s the Caribbean current had become a permanent and vital source of new talent for American teams. In addition to the Senators, the Pittsburgh Pirates and San Francisco Giants established Caribbean connections that remained productive for years. Pirates' scout Howie Haak is credited with "stealing" Roberto Clemente from the Dodgers. Alex Pompez, former owner of the New York Cubans of the Negro Leagues, signed Marichal, Orlando Cepeda, the three Alou brothers, Manny Mota and others for the Giants.

By opening day 1961 the U.S. had invaded the Bay of Pigs, and Cuba's President Castro had permanently ended the exodus of players from his country to the U.S. Among the last Cubans to leave was Bert Campaneris. Campaneris, who broke in with the Kansas City Athletics in 1964, played 19 years in the majors, appeared in three World Series, six league championship series, and stole 649 bases, eighth on the all-time list.

The impact of Hispanic players continued to grow throughout the 1960s, despite the Castro embargo. Luis Arroyo of Puerto Rico led the American League with 29 saves in 1961; another Puerto Rican, Orlando Cepeda, twice led the National League in RBI, and in 1961 hit a league-leading 46 homers. In 1962 Manny Mota, a Dominican, collected the first of his major league record 150 career pinch hits for the San Francisco Giants. The following year the Giants boasted a brotherhood of Dominicans in the outfield: Felipe, Jesus and Matty Alou. In 1966 the top three hitters in the National League—Matty and Felipe Alou and Rico Carty—were from the Dominican Republic. Roberto Clemente, a Puerto Rican, placed fifth. In 1969 Panamanian Rod Carew won the first of his seven American League batting titles.

By the end of the decade, 39 Hispanics—nearly twice the number in 1960—were on the full season rosters of National and American league teams. Among them, Luis Aparicio, Rod Carew, Roberto Clemente and Juan Marichal were destined for the Hall of Fame.

Politics and pitching collided at Yankee Stadium on July 28, 1963 as a group of anti-Castro protestors draped Cuban-born pitcher Camilo Pascual in the Cuban flag. The game was halted briefly, but then Pascual went on to pitch the Minnesota Twins to a 5–1 win over the Yankees.

The return of the running game in the 1960s took its inspiration from the play of Brooklyn Dodger Jackie Robinson. Robinson sent Yankee shortstop Phil Rizzuto flying (right) and the Dodgers stole seven bases in the first four games of the 1947 World Series.

a relatively punchless Chicago White Sox team, led the American League in stolen bases nine straight seasons, from 1956 through 1964. Bert Campaneris of the Athletics followed him with four straight championships. In the 1960s, every stolen base leader in both leagues was black or Hispanic.

Even a few sluggers began to run. Willie Mays led the National League in stolen bases for four straight seasons in the late 1950s. Frank Robinson never stole more than 26 bases in a season, but his speed and aggressive running style were offensive hallmarks, first for the Cincinnati Reds, and starting in 1966 for the Baltimore Orioles.

In every field, there are a few who rise to heroic proportions; in the 1960s, Maury Wills and Lou Brock brought the art of base stealing to new levels, merging their base running skills with new realities of the game. As pitching began to stifle hitting, base running risks became more affordable and desirable. Wills stole 50 bases in 1960 and 35 in 1961, enough to lead the league. Then the Dodgers moved to their new stadium at Chavez Ravine, and Wills was in his heaven.

Crushed rock was mixed into the infield dirt near home plate, providing a hard surface. Wills learned to chop the ball and beat out the high bounce. So did his teammate, Willie Davis. The Dodgers were short on home run punch, and Dodger Stadium—and Dodger pitching—gave few homers to opposing teams. "With the Dodgers," Wills said, "one run is like a mountain."

So Wills had the green light. In 1962, the Dodgers' first season in their new ballpark, Wills electrified baseball by stealing 104 bases to break Cobb's record of 96 in a season, set back in 1915. Willie Davis stole 32, giving the Dodgers a superb base running tandem. Despite injuries, Wills led the

Although Rod Carew is best known for his hitting, he was a terror on the basepaths. The left-handed-hitting Carew perfected the drag bunt and, in 1969, tied major league records by stealing home seven times and by stealing three bases in an inning.

league with 40 stolen bases in 1963. He stole 94 in 1965 as the Dodgers won yet another pennant.

Wills led the National League the first six seasons of the 1960s, and then passed the baton to Lou Brock of the Cardinals, who made stealing a science. Wills believed in taking the longest lead he could; he said a baserunner wasn't taking enough of a lead unless he had to dive back on every pick-off attempt. He used a stylish and elusive hook slide, successful but very hard on his legs. When his thighs became sore, he slid head first.

Brock developed the rolling start. He took modest leads, so that if a pitcher caught him leaning he could still get back, standing. He figured an early start got him further than a long lead, and he was right. He timed pitchers' movements and catchers' throws. When Lou Brock described base stealing, he sounded like a math major—which he was in college. Brock also perfected the quick pop slide, which was easier on his legs and got him on his feet and ready to run in case a throw went wild.

Just as Wills flourished at Dodger Stadium, Brock came into his own when the Cardinals moved into spacious Busch Stadium in 1966. Brock stole 74 bases that season, and Cardinal managers ever since that time have built speed into their strategy, tailoring their offense to fit the ballpark.

Brock ran the Boston Red Sox wild in the 1967 World Series. In the first game, he scored the winning run by singling (his fourth hit), stealing second, and coming around on two ground outs. After tripling and scoring in the bottom of the first in Game 3, Brock beat out a bunt to lead off the sixth. A live-wire runner often panics the defense into mistakes, and Boston pitcher

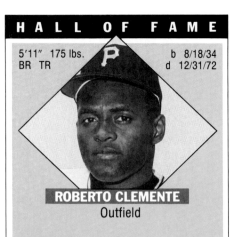

Roberto Clemente was more than the first Hispanic superstar. He was a humanitarian and a folk hero in his native Puerto Rico, as well as in most of Pittsburgh, where he led the Pirates to world championships in 1960 and 1971.

Clemente's critics said he was lazy, a hypochondriac, and too outspoken on racial equality. But 11 weeks after his death in a 1972 New Year's Eve plane crash—he was on a relief mission for victims of a Nicaraguan earthquake—the election committee of the Hall of Fame waived the five-year retirement rule in Clemente's honor.

Clemente was one of the greatest all-around outfielders ever. As the Pirates' right fielder from 1955 to 1972, he hit over .300 thirteen times and led the NL in batting four times, including a career-high .357 in 1967. He ended his 18-year career with a .317 average, 240 home runs, and 3,000 hits—the 3,000th coming in the final game of the 1972 season. An aggressive baserunner, Clemente had nine seasons with ten or more triples, and once hit three triples in a single game.

The winner of 12 Gold Gloves, Clemente was the best right fielder of his era. In 1966 he won the National League's Most Valuable Player Award, as he set career highs with 29 home runs and 119 RBI. In his two World Series, he hit safely in all 14 games, collecting 21 hits, including two homers and seven RBI, for a .362 lifetime Series average.

Stealing home is one of the most exciting, rare and difficult feats in baseball. The trick is to stroll down the baseline as invisibly as you can, then take off when the pitcher begins his motion. Tommy Davis (12) made this a close play as Dodger teammate Don Drysdale screened Pittsburgh catcher Jim Pagliaroni.

Baseball's speed demons make their living with their legs, yet risk injury every time they hit the dirt. Journeyman outfielder Lou Johnson (right, as a Cleveland Indian) got his big break when Dodger star Tommy Davis broke his ankle sliding into second in 1965. Two years later it was Johnson's turn as he broke his ankle sliding into home.

St. Louis' Lou Brock (above and opposite) was a new kind of base-stealer: one who could hit for average and power. In 1967 he became the first player in history to hit at least 20 homers and steal at least 50 bases in a single season.

Lee Stange threw wild trying to pick Brock off first. He dashed to third, then scored on a single by Roger Maris.

Brock stole four bases in the first six games of that Series, but he saved his best for the decisive seventh game. In the fifth inning, he singled, stole second, stole third on ball four to Curt Flood, and scored on Maris' fly out. The Cardinals won behind Bob Gibson, and Brock stole another base to set a World Series record of seven—which he matched in the 1968 Series, although the Cards lost to the Tigers in seven games.

"When you get men with speed thinking more about running, you open up the game," said Bill Rigney, who managed the Giants and Willie Mays. "You worry the opposition to death. This causes that infinitesimal glance by fielders that often can result in a misjudged fly ball or in a man being half a step behind a ground ball."

As the running game developed during the 1960s, a journeyman catcher named Charlie Lau developed a batting style that would later make him baseball's most innovative and admired batting coach. Lau taught George Brett, among others, to hit down on the ball, slash it through the infield and into the outfield gaps, and run like hell. Batters are still doing it, and the running game that was reborn in the 1960s has given baseball an exciting dimension, along with a variety of offensive styles, that had been lacking for too many years. ◗●

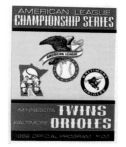

Billy, Ted, Earl and the Lip

Billy Martin punched out the Minnesota Twins' traveling secretary, among others, yet was promoted to manager. Earl Weaver managed 18 minor league teams before getting his chance in the big leagues with the Baltimore Orioles. Ted Williams, slugger turned fisherman, had fended off managing offers for eight years before agreeing to manage the Washington Senators.

In 1969, the first season of divisional play, all three were beginning their first full seasons as American League managers. In the National League, the Chicago Cubs were led by a manager just as tough and combative as Martin and Weaver, but a generation older. Leo Durocher was 63, winding down his colorful, controversial and successful managing career. Martin, 41, and Weaver, 38, were just beginning theirs.

It was a vintage year for managers. Williams was 50, and probably could hit better than almost anyone on the Washington Senators team that he somehow was talked into managing. He had retired as a player in 1960, shortly after his 42nd birthday. Few men ever hit as well as Ted Williams, and none went out in greater style. He batted .316 his final season, tagging 29 home runs. In his final trip to the plate, he drove a homer against a gusting wind at Boston's Fenway Park. He trotted around the bases with his head down, ducked into the dugout, and refused to step out for a bow. Same old Ted.

Then he went fishing. For eight years he fished, earning a lucrative salary from Sears Roebuck for demonstrating fishing equipment. He repeatedly

(Opposite, clockwise from bottom right) Veteran manager Leo Durocher and skippers Earl Weaver, Billy Martin and Ted Williams were near miracle workers in 1969. Collectively their teams played .506 baseball in 1968, .592 in 1969.

When Ted Williams talked batting, Senators—like outfielder Brant Alyea (3), pitcher Bill Denehy (14) and shortstop Toby Harrah—listened.

Ted Williams had the right prescription for all the Senators' hitters in 1969, especially first baseman Mike Epstein (12). Williams insisted Epstein see an eye doctor, and the young slugger returned with new contact lenses and went on to post career highs of .278, 30 home runs and 85 RBI.

said he didn't want to manage. The man who changed his mind was Robert Short, a trucking and hotel magnate who owned the Washington Senators.

The Senators had finished tenth—dead last—in 1968, and Short wanted Williams for his box-office appeal and, maybe, his managing skills. He wooed Williams for months, finally offering him $1.5 million for five years. Williams called Short "the smartest guy I ever met," and accepted the offer.

Williams came to spring training unfamiliar with the Senators' roster, much less the players' skills. He had never been a patient man and he had never gotten along with the press, so many observers expected the worst. But old Teddy Ballgame charmed the writers and inspired the players. "We really do believe we can beat anyone," said pitcher Dick Bosman, and the Senators did, getting off to a fast start.

Bosman posted the league's lowest ERA at 2.19. But Williams' greatest impact was on Washington's hitters. Williams was not only a great hitter himself, but a great hitting coach and theorist. He taught the Senators' one legitimate star slugger, Frank Howard, to swing only at strikes; Howard hit 48 homers, a career high, while cutting way down on strikeouts and coaxing more walks.

He told Ed Brinkman, a good-field-no-hit shortstop, that he could learn to hit if he would do it Williams' way; Brinkman added almost 80 points to his batting average. He got 30 home runs from young first baseman Mike Epstein, and he brought the Senators home fourth, with their first winning record in 17 years.

Durocher went back a long way. As a young shortstop, he had feuded with a Yankee teammate named Babe Ruth. He fit in better as a teammate of Frankie Frisch, Pepper Martin and Dizzy Dean on the Gashouse Gang, the

Umpire Dave Davidson (above) got more abuse than usual from Leo Durocher in this September 1969 game against the Mets. New York won the game 3–2 and moved to within 1½ games of the first-place Cubs in the NL East.

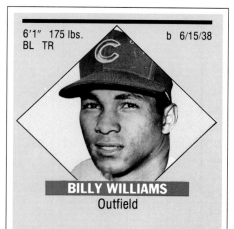

6'1" 175 lbs.   b 6/15/38
BL TR

BILLY WILLIAMS
Outfield

Throughout the 1960s, Billy Williams, Ernie Banks and Ron Santo made the Cubs one of the most powerful teams in all of baseball. Of the three, none was more reliable than Billy Williams.

Few players in the '60s could match his consistency. Breaking in with the Cubs in 1959, Williams won Rookie of the Year honors in 1961, his first full season, hitting .278 with 86 RBI and 25 home runs. That year was his first of 13 consecutive seasons of 20 or more homers. From 1961 to 1972 Williams hit .296, averaging 184 hits, 30 homers, 99 RBI a year, while playing in 161 or more games for eight consecutive seasons. During that span, Williams set a National League record by playing in 1,117 consecutive games, since broken by Steve Garvey with 1,207.

Three times in his career Williams made 200 or more hits, including a league-leading 205 in 1970, when he hit a career-high 42 home runs and led the NL with 137 runs scored. Two years later he led the league in both batting and slugging; his .333 average that season was one of five times he hit .300 or better.

After 16 years with the Cubs, Williams was traded to the Oakland Athletics in 1975 and hit 23 homers as a designated hitter. He retired following the 1976 season, a .290 lifetime hitter with 2,711 hits and 1,475 RBI. His 426 lifetime home runs rank 20th on the all-time list.

turbulent Cardinal champions of 1934. Durocher managed the Brooklyn Dodgers as far back as 1939, and he managed the New York Giants when Bobby Thomson hit his "shot heard 'round the world" homer to win the 1951 pennant. In between, he made headlines with a show biz marriage and Las Vegas connections that earned him a year's suspension by Commissioner Happy Chandler for "misbehavior."

The Lip turned to broadcasting games, and hadn't managed anyone for 11 years when Phil Wrigley hired him to manage the Cubs in 1966. The Cubs hadn't even had a manager for five years, using instead a unique and ineffective system of rotating the team's head coaches. Some baseball people considered the aging Durocher a relic, as bad a choice as the rotation system that preceded him. Yet in 1967 and 1968 he led the Cubs to third place, their highest finish in two decades, and for most of 1969 he had the Cubs on top. They finished second.

Durocher had been a scrappy infielder, and his favorite Cubs were the scrappy double play combination of Glenn Beckert and Don Kessinger. Ron Santo hit 29 homers and drove in 123 runs, and Ernie Banks, 38, had his last good season with 23 and 106. Yet in his autobiography, Durocher said Santo couldn't hit in the clutch and Banks could neither run nor get off a dime in the field. "He never remembered a sign or forgot a newspaperman's name," Durocher wrote of the Cub hero. Same old Leo.

Martin played second base on three Yankee world champions, and was a pet of Casey Stengel. But he tended to get in trouble, and the Yankee front office considered him a bad influence on his good friends Mickey Mantle and Whitey Ford. So when a man somehow wound up flat on the floor after arguing with a few Yankee players at New York's CopaCabana nightclub in

Throughout his playing and managerial career, controversy dogged Billy Martin both on and off the field. In 1957 Yankee general manager George Weiss decided Martin was a bad influence on superstar Mickey Mantle (above, left), and traded Martin to Kansas City. Twelve years later, Martin's tumultuous managerial career began in Minnesota (above, right), where his methods were successful but his madness intolerable.

1957, Martin got blamed, and was traded. He insisted he never saw the guy, much less hit him.

Martin wound up his playing career with Minnesota in 1962. The Twins kept him as a scout, and made him their third-base coach in 1965. He added a running dimension to the Twins' slugging game, coaxed an MVP year out of shortstop Zoilo Versalles, and helped the Twins win their first pennant.

The season was not without controversy. On an airplane trip to Washington, Martin got in an argument with Howard Fox, the Twins' traveling secretary and the right-hand-man to owner Calvin Griffith. As the team checked into a Washington hotel, the argument exploded into a fistfight. The one on the floor this time was Fox, who, Martin says, provoked the fight by throwing a room key at the hapless coach, splitting his lip.

Still, Martin was a darn good baseball man. When the Twins' Denver farm team got off to a bad start in 1968, Griffith asked Martin to take over as manager. He got thrown out of eight games, but his team played superbly. The Twins hired Martin as manager for 1969, and he turned a good team into an excellent one.

The Twins had great hitting. Harmon Killebrew, rebounding from an injury, led the league with 49 homers and 140 runs batted in—including 11 and 34 against Minnesota's closest pursuer, the Oakland Athletics. The Twins went 13–5 in head-to-head competition against the A's, and won the division title by nine games, despite 47 homers from Oakland's Reggie Jackson. At 23, Jackson was in his third of 21 years in the majors, but he never hit more home runs in a season.

Tony Oliva and Rich Reese also hit well for Minnesota, but the team's most versatile weapon was 23-year-old second baseman Rod Carew. He won

his first batting championship at .332. Under Martin's tutelage, he stole home seven times, tying a record set by Brooklyn's Pete Reiser in 1946, when Leo Durocher was the manager.

Martin astutely mixed the power of Killebrew, Reese and Oliva with the speed of Carew, Oliva and Cesar Tovar. Jim Perry, Dave Boswell, Jim Kaat and Ron Perranoski pitched well, although Boswell got badly hurt in a barroom fight in Detroit. His face needed 20 stitches, and the other guy needed seven stitches in his punching hand.

Predictably, the other guy was Boswell's manager and father figure, Billy Martin. As Martin tells it, it was lucky he was around, because he stopped Boswell from attacking the team's pitching coach, Art Fowler. Boswell missed a week, then won six of his next eight starts and wound up 20–12. When the Twins won the American League West Division, Martin was asked how to celebrate this new kind of championship. He said "You split a bottle of champagne and drink the Western half."

The league's eastern half was all Baltimore. The Orioles had been playing well since Earl Weaver took over as manager in mid-season 1968. In 1969 Weaver's team started fast and never slowed down.

He was the youngest manager in the American League, yet one of the most experienced. Billy Martin always said that scrappers make the best managers—particularly infielders, like himself, who are short on talent and have to learn every nook and cranny of baseball to play in the major leagues. Weaver was an infielder who learned every nook and cranny and *still* couldn't make the majors as a player. He got a managing job in the low minors at age 27, worked off-seasons as a winter-league manager, and regularly brought his teams in on top or close to it.

In an effort to boost attendance in the team's first year in Oakland, owner Charlie Finley lured Bay Area native Joe DiMaggio out of retirement and into a job as the Athletics' batting coach. DiMaggio's star appeal didn't pack the seats, but his knowledge may have helped such future stars as Reggie Jackson, Sal Bando and Joe Rudi.

Continued on page 150

The Flake

Even in the hairy and rebellious 1960s, most ballplayers stuck to a close-cropped, conservative image. A happy exception was Moe Drabowsky—college graduate, stockbroker, bullpen wit, and perpetrator of more practical jokes than a nest of snakes.

Snakes were among Drabowsky's favorite props. With the Orioles—Moe pitched for eight teams over 17 years in the big leagues—he walked into the clubhouse one day with a four-foot gopher snake around his neck. "That's fake, isn't it Moe?" asked outfielder Paul Blair. "Of course," replied Drabowsky. "You don't see it moving, do you?" Whereupon the snake raised its head and flicked its tongue, and Blair fled.

Kansas City's expansion franchise drafted Drabowsky from the Orioles before the 1969 season. When the Orioles and Royals met, the Orioles' bullpen crew found goldfish swimming in their water cooler. Cherry bomb fights broke out between players in opposing bullpens; Drabowsky liked fireworks.

Baltimore won the pennant, and on the first day of the World Series, in Baltimore, an airplane circled Memorial Stadium trailing a banner that said "Good luck Birds. Beware of Moe." The next day, as the Orioles were dressing for the game, a messenger delivered a package. Someone opened it, and out slithered a seven-foot black snake.

Drabowsky spent most of his baseball life in bullpens, where time hangs heavy. Drabowsky grilled sausages to keep the crew nourished, and often relieved the boredom by picking up the bullpen telephone. He called a restaurant in Hong Kong and ordered a Chinese dinner, to go. He called Sophia Loren's movie studio, and when he was told that Ms. Loren was on location in Europe he located her hotel and woke her up. "Hello, Sophia?" he said to the sleepy actress, "This is Drabo."

While with the Orioles during a visit to Kansas City, Drabowsky called the K.C. bullpen and imitated the voice of the team's manager, Al Dark. "Get Krausse hot!" he barked. Lew Krausse began warming up, the Oriole bullpen residents roaring with laughter. Moe called again. "Okay, sit him down." He also could imitate the voice of Charlie Finley, who then owned the Kansas City Athletics. Drabowsky called several Athletics' pitchers to renegotiate their salaries.

Staying at the Grant Hotel in Los Angeles, the Orioles encountered a lobby exhibit of Chinese art. At 3 a.m. Drabowsky grabbed a six-foot Buddha, placed it just outside the door of catcher Charlie Lau, knocked hard, and stepped away. Poor Lau stumbled to the door and faced his unblinking visitor. Another time, the Orioles found themselves sharing space with a Shriners' convention at a new hotel—so new that room numbers were written on pieces of paper and tacked to room doors. Moe switched the numbers around.

As a pitcher, Drabowsky was better than he let on. Pitching for the Cubs, he gave up Stan Musial's 3,000th hit—and offered to stick around and help him reach 4,000. When Early Wynn won his 300th game, Moe Drabowsky was the losing pitcher. Not long afterwards, Joe Adcock, then with the Angels, came to Kansas City needing just one homer to reach 300. "I was hoping I wouldn't get into that series," said Moe. "I didn't."

Every flake has his day, and Drabowsky's was

October 5, 1966, the first game of the World Series. The Orioles scored three runs in the first inning on homers by Frank and Brooks Robinson, but the Dodgers knocked out Dave McNally in the third inning. Drabowsky came in and held the lead, yielding just one hit in 6⅔ innings and striking out 11. His brilliant performance set the tone for Oriole pitchers Jim Palmer, Wally Bunker and McNally, who followed with successive shutouts for a Baltimore sweep.

As baseball's biggest flake, Moe Drabowsky was always a great story, but not until Game 1 of the 1966 World Series was he the right story. Drabowsky held the Dodgers to one hit in 6⅔ innings of relief, then distributed quotes to a happy, hungry press.

6'4" 230 lbs.   b 8/17/41
BL TR

BOOG POWELL
First Base

Nicknamed "Boog" by his father because of his penchant for childhood pranks, John Wesley Powell turned down college football scholarships to sign with the Baltimore Orioles. In 14 seasons in Baltimore, Powell hit 303 home runs, a team record since broken by Eddie Murray.

Called up at the end of the 1961 season, Powell hit 15 homers as an outfielder in 1962, his first full season. The following year he became the first Oriole to hit three home runs in a game. In 1964 he hit a career-high 39 homers, with 99 RBI and a league-leading .606 slugging average. In 1969 Powell hit 37 homers, while establishing career highs of 121 RBI and a .304 average. The following season he was named MVP when he hit .297 with 35 homers and 114 RBI.

Powell played in four World Series with the Orioles, hitting .357 in Baltimore's 1966 sweep of Los Angeles. Powell also hit .306 in five American League Championship Series.

A virtual monument at first base, Powell is said to have weighed as much as 280 pounds during his playing days. An agile fielder despite his size, Powell held his own among Orioles' memorable infielders of the 1960s and early 1970s: Brooks Robinson, Luis Aparicio, Jerry Adair, Davey Johnson and Mark Belanger.

One of the most popular Orioles of all time, Powell was traded to Cleveland in 1975. He ended his career with the Dodgers in 1977 having hit 339 home runs.

In 1969—Weaver's second year as manager of the Orioles—second baseman Davey Johnson's batting average went up 38 points from 1968. Fifteen years later, Johnson himself was a manager, as was teammate Frank Robinson.

Martin and Durocher were ferocious umpire baiters, but Weaver was in a class by himself. While managing Elmira, New York, he was thrown out of a game and took third base with him. He relished running feuds with umpires, and while other managers considered that poor policy, Weaver's teams kept winning.

Martin and Weaver seemed a lot alike, but their managing styles differed. Martin was a buddy to his players. Weaver was more old-school. He never socialized with his players and had little to say to them. Martin loved the running game. Weaver played for the home run.

In 1969 Weaver was dealt a straight flush. The Orioles were so good that some observers rated them one of the best teams ever. Frank Robinson's vision had been off since a base running collision in June 1967, but in 1969 he was good as new—.308, 32 homers, 100 RBI. Boog Powell hit 37 homers, Paul Blair 26, Brooks Robinson 23. The defense was at least as good, with Mark Belanger at shortstop, Brooks Robinson at third base, Blair in center field, and a youngster with a managing future of his own—Davey Johnson—at second base.

Weaver knew how to handle pitchers, and he had pitchers to handle. Mike Cuellar had been a hard-luck pitcher at Houston, but with Baltimore he bloomed into a 23-game winner. Dave McNally won his first 15 decisions, tying a record, and a fellow Montanan, U.S. Senator Mike Mansfield, told the Senate that "we are following every game with trepidation."

Jim Palmer, healed at last, won ten straight games in August and September. At 23, he was already talking in orthopedic terms about his joints and muscles—a practice he continued, sometimes to Weaver's irritation, without marring a long and distinguished career. Palmer spent 42 days on the dis-

abled list in 1969, yet finished 16-4, with six shutouts, one a no-hitter. "I'm reserved about success," he said. "I've had to come back about four or five times in the last two years because my arm's been hurt just about everywhere."

The Tigers, defending world champions, tried their best. Willie Horton hit nine homers in nine days. In a September game, Detroit took a 4–2 lead into the ninth, yet lost on successive homers by Robinson, Powell and Robinson. The Orioles won 109 games, and swept the Twins three straight in the first American League Championship Series.

The Twins fired Martin. As other owners would discover, Billy was a winner, but a difficult man to have around. He went on to win a division championship for the Tigers, who fired him, and several pennants for the Yankees, who fired him regularly. Weaver managed the Orioles for 16 years, and won six division championships, four pennants and a World Series.

Ted Williams managed two more seasons in Washington, one in Texas, all dismal. It was just long enough for Martin to rate him "one of the lousiest managers of all time," and for Williams himself to declare: "I wouldn't manage again if you gave me the club and the city it's in."

Following the 1969 season, Williams went hunting for Cape buffalo and greater kudu in Zambia. When told he'd been elected American League Manager of the Year, despite the impressive jobs turned in by Martin and Weaver, Williams said of the honor, "If that's true, it's one more example of how wrong the writers can be." Same Ted Williams. ◑

Baltimore's Earl Weaver was the most successful—and ejectable—manager of his time. Weaver was thrown out 91 times in his 17-year career as a manager, and was even tossed out of both ends of a doubleheader. Here Shag Crawford does the honors in Game 4 of the 1969 World Series.

A Graceful Bow

Ted Williams and Casey Stengel were inducted into the Baseball Hall of Fame in 1966. Everyone expected Stengel to steal the show, including Williams. The Splendid Splinter wrote his acceptance speech in a motel room the night before. He kept it short, but he wowed the crowd. Here is what he said.

"I guess every player thinks about going into the Hall of Fame. Now that the moment has come for me I find it is difficult to say what is really in my heart. But I know it is the greatest thrill of my life. I received 280-odd votes from the writers. I know I didn't have 280-odd close friends among the writers. I know they voted for me because they felt in their minds and some in their hearts that I rated it, and I want to say to them: 'Thank you, from the bottom of my heart.'

Today I am thinking a lot of things. I know I am thinking of my playground director in San Diego, Rodney Luscomb, and my high school coach, Wos Caldwell, my managers, who had such patience with me and helped me so much—fellows like Frank Shellenback, Donie Bush, Joe Cronin and Joe McCarthy. I am thinking of Eddie Collins, who had such faith in me—and to be in the Hall of Fame with him particularly, as well as all those other great ballplayers, is a great honor. I'm sorry Eddie isn't here today.

I'm thinking too of Tom Yawkey. I have always said it: Tom Yawkey is the greatest owner in baseball. I was lucky to have played on the club he owned and I'm grateful to him for being here today.

But I'd not be leveling if I left it at that, because ballplayers are not born great. They're not born great hitters or pitchers or managers, and luck isn't the big factor. No one has come up with a substitute for hard work. I've never met a great player who didn't have to work harder at learning to play ball than anything else he ever did. To me it was the greatest fun I ever had, which probably explains why today I feel both humility and pride, because God let me play the game and learn to be good at it.

The other day Willie Mays hit his 522nd home run. He has gone past me, and he's pushing, and I say to him, 'Go get'em Willie.' Baseball gives every American boy a chance to excel. Not just to be as good as someone else, but to be better. This is the nature of man and the name of the game. I hope that some day Satchel Paige and Josh Gibson will be voted into the Hall of Fame as symbols of the great Negro players who are not here only because they were not given the chance.

As time goes on I'll be thinking baseball, teaching baseball and arguing for baseball to keep it right on top of American sports, just as it is in Japan, Mexico, Venezuela and other Latin and South American countries. I know Casey Stengel feels the same way. I also know I'll lose a dear friend if I don't stop talking. I'm eating into his time, and that is unforgivable. So in closing, I am grateful and know how lucky I was to have been born an American and I had a chance to play the game I loved, the *greatest* game."

Ted Williams—the man many call the greatest hitter ever—performed baseball's most stirring final act when he homered in his last at-bat September 28, 1960 at Fenway Park. Catcher Jim Pagliaroni (29) was the first to offer congratulations.

The Amazin' Mets

Even before they took the field, the New York Mets had the fans in stitches and the Yankees in retreat. They set up their first ticket office at the Martinique Hotel, not far from the Metropolitan Opera House. The sign read simply, METS TICKET OFFICE. An opera patron came by. "Two for *Traviata*,"he said. "First- or third-base side?" replied the clerk.

That was in November 1961. On Thanksgiving Day, the Mets entered a float in the annual Macy's parade. It featured Casey Stengel's name in flowers—and Casey himself aboard, waving to the fans.

The next spring, the Mets assembled for their first spring training. Stengel looked over his charges, and led them on a walk around the bases. "Them are the bases," he said. "We just went around them." A writer asked Stengel, "How do you think you'll do, managing this new team?"

"I don't know how I'll do," he replied. "It ain't been managed yet."

Indeed it had not. The Mets were new, created by expansion. Some said that the players the Mets had assembled were beyond managing. Many, like Gil Hodges and Gus Bell, were too old or infirm. Others, like Rod Kanehl, who played seven positions with an equal lack of grace, were too clumsy. When the Mets selected Giants' catcher Hobie Landrith as their first pick in the expansion draft, writers asked Stengel why.

"Ya gotta start with a catcher, 'cause if you don't you'll have all passed balls," he replied. The Mets used six catchers in their first season, and still had 26 passed balls.

Casey Stengel led the parade welcoming NL baseball back to New York in 1961. He set the tone for the Mets' early years at the news conference that announced his hiring as manager. "It's a great honor for me to be joining the Knickerbockers," he said.

Stengel (37) and the Mets looked for help from every corner, but got little, especially from the bullpen. Met relief pitchers combined for a major league record-low ten saves in 1962. Their total rose to 12 in 1963 and 15 in 1964.

The American League expanded in 1961, adding the Los Angeles Angels and a new Washington Senators franchise to replace the old one, which had moved to Minneapolis–St. Paul. The Mets and the Houston Colt .45s (later Astros) started play in 1962.

So the Mets were not the first expansion team. But they were the worst, and they came to symbolize the humorous futility of a team born raw and thrust into the major leagues. Later, when they succeeded, they were embraced as symbols of baseball's new order, the young and brash overcoming the old and traditional.

In their first season the Mets won 40 games and lost 120, a record that still stands as the worst in baseball history. They lost more than 100 games in each of their first four seasons. Even Houston, the league's other expansion team, consistently drubbed the Mets.

Yet the Mets were an immediate success. They had adoring fans, hungry for National League baseball after the loss of the Giants and Dodgers. They had a wealthy, generous and enthusiastic owner in Mrs. Charles Shipman Payson, the former Joan Whitney. She was worth several hundred million dollars herself, and when she married she chose a man of similar background.

They had a witty and indulgent press, made up of writers and broadcasters who were glad to have some fun after covering the stuffy Yankees. The New York press, for better or worse, is read nationwide, so Mets' misplays became the laughingstock of Peoria and Ponca City as well as New York.

For local appeal, the Mets had the good sense to hire as many old Yankee, Giant and Dodger heroes as they could, and they started at the top, with George Weiss and Casey Stengel.

It was hardly business as usual when the Dodgers played New York at the Polo Grounds (above) in 1962. The Dodgers had come cross-country by plane instead of crosstown by bus, and they were not playing the Giants. Even more unusual was this scene, in which the Mets have two runners on base at the same time.

Weiss had put together the great post-World War II Yankee teams, and Stengel had managed them to ten pennants and seven world championships. Stengel was baseball's most charming, eccentric and quotable figure. But he was 71 and Weiss was 66. Both had been forced into retirement in 1960 by the Yankees' corporate brain trust. Stengel was fired outright. Weiss was put out to pasture as an adviser, at $35,000 a year, under a contract that forbade him to become general manager of any other team.

Four months later, the infant Mets hired Weiss. They called him president, not general manager. For the next five years, he collected $35,000 a year from the Yankees while helping the Mets win thousands of fans from the Yankees, and he did it mostly by picking the right manager—Casey Stengel.

Every clumsy Yankee move was trumped by the Mets. The Yankees abandoned St. Petersburg, where they had held spring training for decades. The Mets moved in. They hired Gus Mauch as their trainer and Red Ruffing as their pitching coach; the former had rubbed down two generations of Yankees, and the latter was one of the Yankees' all-time great pitchers.

In 1964 the Yankees tried to soften their hard, cold image by hiring Yogi Berra—America's baseball teddy bear—as manager. He led the Yankees to the pennant, but they fired him. The Mets promptly hired him, as a coach.

While awaiting the completion of Shea Stadium, the new home that New York was eagerly building for them, the Mets rented the Polo Grounds, the most ancient and hallowed of New York ballparks, home of the Giants from Mathewson to Mays. To get the Polo Grounds back in shape, they hired James K. "Big Jim" Thomson, former stadium manager of both Ebbets Field and Yankee Stadium.

To coach first base, they hired Cookie Lavagetto, the former Dodger

whose double with two out in the ninth inning had ended a World Series no-hit bid by the Yankees' Bill Bevans in 1947. To play first base, they drafted Gil Hodges, the old Dodger slugger. To play third, they picked Don Zimmer, another old Dodger. Hodges' bad knees kept him from playing much, and Zimmer set one of the Mets' first futility records—34 straight times at bat without a hit. But the two veterans added atmosphere and brought in fans.

Not that the Mets were playing for the older generation. Although 71 himself, Stengel had the promotional energy of a rookie. "I guess they want high-class people back there," Stengel said of his appointment. "You can say I'm happy to be going back to the Polar Grounds." He referred to his team as "the Knickerbockers."

Actually, ten names had been considered—Continentals, Skyliners, Mets, Jets, Meadowlarks, Burros, Skyscrapers, Rebels, NYBs and Avengers. Mrs. Payson invited the press in for cocktails, held up a slip of paper, and said, "I like this one. The Mets."

"OK," a writer said. "Let's go, Mets."

Stengel began referring to his team as "the amazin' Mets," and headline writers often did without the final word, as in AMAZINS LOSE 2. Wherever Stengel went—and he rarely rested—he appealed to "the youth of America." It was not clear whether he was looking for players or fans, but he got both. The players weren't much good, but the fans were wonderful.

These were fans of the television age, young men and women who wanted to be part of the show. They have since been emulated elsewhere, but in 1962 they were "the new breed," a name applied by Dick Young of the New York *Daily News.* Unlike old-fashioned Yankee fans, they came not to ooh and aah but to laugh and love—an act that one young couple consummated

under a blanket on a sunny, happy Sunday. An usher led them out despite the woman's assurances. "We're married, and we're Mets fans!" she said.

Mets fan clubs sprung up in improbable places. When President John F. Kennedy made his historic visit to West Berlin in 1963, enthusiastic Germans greeted him with banners—one of which said LET'S GO METS. At Sing Sing prison, 20 men on death row were absorbed in a Mets game when they were told that New York State had abolished the death penalty. "There was no reaction at all," said warden Wilfred L. Denno. "They just kept listening to the ballgame."

At the Polo Grounds, a few fans took to writing on bedsheets and hanging these homemade banners from the railings. Some simply said LET'S GO METS. Others praised—or ridiculed—Mets antiheroes such as Rod Kanehl and Marv Throneberry. PRAY! said one expressive banner. WE DON'T WANT TO SET THE WORLD ON FIRE—WE JUST WANT TO FINISH NINTH said another. Another: TO ERR IS HUMAN, TO FORGIVE IS A METS FAN.

The craze spread. At first, George Weiss disapproved, and had his ushers remove the banners. But the press set up an outcry, and the Mets came to realize that banners were part of the game—on many days, the best part. By 1963, the Mets were promoting an annual Banner Day, complete with parade. Mets players painted up their own banner. It said WE LOVE YOU FANS, and the players carried it around the field.

Fans also led each other in cheers. One was, "Cranberry, Strawberry, We Love Throneberry." The subject of this adulation was Marvin Eugene "Marvelous Marv" Throneberry, a player bad enough to capture the heart and soul of New York.

The Mets provided safe harbor to just about everybody in 1962. Second baseman Charlie Neal (above) was a pretty good fielder caught in a pretty bad situation, as the '62 Mets committed 210 errors, the most since the 1948 Phillies. After setting an all-time record for the lowest team fielding percentage—.967—in '62, the Mets tied their record the following season.

"Marvelous Marv" Throneberry's technique for fielding grounders—eyes on the batter—probably did a lot for sales of Bromo Seltzer at the Polo Grounds in 1963. Despite playing just 116 games, Throneberry paced NL first baseman with 17 errors.

Throneberry had spent three years on the Yankees' bench after hitting 82 home runs in two seasons at Denver, where the air is thin. He had been traded from New York to Kansas City to Baltimore, and early in the 1962 season he came to the Mets in exchange for Hobie Landrith, the catcher whom the Mets had so eagerly drafted.

Stengel needed a first baseman with power. Throneberry fit that description—he stood where a first baseman is supposed to stand, and he hit 16 home runs. But when a ball was ready to be dropped, Throneberry always seemed to drop it, and when a Met rally needed killing, Marv was the hit man.

Throneberry couldn't understand why the fans laughed at him. "I am a sweet hitter," he said. "Not really a great hitter. Just a sweet hitter."

On June 17, 1962, the Cubs came to New York and scored four runs in the first inning with the help of an interference call against Throneberry, who stood in the baseline when he should have stepped out of the runner's way. But in the bottom of the first, the Mets showed off the skill of three veterans they had acquired since the draft. Richie Ashburn, the former Phillie star, bunted for a single. Gene Woodling, the former Yankee, walked. Frank Thomas, the former Pirate slugger, singled Ashburn home.

Throneberry, the epitome of young muscle, slashed a drive off the right field wall. Woodling and Thomas scored, and Throneberry pulled into third base. But Ernie Banks, the Cubs' first baseman, called for the ball and stepped on first, claiming Throneberry had failed to touch the base. The umpire, Dusty Boggess, agreed; Throneberry was out. Stengel stormed out of the dugout, but was quieted by his first-base coach, Cookie Lavagetto. "Don't argue too much, Case," Lavagetto said. "I think he missed second base, too."

With Landrith gone, the Mets worked their way through a succession

The Mets' over-30 crowd (left) seemed pretty excited the day before the team's 1962 season opener. Whooping it up at the Polo Grounds are, from left to right, outfielder Frank Thomas, 33, first baseman Gil Hodges, 38, third baseman Don Zimmer, 31, and pitcher Roger Craig, 31.

In 1964 this Johnny Hero doll was just one example of how the Mets did better in the marketplace than they did on the field.

of catchers. One was Clarence "Choo Choo" Coleman, who had caught for Philadelphia. A Phillies' pitcher, asked to name the toughest man in the league to pitch to, answered "Coleman"—not referring to his batting prowess. Stengel disagreed. "He can handle a low-ball pitcher because he crawls on his belly like a snake," Stengel said of young Coleman.

As for himself, Coleman said little beyond "Yeah, bub." Ralph Kiner, the great slugger turned Mets radio announcer, faced the prospect of interviewing Coleman, and figured his nickname, at least, would be worth a story.

"Choo Choo, where did you get your nickname?" Kiner asked.

"Dunno," Coleman replied.

Although Stengel was never at a loss for words, he rarely remembered names. At midseason, the Mets acquired catcher Joe Pignatano from the Giants. Pignatano took the train to New York from Philadelphia, where the Giants had been playing. He put on his new Mets uniform, stepped into the dugout and introduced himself to Stengel. It was several hours before game time, and Stengel and Pignatano were shooting the breeze. Sportswriter Jack Lang came by, greeted Pignatano, and asked Stengel who would catch that night. "I'll catch that new kid we just got from the Giants if he ever gets here," Stengel answered.

He also tried Harry Chiti, a catcher acquired from Cleveland's farm system for a "player to be named later." *Later* came after Stengel watched Chiti play 15 games, and the player Stengel named was Harry Chiti. He was returned to Jacksonville, traded for himself. A strong young catcher named Greg Goossen came up in 1965, and Stengel, putting the best face on things, said, "We have this fine young catcher named Goossen who is only 20 years old, and in 10 years he has a chance to be 30."

Continued on page 164

The Duke Goes Home

Donald Edwin Snider was born in Los Angeles, belonged to Brooklyn, but somehow seemed far from home in either setting. Although Brooklyn fans loved their Duke, Snider never fit the Dodger image. He was too Californian. Handsome, and prematurely gray at the temples, he looked more like an up-and-coming banker than a ballplayer. Dodger haters liked to say that the Duke was aloof, that he played only for money, that his heart belonged in the avocado fields of California, not the outfield of Brooklyn. And Snider could also be arrogant. In 1955 he blasted Dodger fans, saying, "They're the worst fans in the world. They don't deserve a pennant."

In 1957 Dodger owner Walter O'Malley announced plans to move the team to Los Angeles. Snider should have been thrilled; he was crushed. In their own peculiar ways, Snider and the Borough of Brooklyn had adopted each other. In 1947 Snider had roomed with Gil Hodges in a house on Bedford Avenue, two blocks from Ebbets Field. Brooklyn became Snider's summer home.

In 1958, when the Willard Mullin cartoon bum was deemed too down-and-out for LA, the team appropriated a baseball with a halo of sunbeams as its insignia. Four years later, the team moved into Dodger Stadium. The Duke of Flatbush in Chavez Ravine? Something in the sound of it didn't travel well.

The shock of leaving Brooklyn was nothing compared with what Snider must have felt when he first saw the Los Angeles Coliseum, the Dodgers' temporary home through 1961. The right field line measured 390 feet; in Ebbets Field it was 297. And Snider was a left-handed hitter. With a 40-foot left field screen a mere 250 feet from home plate and an interminably distant center field, the Coliseum promised high drama for fans and pitchers alike.

Snider adjusted, hitting .312 in 1958 and .308 with 23 homers in 1959.

By the time the 1960s arrived, Snider was 33 years old. The '60s belonged to Sandy Koufax, Don Drysdale, Maury Wills, big Frank Howard, and the Davis speedsters, Tommy and Willie. By 1962, Snider, the Dodger captain, was a full-time role player. He appeared in only 80 games in 1962, including the 165th of the season, the third and deciding game of a pennant playoff against, of all teams, the San Francisco Giants.

Snider was the only player on the 1962 Dodgers who had appeared in the previous playoff between these two teams, the 1951 cliffhanger known as the Miracle of Coogan's Bluff. As in '51, the Dodgers took a 4–1 lead into the ninth. "It all looked too familiar," Snider wrote in his autobiography. "There was too much 1951 and I didn't like the symptoms." Only this time the Dodgers fell victim to a self-inflicted mud slide, not a two-out, three-run homer. A couple of scratch singles, an error, a couple of walks: 5–4 Giants. Same as '51.

The loss haunted both management and players all winter. By 1963 the front office was ready to shed any remnant of their carpetbagger image and its jinx-ridden legacy. On April 1, 1963, the Los Angeles Dodgers held an estate sale, and for $40,000 the New York Mets purchased the last vestige of the Dodgers' Brooklyn origins: Duke Snider. Six years after the franchise had settled in LA, the Dodger transition was complete.

The roster of the New York Mets was already well stocked with ex-Dodgers when Snider joined the club for the opening of the 1963 season. Gil Hodges, Charlie Neal, Roger Craig, Larry Burright, Tim Harkness, Norm Sherry: all were former Dodgers playing for the worst team in baseball. If the sight of Gil Hodges in a home uniform

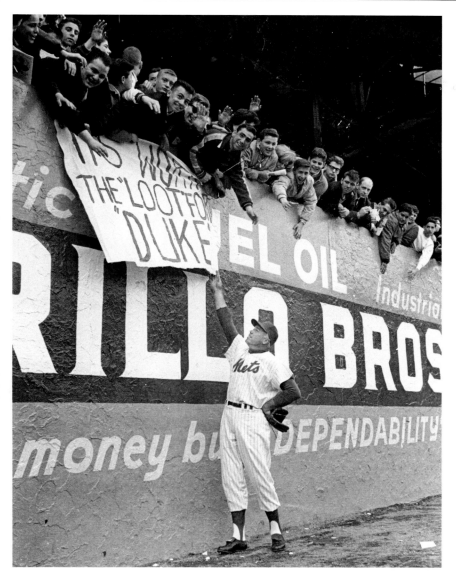

Snider, known as "The Silver Fox," returned to New York in 1963 to spend his golden years before fans who remembered the grace with which he roamed the outfield at Ebbets Field when he was a Brooklyn Dodger.

DUKE SNIDER

Outfield
Brooklyn Dodgers 1947–1957
Los Angeles Dodgers 1958–1962
New York Mets 1963
San Francisco Giants 1964
Hall of Fame 1980

GAMES	**2,143**
AT BATS	**7,161**
BATTING AVERAGE	
Career	**.295**
Season High	**.341**
SLUGGING AVERAGE	
Career	**.540**
Season High	**.647**
HITS	
Career	**2,116**
Season High	**199**
DOUBLES	
Career	**358**
Season High	**39**
TRIPLES	
Career	**85**
Season High	**10**
HOME RUNS	
Career	**407**
Season High	**43**
TOTAL BASES	**3,865**
EXTRA BASE HITS	**850**
RUNS BATTED IN	
Career	**1,333**
Season High	**136**
RUNS	
Career	**1,259**
Season High	**132**
WORLD SERIES	**1949, 1952**
	1953, 1955, 1956, 1959

at the Polo Grounds seemed ludicrous, that of Duke Snider in one was sacrilege.

Snider played one year for the Mets. He hit 14 home runs, including one off Don Drysdale in his first at-bat as a Met in Dodger Stadium. In April 1964 the team made Snider expendable, and the Giants purchased his contract for the final season of his career. Once again, The Duke of Flatbush was back on the West Coast, if not quite home.

Utility infielder Rod Kanehl (above) was a favorite both of Met fans and manager Casey Stengel because of his hustling style of play. Kanehl captured the fans' fancy early in the 1962 season by scoring from second on a passed ball, and here he beats the tag of Bill White, St. Louis first baseman and future president of the National League.

Players came and went. Evans Killeen, a promising pitcher, cut his thumb while shaving, and never came back. Grover Powell injured his pitching arm while combing his hair. The Mets had two pitchers named Bob Miller, one right-handed and the other a lefty, and roomed them together as a favor to hotel switchboard operators.

Still, Stengel couldn't remember their names—or name. He called the bullpen one day and told Pignatano to warm up Nelson. The team had no one named Nelson, except a play-by-play broadcaster, and Pignatano said so, but Stengel insisted. Pignatano later related the incident to sportswriters: "So I just took a baseball and put it on the rubber and said to the guys in the bullpen, 'He wants Nelson.' Bob Miller got up immediately and grabbed the ball. 'He always calls me Nelson,' Miller said."

The Mets went for a veteran team in hopes the familiar old players would draw fans and might still have a little zip. But the team lost and lost. Heading for their glorious inaugural on opening day of 1962, a dozen of them got stuck in a hotel elevator. They lost, in St. Louis, and flew home to a ticker-tape parade. When Stengel was told that it was the first big parade in New York since astronaut John Glenn was honored, he said, "We ain't never gonna get that high. I'll settle for ninth place right now."

They lost their first nine games, won a few, and then lost 17 straight. Their pitchers—and fielders—yielded ten or more runs 23 times in that inglorious maiden season.

After the Mets lost their opener in 1963, Stengel said, "We're still frauds. We're cheating the public." Whereupon the Mets lost seven more games before finally winning. In 1964 they lost 16 of their first 19, settling into last place for good on April 23. "We're gonna finish 30th," Stengel said. He meant tenth

Mets vs Yankees

Fans usually flock to see winning teams and to avoid losers, but in the 1960s the Mets turned the tables on the Yankees.

| METS | | | YANKEES | |
Position in Standings	Home Attendance	Year	Home Attendance	Position in Standings
10th	922,530	**1962**	1,493,574	1st
10th	1,080,108	**1963**	1,308,920	1st
10th	1,732,597	**1964**	1,305,638	1st
10th	1,768,389	**1965**	1,213,552	6th
9th	1,932,693	**1966**	1,124,648	10th
10th	1,565,492	**1967**	1,141,714	9th
9th	1,781,657	**1968**	1,125,124	5th
1st	2,175,373	**1969**	1,067,996	5th

Divisional play began in 1969. The Yankees finished fifth in a six-team division.

Met fans were a new breed—young, fanatical and fashion-conscious.

for the third straight year, and by that standard the Mets finished 40th in 1965, 49th (ninth place!) in 1966, and 59th (last again) in 1967.

Yet the fans kept coming. The Mets moved into Shea Stadium in 1964, finished last, and drew 1.7 million, more than any other major league team except the Los Angeles Dodgers. The Yankees finished first and drew only 1.3 million. The old order was changing; 1965 and 1966 marked the first time in 20 years New York had gone two seasons in a row without a pennant.

The Mets' best pitchers piled up the worst records, simply because they pitched so much. Roger Craig, a good pitcher who later became a very good manager, won ten games in 1962, a quarter of the team's total. But he lost 24, and the next year he lost 18 straight en route to a record of 5–22. "The losing doesn't bother me," Craig said. "It's the not winning that hurts." Five of his losses were by 1–0 scores.

The Mets uncharacteristically swept a doubleheader on May 12, 1962. Craig Anderson, pitching in relief, was the winning pitcher in both games, bringing his record to 3–1. He never won another game, losing 16 straight in 1962, two in 1963, and one in 1964 to bow out of the major leagues with a 19-game losing streak.

One Met pitcher, Ken MacKenzie, did register a winning record (5–4) in 1962. He was a Yale graduate. "I have taken a survey and I find that I am the lowest paid alumnus in the entire Yale class of 1956," he said. Stengel brought him in to relieve one day, handed him the ball and said, "Pretend they're the Harvards."

So suspect were the Mets' pitching and defense that when the Mets beat the Cubs 19–1 in an unusual game early in 1964, a fan called a newspaper

Met first baseman Gil Hodges pleaded with pitcher Bob Miller to get a grip on things, but in 1962 Miller would have been better off keeping his hands off the ball. He went 1-12 with a 4.89 ERA that season.

in Waterbury, Connecticut. "Hey, I hear the Mets scored 19 runs today," the fan said.

"That's right," the operator replied.

"But did they win?" the fan asked.

In 1964 the Mets' losses boiled over in criticism of Stengel. Howard Cosell, an aggressive young announcer for New York's WABC, repeatedly suggested that Stengel was more entertainer than manager, more interested in his own reputation than in the success of the Mets. Jackie Robinson was quoted as saying that Stengel dozed on the bench. "You'd think they was trying to put me in a museum," Casey said.

Weiss signed Stengel for another year. At midseason—July 24, 1965—Stengel partied deep into the night at Toots Shor's. The next day, the Mets were staging a double promotion—Oldtimers' Day, coupled with celebration of Stengel's 75th birthday.

Stengel spent the night at a friend's home, not far from the ballpark. He complained of pain during the night and was taken to a hospital, where X-rays disclosed a broken hip. Coach and former New York Giant catcher Wes Westrum took over the team, and Stengel soon decided to retire. "I got this limp," he said, "and if I can't walk out there to take the pitcher out, I can't manage." Stengel had been in professional baseball since 1910, and he had managed for 25 years.

Some fans thought Berra should have gotten the managing job, but Westrum's syntax had that Stengelese edge. "Boy, when they made him they threw away the molding," he said of Stengel. After a close game, Westrum said, "Whew! That was a real cliffdweller!"

The Mets were awful in 1966, but they were beginning to spot their line-

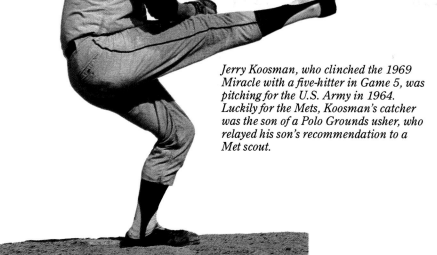

Jerry Koosman, who clinched the 1969 Miracle with a five-hitter in Game 5, was pitching for the U.S. Army in 1964. Luckily for the Mets, Koosman's catcher was the son of a Polo Grounds usher, who relayed his son's recommendation to a Met scout.

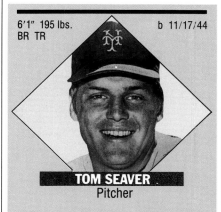

6'1" 195 lbs. b 11/17/44
BR TR

TOM SEAVER
Pitcher

After graduating from Fresno High School in 1962, Tom Seaver joined the Marines; pitched in a semipro league in Alaska and in college at the University of Southern California; was drafted by the Dodgers and offered a contract by the Braves; was signed by the Mets; and won 16 games and the NL Rookie of the Year Award in 1967—all before his 23rd birthday. By 1969, Seaver was known as "Tom Terrific," winner of 25 games and the Cy Young Award for the world champion Mets.

In 11 full seasons with the Mets, Seaver won 20 or more games four times, five times leading the league in strikeouts, three times in ERA, and twice in wins and winning percentage. He added his second and third Cy Young awards in 1973 and 1975.

Seaver was 7–3 in June 1977, when a falling out with Mets' ownership brought about his trade to Cincinnati. He finished the year at 21–6, and remained with the Reds through the 1982 season, winning a league-leading 14 games in 1981 and pitching a 4–0 no-hitter against the St. Louis Cardinals in 1978.

Traded back to New York in 1983, Seaver was signed by the White Sox when the Mets failed to protect him in the 1984 compensation draft. He ended his career in 1986 with the pennant-winning Boston Red Sox. In 20 years, Seaver won 311 games, had a .603 winning percentage, a 2.86 ERA, and struck out 3,640 batters, third on the all-time list.

up with young players of genuine promise—Cleon Jones, Jerry Grote, Bud Harrelson, Ron Hunt. Pitcher Tug McGraw, 21, threw hard, if erratically.

The brightest Met prospect was a bright and articulate young pitcher who had starred at the University of Southern California. The Braves had paid him a $50,000 bonus, but the contract was voided because it violated baseball's rule against signing college players during their season. To solve the problem, the commissioner's office set up a drawing. Any team willing to pay the $50,000 bonus was allowed to participate. The Mets entered, and won. Their prize was Tom Seaver.

Seaver pitched a season in the minor leagues, then joined the Mets in 1967. He was a sensation, the NL Rookie of the Year, with 16 wins, 13 losses and a 2.76 ERA—far and away the best record ever by a Met pitcher.

Seaver won 16 games again in 1968 but was overshadowed by another rookie, Jerry Koosman, who shut out the Giants as the Mets won their home opener for the first time. Koosman posted seven shutouts for the season, more than any National League rookie since Grover Cleveland Alexander in 1911. Koosman won 19 games and finished one point behind Cincinnati's Johnny Bench in the voting for Rookie of the Year. Another Met rookie, Nolan Ryan, threw harder than either Seaver or Koosman, but missed most of the season because of blisters on his pitching hand.

The Mets were showing promise. Whitey Herzog was putting together a strong player development program. Gil Hodges, the longtime Dodger first baseman, was hired away from the Washington Senators and became the Mets' manager in 1968. But the team continued to founder, finishing last in 1967 and ninth in 1968. Hodges ran a strict spring training camp in 1969 and predicted the Mets would win 85 games, but few took him seriously. The

Continued on page 170

A Cincinnati Centennial

On June 1, 1869, the Cincinnati Red Stockings—a club whose members were all paid to play baseball—defeated the Mansfield Independents 48–14, and the all-salaried baseball team was born. The history of professional baseball, its milestones and innovations, parallels the history of the Cincinnati team. One hundred years before Sparky Anderson's "Big Red Machine," Aaron Champion, a local attorney and sports promoter, popularized in Cincinnati an idea that changed the game—and a nation—forever.

Champion's Red Stockings—taking their name from the color of their socks, as was customary at the time—were managed by Harry Wright. The team won all its 52 games in 1869, and ran up an incredible 130–0–1 record before its first loss, in June 1870. As Wright's professionals barnstormed the country, their influence proved immeasurable: amateurs everywhere wanted nothing less than to sign contracts to play for pay; and from coast to coast, moneyed promoters, inspired by Champion's success, were waiting to accommodate them.

The first player Wright recruited was his brother George, a shortstop. And for good reason. At 5′9″ and 150 pounds, George Wright was a 19th-century Pete Rose, the best baseballer in the country, the player fans came to see. In 1869 he batted .518, hit 52 homers, scored 339 runs, and was paid the handsome sum of $1,400—high on the team.

Cincinnati's success in league play, however, left something to be desired. In 1876, playing in the newly formed National Baseball League, the Reds finished last with a 9–56 record. Cincinnati was expelled from the league in 1880 for violating the ban on selling beer at games. The team moved to the American Association, rejoining the National League when the ban was lifted in 1890.

By the turn of the century, and for the next 50 years, the team's official name was the Reds. In 1953, with the fear of communism sweeping the country, management advisedly assumed its former name, Red Stockings, switching to Redlegs from 1955 to 1958. By 1959 Senator Joe McCarthy's "red scare" had subsided and the team once again became the Reds.

Throughout the 20th century, the Reds were involved in some of the game's most unusual moments. On May 2, 1917, Fred Toney of the Reds and Hippo Vaughn of the Cubs hooked up in baseball's only double no-hit game. The Reds won it when Vaughn allowed the game's only hit in the tenth inning. On October 2, 1920, Cincinnati beat Pittsburgh two games out of three in baseball's last triple-header. Eighteen seasons later, in 1938, the Reds' Johnny Vander Meer pitched baseball's only back-to-back no-hitters, beating the Braves 3–0 on June 11 and the Dodgers 6–0 four days later.

Cincinnati won its first World Series in 1919, beating the favored Chicago White Sox five games to three. The following season, eight White Sox players were accused of having thrown the Series, leading to what has since become known as the Black Sox Scandal.

Under general manager Larry MacPhail, the Reds helped modernize baseball in the 1930s. In 1934, Cincinnati became the first major league team to fly to an away game. The following season the Reds played the first night game in major league history. After establishing baseball's first national radio hookup, Cincinnati appeared in baseball's first televised game against the Dodgers on August 26, 1939. Three decades later, Cincinnati's Pete Rose collected the 1,000th of his career record 4,256 hits. Baseball's second 100 years was officially under way.

Cincinnati baseball through the years: (opposite) the 1869 Red Stockings; (top) the 1895 Red Stockings; (left) H.M. Mott-Smith's painting of baseball's first night game—which was played at Crosley Field in Cincinnati in 1935; (above) the Reds went first into baseball's second century.

Unfamiliarity with being on base led Met players into embarassing situations like this one in 1962. Frank Thomas (25) makes it back to third in time to see teammate Charlie Neal already there. Thomas, having already touched third once, had squatter's rights, so Neal had to race back to second. Witnessing this comedy of errors were Phillies' first baseman Don Demeter (24), catcher Sammy White (9), shortstop Ruben Amaro and umpire Dusty Boggess, the man who had to sort it all out.

In 1966 hitters got their first look at Nolan Ryan. Ryan struck out six in three innings of work, then tried pickle brine as a solution to his blister problem.

Justice rarely smiled on the Mets, and so on this play shortstop Roy McMillan (opposite, 11), known for his good glove, got charged for the error while second baseman Chuck "Iron Hands" Hiller (2) got off scot-free. The play came in a rare doubleheader sweep for the Mets in 1965, in which the Cubs were the embarrassed victims.

Cardinals, runaway winners in 1967 and 1968, were considered shoo-ins. Jimmy the Greek posted the Mets at 75 to 1.

Baseball celebrated its centennial in 1969. The All-Star Game was held in Washington, DC, and President Richard M. Nixon held a White House reception the night before for players, officials, sportswriters and an impressive collection of old-time stars who had been voted baseball's "greatest living players."

With the leagues expanded to 12 teams each, baseball now had four pennant races. The Chicago Cubs, under Leo Durocher, were the surprise pace-setters of the National League East. The Mets, under Hodges, were a close second. It was amazin'.

On July 8 the Cubs came to New York to pad their slim lead. "The Cubs are gonna shine in '69," sang Cubs' first baseman Ernie Banks. It was the first truly crucial game in Met history, and 55,096 came to see it.

Chicago's Ferguson Jenkins dueled Jerry Koosman, and the Cubs led 3-1 as the Mets came up in the ninth. Don Young, playing center field for the Cubs because of his alleged defensive skills, misplayed two balls like a regular Met. Cleon Jones doubled two runs home, and Ed Kranepool, the last of the original Mets, singled in the winning run.

The next night, with an even larger crowd on hand, Seaver took a perfect game into the last of the ninth. He retired the first batter, but the next, rookie Jimmy Qualls, singled sharply. Seaver got the next two outs, and as he emerged from postgame interviews he spotted his wife, Nancy, in tears. "What are you crying for?" he asked. "We won 4–0."

The Cubs took the series finale, but the Mets were in the race to stay.

Met second baseman Al Weis (6) fought to a draw in this collision with Cub outfielder Jim Qualls, but in the 1969 World Series the light-hitting Weis would deliver two crushing blows to the Baltimore Orioles. His two-out single in the ninth inning gave the Mets a 2–1 win in Game 2, and his home run in the seventh inning of Game 5 tied the score, and the Mets went on to finish the Miracle, 5–3.

The Miracle Mets were a nationwide sensation, and drew fans from all walks of life, including former First Lady Jacqueline Kennedy Onassis (center), who showed up at Shea with son John-John (left) and daughter Caroline (far right).

A week later they traveled to Chicago and again won two of three, pulling within 3½ games of first place.

The Mets got help from unexpected quarters. Bud Harrelson, like many players of the Vietnam era, missed two weeks for Army Reserve summer camp, but a White Sox castoff named Al Weis filled in admirably at shortstop. Tommie Agee, a disappointment in 1968, provided power at the plate and defensive skill in center field. Cleon Jones played alongside Agee, as he had when they were high school classmates in Alabama, and led the league in batting much of the year. For home run help, the Mets acquired veteran first baseman Donn Clendenon from Houston.

In early August the Mets slumped and the Cubs pulled 9½ games ahead. Leo Durocher had a strong team, with sluggers Billy Williams, Ron Santo and Ernie Banks in the middle of the lineup. Many said the race was over, but Hodges' team righted itself. Agee hit a homer in the 14th inning for a 1–0 win over the Giants' Juan Marichal, who had beaten the Mets the first 19 times he pitched against them. The Cardinals' Steve Carlton set a record by striking out 19 Mets, but Ron Swoboda hit two two-run homers off Carlton and New York won, 4–3.

With 40,450 on hand, Seaver won his 20th game, downing the Phillies 5–1 and pulling the Mets within four games of first place. They closed the gap to 2½ and were about to host the Cubs for two games at Shea Stadium.

Cubs' starter Bill Hands decked Agee in the first inning, and Koosman responded by drilling Santo in the elbow. Agee hit a two-run homer and later doubled and scored on a single by Wayne Garrett. Koosman struck out 13, and the Mets won, 3–2. Seaver beat Jenkins the next day, and then the Mets took first place by sweeping a doubleheader from Montreal.

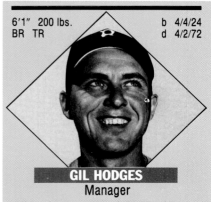

6'1" 200 lbs.   b 4/4/24
BR TR   d 4/2/72

GIL HODGES
Manager

Gil Hodges managed the Washington Senators from tenth place in 1963 to sixth place in 1967. But a repeat performance seemed unlikely when Hodges was signed to manage the New York Mets in 1968. Following a ninth-place finish that first season, Hodges performed the unimaginable, taking the Mets to their first world championship in 1969. During New York's victory parade, one writer remarked, "Hodges was typecast for the role. He was the Mets' first first baseman, the guy who was forced to teach Throneberry."

Born Gilbert Raymond Hodge, the son of a coal miner in Princeton, Indiana, Hodges was drafted as a third baseman by the Dodgers in 1943, served with the Marines in World War II, then spent the 1947 season learning to be a catcher. When Brooklyn brought up Roy Campanella in 1948, Hodges shifted to first base, where he became a Gold Glove fielder.

Hodges played 16 years for the Dodgers, the most memorable 12 in Brooklyn, where in 1950 he hit four home runs in one game. He hit 30 or more homers six times with Brooklyn and drove in 100 or more runs for seven consecutive seasons, 1949 to 1955. In 1954 he set career highs with 42 homers, 130 RBI and a .304 batting average. Hodges retired in 1963 with a .273 career average and 370 homers.

After managing the Mets to third-place finishes in 1970 and 1971, Hodges died of a heart attack in spring training in 1972.

The Mets were on a ten-game winning streak while Chicago lost eight in a row. Durocher snarled and cursed, but he could not make the Cubs win. The two teams passed one another like cars speeding in opposite directions, and the Mets coasted home by eight games. They won 38 of their last 49 games, mostly on superb pitching. Seaver won his last ten games and came in at 25–7 with a 2.21 ERA. Koosman, after a slow start, won eight of his last nine; for the season he was 17–9, 2.28. Rookie Gary Gentry won 13 games, and veteran Don Cardwell won five in a row when the race was close. Tug McGraw and veteran Ron Taylor pitched well in relief.

In the first National League Championship Series, the Mets, an expansion team, faced the Atlanta Braves, an old team in a new city. Both teams came in hot; the Braves had won their last ten games, 17 of their last 20. Jones paced the Mets with a .340 average and Agee had 26 homers, but the Mets' lineup was puny compared with that of the Braves. Atlanta had Orlando Cepeda, Felipe Alou, Rico Carty and—most of all—Hank Aaron, who had led the National League with 44 home runs.

New York had an edge in pitching, although Phil Niekro won 23 games for Atlanta, Ron Reed 18, and reliever Cecil Upshaw six, plus 27 saves. In the playoffs, however, the Mets suffered a pitching slump. Seaver was knocked out of the first game, and Koosman was KO'd in the second. Gentry didn't make it through the third inning of Game 3. Aaron homered in every game.

But the Mets, for once, hit like crazy: in three games 37 hits, six homers, 27 runs. They swept the Braves, and put on their underdog clothes for a World Series against the Baltimore Orioles, who had coasted to the pennant, swept the playoffs from Minnesota, and graciously accepted praise as baseball's best team since the 1961 Yankees.

Continued on page 177

Shea Stadium

Designed by the same architectural firm—Prager-Kavanaugh-Waterbury—that built Dodger Stadium, Shea Stadium is everything the Dodgers' park is not. It's loud and it's raucous. The constant air traffic in and out of nearby La Guardia Airport is only a partial source of noise. Mets' fans are some of the most vocally loyal in all of baseball.

Shea Stadium is located in Flushing Meadow Park, adjacent to the site of the 1939 and the 1964 World's Fairs. Because the park has no bleachers and is open beyond the outfield fences, winds can play havoc with fly balls hit to the outfield, particularly in early April and late September, when the grandstand can feel like the coldest place on earth.

The park has undergone relatively few changes since it was opened in 1964. Seating comprises five tiers, including the press and club level, and 96 percent of all seats are located in foul territory. Built at a cost of $28.5 million and financed through New York City bonds, Shea is the first stadium ever built that allowed for conversion from baseball to football configurations by means of underground tracks on which motor-operated stands are moved. The scoreboard in right center field—86 feet high by 175 feet long—is the largest in the major leagues.

Although hurried New Yorkers simply call it Shea, the park's official name is the William A. Shea Municipal Stadium. Shea was the New York attorney who, conniving with former front office genius Branch Rickey, threatened the American and National leagues by inventing the Continental League. Shea agreed to disband his new league—which existed only on paper—if the National League granted the city of New York a franchise. And it was Walter O'Malley, the Dodger owner who moved his team from Brooklyn to Los Angeles in 1958, whose approval of the franchise had the greatest influence among his fellow owners.

While their new park was under construction, the Mets played their first two seasons in the hallowed Polo Grounds, former home of the New York Giants. While many former Dodger fans expressed their eternal allegiance by refusing to root for a team that called the Polo Grounds home, the opening of Shea Stadium on April 17, 1964, served to unite the city of New York. Pregame music at that historic opening was provided by groups as diverse as Guy Lombardo and his Royal Canadians and the New York Sanitation Department Band. The only thing to mar opening day—besides another Mets' loss—was a massive traffic jam that resulted from 3,000 commuters having parked their cars in Shea's parking lots earlier that morning. The park was virtually inaccessible by automobile. Fans bound for the afternoon game abandoned their cars, left their worries to the guys behind them, and walked.

The Mets drew 1.7 million fans that first year, and immediately someone suggested improvements to the new park. A proposal was made to add 15,000 seats and enclose the field beneath a dome, but a study of the stadium's structure showed the plan was unfeasible.

Shea has been the site of two of baseball's longest games: a 23-inning Met loss in 1964 and a 25-inning Met loss in 1974; in each instance Ed Sudol was the home plate umpire. But no moment in Shea Stadium's history lives as warmly in the hearts of Mets fans as the team's 1969 World Series victory over the Orioles—although the retirement of Tom Seaver's Number 41 on July 24, 1988, comes tearfully close.

Shea Stadium

126th Street and
   Roosevelt Avenue
Flushing, New York

Built 1964

New York Mets, NL
   1964–present
New York Yankees, AL
   1974–1975

Seating Capacity 55,601

Style
Grass surface, symmetrical,
   multipurpose

Height of outfield fence
8 feet, foul pole to foul pole

Dugouts
Home, 1st base
Visitors, 3rd base

Bullpens
Outfield, recessed
Home, right field
Visitors, left field

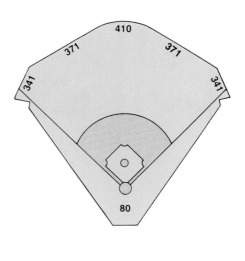

Seaver opened the Series for the Mets and yielded a leadoff homer to Baltimore's Don Buford. With two out in the fourth, the Orioles scored three runs on a walk, three singles and a double. Southpaw Mike Cuellar subdued the New York hitters, and Brooks Robinson snuffed out a threat with a nifty play at third base: 4–1, Baltimore.

Dave McNally, another Oriole lefty, pitched almost as well as Cuellar in the second game, but Koosman pitched better. Clendenon homered for New York in the fourth. Baltimore didn't get a hit until the seventh, when Paul Blair singled, stole second, and scored on a single by Brooks Robinson. With two out in the Met ninth, Ed Charles, Jerry Grote and Al Weis singled for a run. Koosman got through the bottom of the inning with help from Taylor: 2–1, New York.

The Series moved to Shea. Two spectacular catches by Agee helped Gentry and Ryan shut out the Orioles, and Gentry doubled two runs home as the Mets cuffed Jim Palmer, 5-0.

The next day was Moratorium Day, a big nationwide protest against the Vietnam War. Protesters handed out fliers quoting Seaver in strong opposition to American involvement in the conflict. Seaver also had a strong opposition to the Birds, and he took a 1-0 lead into the ninth. With one out, Frank Robinson singled and Boog Powell singled him to third. Brooks Robinson hit a liner to right center that looked like a sure hit, particularly with Ron Swoboda in right field. Of Swoboda's fielding, Casey Stengel had once said, "He's a little weak on balls in the air. He leaps after them when they ain't there."

Swoboda dived, skidded and caught the ball. Frank Robinson scored after the catch to tie the game, but Elrod Hendricks flied to Swoboda to end the inning. In the Met tenth, Don Buford, the Oriole left fielder, misjudged

Game 5 of the 1969 World Series had the Orioles once again going in the wrong direction. Shortstop Mark Belanger (above) just got back ahead of Met catcher Jerry Grote, but the Mets tagged the Orioles out once more, 5–3.

Rookie manager Earl Weaver's main gripe in the 1969 World Series (opposite) was with his Oriole hitters, but he found time to yell at the umpires too. The Orioles hit .146 against the precocious Met pitching staff. The next year Baltimore doubled its Series average to .292 and beat Cincinnati in five games.

"All the News That's Fit to Print"

The New York Times

LATE CITY EDITION

Weather: Variable cloudiness today. Mostly fair tonight and tomorrow. Temp. range: today 61-50; Thurs. 64-47. Full U.S. report on Page 94.

VOL. CXIX...No. 40,809 © 1969 The New York Times Company. NEW YORK, FRIDAY, OCTOBER 17, 1969 10 CENTS

PRESIDENT IS FIRM ON PUSHING POLICY TO CURB INFLATION

He Will Address Nation on Radio Today—Burns Says 'We Will Not Budge'

SURTAX MEASURE GAINS

Nixon Meets With Leaders of Congress to Press His Views on the Economy

By EILEEN SHANAHAN
Special to The New York Times

WASHINGTON, Oct. 16—The Nixon Administration pledged today to "persevere" in its anti-inflationary policies until they yield results.

"We in this Administration will very definitely persevere in the present policy of restraint," Dr. Arthur F. Burns, counselor to the President, said. "We will not budge from it."

President Nixon will explain his anti-inflationary policies to the American people tomorrow, the White House announced, in a radio address on the subject at 4 P.M.

Continuation of the anti-inflationary policies, so far as the Federal budget is concerned, will require not only a strict rein on federal expenditures but also a continuation of the income tax surcharge, at the reduced rate of 5 per cent, from January through next June, Dr. Burns said. The present rate is 10 per cent.

Sees Congressional Chiefs

Both these points were made by President Nixon in a meeting this morning with Congressional leaders and the ranking Democrats and Republicans on the Congressional tax and appropriations committees, Dr. Burns disclosed at a briefing.

The Senate Finance Committee, meanwhile, voted the surtax extension as requested. Its chairman, Senator Russell B. Long, Democrat of Louisiana, said that the vote had not been influenced by the President's statements. [Page 18.]

Monetary restraint as well as budgetary restraint "will continue for the present," Dr. Burns said.

But, at the same time, he predicted that interest rates would "move down sometime soon."

Paul W. McCracken, chair-

Continued on Page 19, Column 1

PROCACCINO VOWS JAIL FOR MAFIOSI

Pledges an 'Unprecedented Attack' on Syndicate

By DOUGLAS ROBINSON

Controller Mario A. Procaccino pledged yesterday that if elected he would unleash an "unprecedented attack" on the Mafia and said he was fully aware of its "infiltration into legitimate businesses and into labor unions."

In his first formal campaign statement on organized crime, which he coupled with a scathing attack on Mayor Lindsay, the Democratic candidate for Mayor promised to jail Mafia men.

"It is claimed there are about 5,000 members of the Mafia in these United States, 5,000 punks or bums or whatever you want to call them, who have besmirched the reputations of millions of decent, honest, hard-working Italian-Americans," he said.

"I will fight them, I will beat them, and put them behind bars."

Mr. Procaccino made known his stand on organized crime in a short statement and in a lengthy position paper distributed at a news conference

Continued on Page 50, Column 3

NEWS INDEX

Nixon's Draft Lottery Plan Approved by House Panel

Laird Praises 31-0 Vote on Proposal to Induct 19-Year-Olds First

By JOHN W. FINNEY
Special to The New York Times

WASHINGTON, Oct. 16—The House Armed Services Committee unexpectedly approved today, 31 to 0, the Administration's proposal of drafting 19-year-olds first through a random selection, or lottery, system.

The committee, however, refusing to go beyond this reform, rejected a proposal by a committee minority to end deferments for college students.

In an informal discussion with Pentagon newsmen, Defense Secretary Melvin R. Laird described the House committee's action as "a most heartening step to eliminate some of the inequities in the draft." He expressed hope that a lottery system could be inaugurated early next year.

The House committee had been regarded as the main obstacle to implementation of a lottery selection system, which was specifically prohibited in the 1967 draft law. But it is not certain whether the way

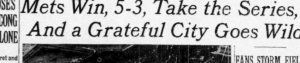

Associated Press
Melvin R. Laird

is now clear for Congressional approval of the lottery this session.

With the unanimous approval of the House committee, the lottery proposal is certain to be approved by the House, perhaps as early as next week. What remained uncertain was whether the Senate Armed Services Committee, and thus

Continued on Page 23, Column 1

Moratorium Backers Say Nixon Will Have to React

By JOHN HERBERS

Some of the prominent supporters of Wednesday's Vietnam moratorium say that the massive outpourings of Americans opposed to the war will force President Nixon to alter his policy, even though the White House insists it will not.

This was the central issue emerging from the moratorium—whether mass demonstrations of unprecedented size will, or should, precipitate a major change in the nation's Vietnam policy.

In Washington, leaders of the moratorium were attempting to puzzle out what they had accomplished. "I think it was a good start," Sam Brown, one of the prime movers, remarked.

A number of newspapers around the country expressed concern in editorials that the country seemed to be moving into an era in which foreign policy was being made in the streets rather than through established channels of government.

Harriman Sums It Up

Supporters of the moratorium, however, said such a procedure was both proper and effective—a view summed up by W. Averell Harriman Wednesday night at a rally of 15,000 in East Meadow, L. I., and repeated yesterday by a number of prominent political leaders.

"I've been working for peace for four years," said Mr. Harriman, former chief negotiator at the Paris peace talks. "Now you've started something and nobody can stop you. President Nixon said he wouldn't pay attention to your voices. Now he's going to have to pay attention."

In Washington, Mike Mansfield of Montana, the Senate

Continued on Page 20, Column 3

A 'RESIDUAL FORCE' IN VIETNAM HINTED

Laird Sees Need to Maintain Small Group to Train and Advise After the War

By WILLIAM BEECHER
Special to The New York Times

WASHINGTON, Oct. 16—Secretary of Defense Melvin R. Laird said today that he expected the United States to maintain several thousand military men for training and advisory duty in South Vietnam after the fighting had ended.

But Mr. Laird, speaking at an informal news conference in the Pentagon, said he did not want to give the impression that the Nixon Administration contemplated keeping in Vietnam for any indefinite period anything like the 300,000 men in Europe or the 50,000 in South Korea.

The Secretary got into the matter of postwar planning while answering questions about the next defense budget, currently under preparation. He asserted that the Administration was trying to give more realistic planning guidance to the armed services in drawing up their budget proposals.

The premise in previous budget guidance, he said, has been to provide forces to fight two major wars and one brushfire war simultaneously, but

Continued on Page 3, Column 5

$500-Million Development Plan For Brooklyn Shown by Mayor

By DAVID K. SHIPLER

Mayor Lindsay yesterday unveiled a master plan designed to remake downtown Brooklyn with $500-million worth of office buildings, department stores and apartment houses connected by an underground network of pedestrian passages.

Unlike some ambitious plans, this one appears likely to be realized, planners say, since numerous private investors are anxious to build there.

Six major department stores, including Alexander's and S. Klein, have expressed interest, according to Jonathan Barnett, director of the City Planning Department's Urban Design Group. A $14-million office building has already been scheduled for construction by private builders.

Downtown Brooklyn is now

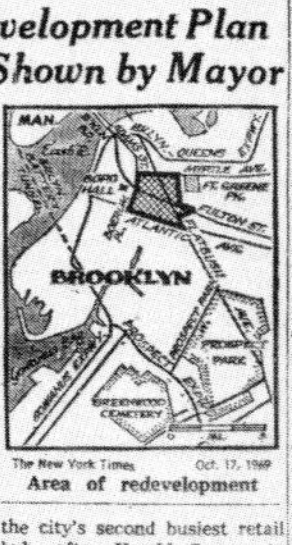

The New York Times Oct. 17, 1969
Area of redevelopment

the city's second busiest retail hub, after Herald Square in Manhattan.

But for several blocks on each side of Fulton Street, which is well developed with some major department stores,

Continued on Page 52, Column 4

HANOI PROPOSES U.S. AND VIETCONG NEGOTIATE ALONE

Calls, in Paris, for Secret and Immediate Talks—Plan Is Barred in Washington

By HENRY GINIGER
Special to The New York Times

PARIS, Oct. 16 — North Vietnam today proposed direct and secret peace talks, to begin immediately, between the United States and the South Vietnamese Communist forces.

The proposal, which would eliminate the South Vietnamese Government as a party to a settlement, was countered by the United States. Its chief delegate to the Paris peace talks, Henry Cabot Lodge, called for secret talks among all four participants at the conference here.

[In Washington, the White House said that "We would not meet alone with the Vietcong" but that the United States was ready to meet "with all the parties together in any format."

[In Saigon, allied spokesmen reported that 82 Americans were killed in battle last week; one of the lowest levels of the last three years. Page 3.]

Move Believed Tactical

North Vietnam has sought before to bring together the United States and the Vietcong without the Saigon Government. The latest move at the peace conference appeared to be a tactical one designed to take advantage of antiwar feelings in the United States, which reached a high point yesterday.

Hanoi's move followed the peace moratorium in the United States, which the North Vietnamese chief delegate, Xuan Thuy, and the Vietcong chief delegate, Mrs. Nguyen Thi Binh, hailed.

Mr. Thuy said President Nixon had not lived up to his promises of peace and now had to face "a movement of protest of the American people, a movement of national character, vigorous and widespread and without precedent in the United States."

In an unusually strong attack on the Saigon Government, Mr. Thuy referred to it as "traitorous" and warned that "as long

Continued on Page 3, Column 1

BOY AND GIRL DIE IN ANTIWAR PACT

Commit Suicide in Jersey After Moratorium Rally

By BERNARD WEINRAUB
Special to The New York Times

BLACKWOOD, N. J., Oct. 16—Two high school classmates who had attended the Vietnam Moratorium at nearby Glassboro State College yesterday were found dead this morning in a locked car cluttered with 24 notes urging peace and brotherhood for mankind.

The teen-agers, whose deaths were ruled suicides, were Craig Badiali, the president of the Highland Regional High School Dramatic Society, and Joan Fox, a cheerleader at the high school. The bodies of the two 17-year-olds were found in the front seat of a blue 1962 Ford Falcon owned by the Badiali family.

This morning the dead youth's 21-year-old brother Bernard Jr. said:

"My brother died for his convictions. He was against the war."

Thomas R. Daley, the medical investigator for the Camden County Medical Examiner's Office, gave the following account of the suicides in this community 10 miles from Philadelphia:

"They hooked a vacuum cleaner hose to the exhaust and drilled a hole through the rear floor of the car and brought the hose in through there.

"We found 24 notes in the car addressed to parents and close friends," he went on. "The

Continued on Page 22, Column 4

Mets Win, 5-3, Take the Series, And a Grateful City Goes Wild

The New York Times (by Michael Evans)
JUBILEE: Broad and Wall Streets at 4 P.M. yesterday after Mets stock hit all-time high

FANS STORM FIELD

Thousands Rip Up Turf After a Late Rally Defeats Orioles

By JOSEPH DURSO

The Mets entered the promised land yesterday after seven years of wandering through the wilderness of baseball.

In a tumultuous game before a record crowd of 57,397 in Shea Stadium, they defeated the Baltimore Orioles, 5-3, for their fourth straight victory of the 66th World Series and captured the championship of a sport that had long ranked them as comical losers.

They did it with a full and final dose of the magic that had spiced their unthinkable climb from ninth place in the

Thumbnail sketches and pictures of all the Mets will be found on Page 57.

National League — 100-to-1 shots who scraped and scrounged their way to the pinacle as the waifs of the major leagues.

At 3:17 o'clock on a cool and often sunny afternoon, their impossible dream came true when Cleon Jones caught a fly ball hit by Dave Johnson to left field. And they immediately touched off one of the great, riotous scenes in sports history, as thousands of persons swarmed from their seats and tore up the patch of ground where the Mets had made history.

Lovable Winners Now

It was 10 days after they had won the National League pennant in a three-game sweep of the Atlanta Braves. It was 22 days after they had won the Eastern title of the league over the Chicago Cubs. It was eight years after they had started business under Casey Stengel as the lovable losers of all sports.

They reached the top, moreover, in the best and most far-fetched manner of Met baseball.

They spotted the Orioles three runs in the third inning when Dave McNally and Frank Robinson hit home runs off Jerry Koosman.

But then they stormed back with two runs in the sixth inning on a home run by Donn Clendenon, another in the seventh on a home run by Al Weis and two more in the eighth on two doubles and two errors.

The deciding run was batted

Continued on Page 58, Column 4

3 AMERICANS GET NOBEL IN MEDICINE

Share Prize for Discoveries Concerning Reproductive Mechanism of Viruses

By JOHN M. LEE
Special to The New York Times

STOCKHOLM, Oct. 16—Three American scientists were jointly awarded the 1969 Nobel Prize in Physiology or Medicine today for their discoveries concerning viruses and viral diseases.

The winners are:

Dr. Max Delbrück, 63-year-old professor of biology at the California Institute of Technology, Pasadena.

Dr. Alfred D. Hershey, 60, director of the Carnegie Institution's genetics research unit, Cold Spring Harbor, L. I.

Dr. Salvador E. Luria, 57, Sedgwick Professor of Microbiology, Massachusetts Institute of Technology, Cambridge.

The three men, who will

Continued on Page 24, Column 4

A Paper Blizzard Wraps City in a Blanket of Joy

By WILLIAM BORDERS

With the kind of jubilation it reserves for its special heroes, New York yesterday went pleasantly mad over the Mets.

From the sleek skyscrapers of Wall Street, where a spontaneous tickertape blizzard greeted the World Series victory, to the undistinguished bars of a hundred neighborhoods, where the toasts were in draft beer, the shouted cry was:

"We're Number One!"

Teachers suspended classes, because their transistor-equipped students were not paying attention anyway; bosses closed offices early for the same reason, and even policemen shrugged happily as they despaired of keeping order in the streets.

Celebrators, wading through paper that was ankle-deep in Wall Street and midtown Manhattan, hopelessly clogged traffic during the evening rush, an hour after the game ended.

But the mood was happy, and even the stalled motorists seemed not to mind.

The news from Shea Stadium occasioned largesse on the part of some New Yorkers, like the Madison Avenue bus driver who stopped collecting fares, informing startled passengers: "Everyone on free!"

It was a sign of hope for others, like Isaac Stern, the violinist, who said:

"If the Mets can win the Series, anything can happen—even peace."

In the financial district, where the police were forced to close part of Broad Street for an hour because of the crowds, old-timers compared the celebration to that honoring Col. Charles A. Lindbergh in 1927, after his solo flight across the Atlantic.

Shoulder to shoulder, the tycoons and the clerks poured out of their offices and into the narrow streets to cheer their team. From windows high above them, secretaries threw whatever paper was handy — tickertape, stationery, or shredded computer cards.

There, as in midtown, the

Continued on Page 60, Column 3

Associated Press
THE IMPOSSIBLE DREAM: Ed Charles dances for joy as Jerry Koosman, pitcher, jumps on Jerry Grote after last out

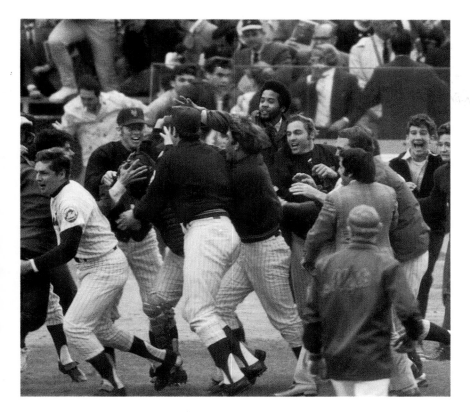

Most of the 57,397 fans at Shea Stadium joined in the Mets' celebration after winning the 1969 World Series over the Baltimore Orioles. Met pitcher Tom Seaver (left) heads for the clubhouse, while at the center of the pack is pitcher Jerry Koosman, whose five-hitter led the Mets to a 5–3 win and a world championship in Game 5. Koosman allowed just seven hits in 17⅔ innings pitched in the Series.

Two architects of the Miracle—pitchers Tom Seaver (left) and Gary Gentry (right) survey the damage at Shea Stadium after fans stormed the field to celebrate the Mets' Series-clinching 5–3 win over the Orioles on October 16, 1969. Gentry, 23, helped blank Baltimore in Game 3, while Seaver, 24, won Game 4.

Jerry Grote's short fly, and Grote wound up on second base. Rod Gaspar ran for Grote. J.C. Martin bunted, and the throw to first base hit him on the wrist and ricocheted into right field as Gaspar scored the winning run: 2–1, Mets.

The Orioles opened the fifth game by bombing Koosman. McNally, the Baltimore pitcher, hit a two-run homer in the third inning, and two outs later Frank Robinson homered. But Koosman allowed only one more hit. Clendenon hit his third homer of the Series. Weis homered—his only home run at Shea Stadium all season. With the score tied, the Mets scored two in the eighth on doubles by Jones and Swoboda, followed by two Oriole errors.

Three outs to go. Koosman walked Frank Robinson. Powell forced Robinson at second. Brooks Robinson flied to Swoboda. The final out was a soft fly to Cleon Jones, hit by a man with the Mets in his future, Davey Johnson—5–3, New York, for a 4–1 World Series upset.

Casey Stengel was there to enjoy it. "I'm very proud of these fellas, which did such a splendid job, and if they keep improving like this they can keep going to Christmas," Casey said.

"The Mets are amazin'." ⑩

Rarely has the taste of victory been so sweet as it was at Shea Stadium on October 16, 1969. The Mets' world championship was an impossible ending to an improbable decade, and it started an impromptu version of a New York City specialty—a ticker-tape parade.

1960s Statistics

1960

American League

	W	L	PCT	GB
New York	97	57	.630	—
Baltimore	89	65	.578	8
Chicago	87	67	.565	10
Cleveland	76	78	.494	21
Washington	73	81	.474	24
Detroit	71	83	.461	26
Boston	65	89	.422	32
Kansas City	58	96	.377	39

Most Valuable Player	R.Maris, NY
Rookie of the Year	R.Hansen, BAL

League Leaders

Batting	P.Runnels, BOS	.320
Runs	M.Mantle, NY	119
Home Runs	M.Mantle, NY	40
RBI	R.Maris, NY	112
Steals	L.Aparicio, CHI	51
Wins	J.Perry, CLE	18
	C.Estrada, BAL	18
Saves	M.Fornieles, BOS	14
	J.Klippstein, CLE	14
ERA	F.Baumann, CHI	2.67
Strikeouts	J.Bunning, DET	201

World Series
Pittsburgh (NL) def. New York (AL) 4-3

All-Star Games
July 11 at Kansas City — NL 5 - AL 3
July 13 at New York — NL 6 - AL 0

Record Setters
Most home runs, team, 154-game season, AL — 193, NY
Most RBI in a World Series — 12, B.Richardson, NY (AL)

National League

	W	L	PCT	GB
Pittsburgh	95	59	.617	—
Milwaukee	88	66	.571	7
St. Louis	86	68	.558	9
Los Angeles	82	72	.532	13
San Francisco	79	75	.513	16
Cincinnati	67	87	.435	28
Chicago	60	94	.390	35
Philadelphia	59	95	.383	36

Most Valuable Player	D.Groat, PIT
Cy Young	V.Law, PIT*
Rookie of the Year	F.Howard, LA

(*only one Cy Young Award was given until 1967)

League Leaders

Batting	D.Groat, PIT	.325
Runs	B.Bruton, MIL	112
Home Runs	E.Banks, CHI	41
RBI	H.Aaron, MIL	126
Steals	M.Wills, LA	50
Wins	E.Broglio, StL	21
	W.Spahn, MIL	21
Saves	L.McDaniel, StL	26
ERA	M.McCormick, SF	2.70
Strikeouts	D.Drysdale, LA	246

1961

American League

	W	L	PCT	GB
New York	109	53	.673	—
Detroit	101	61	.623	8
Baltimore	95	67	.586	14
Chicago	86	76	.531	23
Cleveland	78	83	.484	30½
Boston	76	86	.469	33
Minnesota	70	90	.438	38
Los Angeles	70	91	.435	38½
Kansas City	61	100	.379	47½
Washington	61	100	.379	47½

Most Valuable Player	R.Maris, NY
Cy Young	W.Ford, NY
Rookie of the Year	D.Schwall, BOS

League Leaders

Batting	N.Cash, DET	.361
Runs	M.Mantle, NY	132
	R.Maris, NY	132
Home Runs	R.Maris, NY	61
RBI	R.Maris, NY	142
Steals	L.Aparicio, CHI	53
Wins	W.Ford, NY	25
Saves	L.Arroyo, NY	29
ERA	D.Donovan, WAS	2.40
Strikeouts	C.Pascual, MIN	221

World Series
New York (AL) def. Cincinnati (NL) 4-1

All-Star Games
July 11 at San Francisco — NL 5 - AL 4
July 31 at Boston — NL 1, AL 1 (called after nine innings, rain)

Record Setters
Most pinch-hits, season, AL — 24, D.Philley, BAL
Most home runs by a shortstop, career — 277, E.Banks, CHI, 1953-1961
Most home runs, 162-game season — 61, R.Maris, NY (AL)
Most home runs by a switch-hitter, season — 54, M.Mantle, NY (AL)
Most home runs by a team, season — 240, NY (AL)
Most home runs by two teammates, season — 115, R.Maris (61) and M.Mantle (54), NY (AL)
Most consecutive games won by a relief pitcher, season, AL — 12, L.Arroyo, NY (AL)

National League

	W	L	PCT	GB
Cincinnati	93	61	604	—
Los Angeles	89	65	.578	4
San Francisco	85	69	.552	8
Milwaukee	83	71	.539	10
St. Louis	80	74	.519	13
Pittsburgh	75	79	.487	18
Chicago	64	90	.416	29
Philadelphia	47	107	.305	46

Most Valuable Player	F.Robinson, CIN
Rookie of the Year	B.Williams, CHI

League Leaders

Batting	R.Clemente, PIT	.351
Runs	W.Mays, SF	129
Home Runs	O.Cepeda, SF	46
RBI	O.Cepeda, SF	142
Steals	M.Wills, LA	35
Wins	J.Jay, CIN	21
	W.Spahn, MIL	21
Saves	R.Face, PIT	17
	S.Miller, SF	17
ERA	W.Spahn, MIL	3.02
Strikeouts	S.Koufax, LA	269

Records listed in **Record Setters** still stand as of publication date.

1960s Statistics

1962

American League

	W	L	PCT	GB
New York	96	66	.593	—
Minnesota	91	71	.562	5
Los Angeles	86	76	.531	10
Detroit	85	76	.528	10½
Chicago	85	77	.525	11
Cleveland	80	82	.494	16
Baltimore	77	85	.475	19
Boston	76	84	.475	19
Kansas City	72	90	.444	24
Washington	60	101	.373	35½

Most Valuable Player — M.Mantle, NY
Rookie of the Year — T.Tresh, NY

League Leaders

Batting	P.Runnels, BOS	.326
Runs	A.Pearson, LA	115
Home Runs	H.Killebrew, MIN	48
RBI	H.Killebrew, MIN	126
Steals	L.Aparicio, CHI	31
Wins	R.Terry, NY	23
Saves	D.Radatz, BOS	24
ERA	H.Aguirre, DET	2.21
Strikeouts	C.Pascual, MIN	206

World Series
New York (AL) def. San Francisco (NL) 4-3

All-Star Games
July 10 at Washington — NL 3 - AL 1
July 30 at Chicago — AL 9 - NL 4

Record Setters
Most seasons batting .300 or over, NL since 1900 — 17, S.Musial, StL, 1942-44, 1946-58, 1962
Hitless season involving the most at-bats — 70, B.Buhl, MIL, CHI (NL)
Most consecutive innings pitched without a walk — 84 1/3, B.Fischer, KC
Most strikeouts, extra-inning game — 21 (16 innings), T.Cheney, WAS

National League

	W	L	PCT	GB
San Francisco	103	62	.624	—
Los Angeles	102	63	.618	1
Cincinnati	98	64	.605	3½
Pittsburgh	93	68	.578	8
Milwaukee	86	76	.531	15½
St. Louis	84	78	.519	17½
Philadelphia	81	80	.503	20
Houston	64	96	.400	36½
Chicago	59	103	.364	42½
New York	40	120	.250	60½

Most Valuable Player — M.Wills, LA
Cy Young — D.Drysdale, LA
Rookie of the Year — K.Hubbs, CHI

League Leaders

Batting	T.Davis, LA	.346
Runs	F.Robinson, CIN	134
Home Runs	W.Mays, SF	49
RBI	T.Davis, LA	153
Steals	M.Wills, LA	104
Wins	D.Drysdale, LA	25
Saves	R.Face, PIT	28
ERA	S.Koufax, LA	2.54
Strikeouts	D.Drysdale, LA	232

1963

American League

	W	L	PCT	GB
New York	104	57	.646	—
Chicago	94	68	.580	10½
Minnesota	91	70	.565	13
Baltimore	86	76	.531	18½
Cleveland	79	83	.488	25½
Detroit	79	83	.488	25½
Boston	76	85	.472	28
Kansas City	73	89	.451	31½
Los Angeles	70	91	.435	34
Washington	56	106	.346	48½

Most Valuable Player — E.Howard, NY
Rookie of the Year — G.Peters, CHI

League Leaders

Batting	C.Yastrzemski, BOS	.321
Runs	B.Allison, MIN	99
Home Runs	H.Killebrew, MIN	45
RBI	D.Stuart, BOS	118
Steals	L.Aparicio, BAL	40
Wins	W.Ford, NY	24
Saves	S.Miller, BAL	27
ERA	G.Peters, CHI	2.33
Strikeouts	C.Pascual, MIN	202

World Series
Los Angeles (NL) def. New York (AL) 4-0

All-Star Game
July 9 at Cleveland — NL 5 - AL 3

Record Setters
Most consecutive seasons with the same team — 22, S.Musial, StL (tied with C.Anson)
Most home runs by a catcher, career, AL — 306, Y.Berra, NY, 1946-1963
Most shutouts by a left-hander, season, NL — 11, S.Koufax, LA
Most World Series hits, career — 71, Y.Berra, NY (AL), 1947, 1949, 1950-53, 1955-58, 1960-63

National League

	W	L	PCT	GB
Los Angeles	99	63	.611	—
St. Louis	93	69	.574	6
San Francisco	88	74	.543	11
Philadelphia	87	75	.537	12
Cincinnati	86	76	.531	13
Milwaukee	84	78	.519	15
Chicago	82	80	.506	17
Pittsburgh	74	88	.457	25
Houston	66	96	.407	33
New York	51	111	.315	48

Most Valuable Player — S.Koufax, LA
Cy Young — S.Koufax, LA
Rookie of the Year — P.Rose, CIN

League Leaders

Batting	T.Davis, LA	.326
Runs	H.Aaron, MIL	121
Home Runs	H.Aaron, MIL	44
	W.McCovey, SF	44
RBI	H.Aaron, MIL	130
Steals	M.Wills, LA	40
Wins	S.Koufax, LA	25
	J.Marichal, SF	25
Saves	L.McDaniel, CHI	22
ERA	S.Koufax, LA	1.88
Strikeouts	S.Koufax, LA	306

1960s Statistics

1964

American League

	W	L	PCT	GB
New York	99	63	.611	—
Chicago	98	64	.605	1
Baltimore	97	65	.599	2
Detroit	85	77	.525	14
Los Angeles	82	80	.506	17
Cleveland	79	83	.488	20
Minnesota	79	83	.488	20
Boston	72	90	.444	27
Washington	62	100	.383	37
Kansas City	57	105	.352	42

Most Valuable Player   B.Robinson, BAL
Cy Young   D.Chance, LA
Rookie of the Year   T.Oliva, MIN

League Leaders

Batting	T.Oliva, MIN	.323
Runs	T.Oliva, MIN	109
Home Runs	H.Killebrew, MIN	49
RBI	B.Robinson, BAL	118
Steals	L.Aparicio, BAL	57
Wins	D.Chance, LA	20
	G.Peters, CHI	20
Saves	D.Radatz, BOS	29
ERA	D.Chance, LA	1.65
Strikeouts	A.Downing, NY	217

World Series
St. Louis (NL) def. New York (AL) 4-3

All-Star Game
July 7 at New York — NL 7 - AL 4

Record Setters
Most hits by a rookie, season, AL — 217, T.Oliva, MIN
Most consecutive seasons leading league in steals — 9, L.Aparicio, CHI, BAL, 1956-64
Most strikeouts by a relief pitcher, season — 181, D.Radatz, BOS
Most World Series runs scored, career — 42, M.Mantle, NY (AL), 1951-53, 1955-58, 1960-64
Most World Series home runs, career — 18, M.Mantle, NY (AL)
Most World Series RBI, career — 40, M.Mantle, NY (AL)
Most World Series wins, career — 10, W.Ford, NY (AL), 1950, 1953, 1955-58, 1960-64
Most World Series strikeouts, career — 94, W.Ford, NY (AL)

National League

	W	L	PCT	GB
St. Louis	93	69	.574	—
Cincinnati	92	70	.568	1
Philadelphia	92	70	.568	1
San Francisco	90	72	.556	3
Milwaukee	88	74	.543	5
Los Angeles	80	82	.494	13
Pittsburgh	80	82	.494	13
Chicago	76	86	.469	17
Houston	66	96	.407	27
New York	53	109	.327	40

Most Valuable Player   K.Boyer, StL
Rookie of the Year   R.Allen, PHI

League Leaders

Batting	R.Clemente, PIT	.339
Runs	R.Allen, PHI	125
Home Runs	W.Mays, SF	47
RBI	K.Boyer, StL	119
Steals	M.Wills, LA	53
Wins	L.Jackson, CHI	24
Saves	H.Woodeshick, HOU	23
ERA	S.Koufax, LA	1.74
Strikeouts	B.Veale, PIT	250

1965

American League

	W	L	PCT	GB
Minnesota	102	60	.630	—
Chicago	95	67	.586	7
Baltimore	94	68	.580	8
Detroit	89	73	.549	13
Cleveland	87	75	.537	15
New York	77	85	.475	25
California	75	87	.463	27
Washington	70	92	.432	32
Boston	62	100	.383	40
Kansas City	59	103	.364	43

Most Valuable Player   Z.Versalles, MIN
Rookie of the Year   C.Blefary, BAL

League Leaders

Batting	T.Oliva, MIN	.321
Runs	Z.Versalles, MIN	126
Home Runs	T.Conigliaro, BOS	32
RBI	R.Colavito, DET	108
Steals	B.Campaneris, KC	51
Wins	M.Grant, MIN	21
Saves	R.Kline, WAS	29
ERA	S.McDowell, CLE	2.18
Strikeouts	S.McDowell, CLE	325

World Series
Los Angeles (NL) def. Minnesota (AL) 4-3

All-Star Game
July 13 at Minnesota — NL 6 - AL 5

Record Setters
Oldest person to play in a major league game — 59 years, 2 months, 18 days, S.Paige, KC, September 25, 1965
Most home runs in a month, NL — 17, W.Mays, SF, August
Most games won by a left-hander, career— 363, W.Spahn, BOS, MIL, NY, SF (NL), 1942, 1946-1965
Most shutouts by a left-hander, career, NL — 63, W.Spahn
Most no-hit games, career, NL — 4, S.Koufax, LA, 1962, 1963, 1964, 1965
Most strikeouts, season, NL since 1900 — 382, S.Koufax, LA
Most ten-or-more-strikeout games, season, NL — 21, S.Koufax, LA

National League

	W	L	PCT	GB
Los Angeles	97	65	.599	—
San Francisco	95	67	.586	2
Pittsburgh	90	72	.556	7
Cincinnati	89	73	.549	8
Milwaukee	86	76	.531	11
Philadelphia	85	76	.528	11½
St. Louis	80	81	.497	16½
Chicago	72	90	.444	25
Houston	65	97	.401	32
New York	50	112	.309	47

Most Valuable Player   W.Mays, SF
Cy Young   S.Koufax, LA
Rookie of the Year   J.Lefebvre, LA

League Leaders

Batting	R.Clemente, PIT	.329
Runs	T.Harper, CIN	126
Home Runs	W.Mays, SF	52
RBI	D.Johnson, CIN	130
Steals	M.Wills, LA	94
Wins	S.Koufax, LA	26
Saves	T.Abernathy, CHI	31
ERA	S.Koufax, LA	2.04
Strikeouts	S.Koufax, LA	382

Records listed in **Record Setters** still stand as of publication date.

1960s Statistics

1966

American League

	W	L	PCT	GB
Baltimore	97	63	.606	—
Minnesota	89	73	.549	9
Detroit	88	74	.543	10
Chicago	83	79	.512	15
Cleveland	81	81	.500	17
California	80	82	.494	18
Kansas City	74	86	.463	23
Washington	71	88	.447	25½
Boston	72	90	.444	25
New York	70	89	.440	26½

Most Valuable Player   F.Robinson, BAL
Rookie of the Year   T.Agee, CHI

League Leaders

Batting	F.Robinson, BAL	.316
Runs	F.Robinson, BAL	122
Home Runs	F.Robinson, BAL	49
RBI	F.Robinson, BAL	122
Steals	B.Campaneris, KC	52
Wins	J.Kaat, MIN	25
Saves	J.Aker, KC	32
ERA	G.Peters, CHI	1.98
Strikeouts	S.McDowell, CLE	225

World Series
Baltimore (AL) def. Los Angeles (NL) 4-0

All-Star Game
July 12 at St. Louis — NL 2 - AL 1

Record Setters
Most pinch-hit home runs, career, NL — 18, J.Lynch, CIN, PIT, 1957-66
Most consecutive seasons, 100 or more RBI, NL — 8, W.Mays, SF, 1959-1966 (tied with M.Ott)
Most wins by a left-hander, season, NL since 1900 — 27, S.Koufax, LA (tied with S. Carlton)
Most consecutive seasons leading league in ERA — 5, S.Koufax, LA, 1962-66
Most ten-or-more-strikeout games, career, NL — 97, S.Koufax, LA, 1955-66
Most strikeouts by a relief pitcher in a World Series game — 11, M.Drabowsky, Baltimore, Game 1

National League

	W	L	PCT	GB
Los Angeles	95	67	.586	—
San Francisco	93	68	.578	1½
Pittsburgh	92	70	.568	3
Philadelphia	87	75	.537	8
Atlanta	85	77	.525	10
St. Louis	83	79	.512	12
Cincinnati	76	84	.475	18
Houston	72	90	.444	23
New York	66	95	.410	28½
Chicago	59	103	.364	36

Most Valuable Player   R.Clemente, PIT
Cy Young   S.Koufax, LA
Rookie of the Year   T.Helms, CIN

League Leaders

Batting	M.Alou, PIT	.342
Runs	F.Alou, ATL	122
Home Runs	H.Aaron, ATL	44
RBI	H.Aaron, ATL	127
Steals	L.Brock, StL	74
Wins	S.Koufax, LA	27
Saves	P.Regan, LA	21
ERA	S.Koufax, LA	1.73
Strikeouts	S.Koufax, LA	317

1967

American League

	W	L	PCT	GB
Boston	92	70	.568	—
Detroit	91	71	.562	1
Minnesota	91	71	.562	1
Chicago	89	73	.549	3
California	84	77	.522	7½
Baltimore	76	85	.472	15½
Washington	76	85	.472	15½
Cleveland	75	87	.463	17
New York	72	90	.444	20
Kansas City	62	99	.385	29½

Most Valuable Player   C.Yastrzemski, BOS
Cy Young   J.Lonborg, BOS
Rookie of the Year   R.Carew, MIN

League Leaders

Batting	C.Yastrzemski, BOS	.326
Runs	C.Yastrzemski, BOS	112
Home Runs	H.Killebrew, MIN	44
	C.Yastrzemski, BOS	44
RBI	C.Yastrzemski, BOS	121
Steals	B.Campaneris, KC	55
Wins	J.Lonborg, BOS	22
	E.Wilson, DET	22
Saves	M.Rojas, CAL	27
ERA	J.Horlen, CHI	2.06
Strikeouts	J.Lonborg, BOS	246

World Series
St. Louis (NL) def. Boston (AL) 4-3

All-Star Game
July 11 at California — NL 2 - AL 1

Record Setters
Most consecutive seasons, 100 or more runs scored, NL — 13, H.Aaron, MIL, ATL, 1955-67
Highest winning percentage, 200 or more wins — .690, W.Ford, NY (AL), 1950, 1953-67
Lowest ERA by a left-hander, 200 or more wins — 2.74, W.Ford, NY (AL)
Most team strikeouts, pitching staff, season, AL — 1,189, CLE
Most strikeouts in an All-Star Game — 6, F.Jenkins, CHI (tied with C.Hubbell, J.Vander Meer and L.Jansen)

National League

	W	L	PCT	GB
St. Louis	101	60	.627	—
San Francisco	91	71	.562	10½
Chicago	87	74	.540	14
Cincinnati	87	75	.537	14½
Philadelphia	82	80	.506	19½
Pittsburgh	81	81	.500	20½
Atlanta	77	85	.475	24½
Los Angeles	73	89	.451	28½
Houston	69	93	.426	32½
New York	61	101	.377	40½

Most Valuable Player   O.Cepeda, SF
Cy Young   M.McCormick, SF
Rookie of the Year   T.Seaver, NY

League Leaders

Batting	R.Clemente, PIT	.357
Runs	H.Aaron, ATL	113
	L.Brock, StL	113
Home Runs	H.Aaron, ATL	39
RBI	O.Cepeda, StL	111
Steals	L.Brock, StL	52
Wins	M.McCormick, SF	22
Saves	T.Abernathy, CIN	28
ERA	P.Niekro, ATL	1.87
Strikeouts	J.Bunning, PHI	253

1960s Statistics

1968

American League	W	L	PCT	GB
Detroit	103	59	.636	—
Baltimore	91	71	.562	12
Cleveland	86	75	.534	16½
Boston	86	76	.531	17
New York	83	79	.512	20
Oakland	82	80	.506	21
Minnesota	79	83	.488	24
California	67	95	.414	36
Chicago	67	95	.414	36
Washington	65	96	.404	37½

Most Valuable Player — D.McLain, DET
Cy Young — D.McLain, DET
Rookie of the Year — S.Bahnsen, NY

League Leaders

Batting	Carl Yastrzemski, BOS	.301
Runs	Dick McAuliffe, DET	95
Home Runs	Frank Howard, WAS	44
RBI	K.Harrelson, BOS	109
Steals	B.Campaneris, OAK	62
Wins	D.McLain, DET	31
Saves	A.Worthington, MIN	18
ERA	L.Tiant, CLE	1.60
Strikeouts	S.McDowell, CLE	283

World Series
Detroit (AL) def. St. Louis (NL) 4-3

All-Star Game
July 9 at Houston — NL 1 - AL 0

Record setters
Lowest batting average to lead league — .301, C.Yastrzemski, BOS
Most career home runs by a switch-hitter — 536, M.Mantle, NY (AL), 1951-68
Most team strikeouts, hitters — 1,203, NY (NL)
Lowest ERA, 300 or more innings — 1.12, B.Gibson, StL
Highest World Series batting average, 20 or more games—.391, L.Brock, StL, 1964, 1967, 1968
Most career World Series stolen bases — 14, L.Brock, StL (tied with E.Collins)
Most strikeouts in a World Series game — 17, B.Gibson, StL
Most strikeouts in a World Series — 35, B.Gibson, StL
Most career All-Star Game strikeouts — 19, D.Drysdale, LA (NL), 1952, 1962-65, 1967-68

National League	W	L	PCT	GB
St. Louis	97	65	.599	—
San Francisco	88	74	.543	9
Chicago	84	78	.519	13
Cincinnati	83	79	.512	14
Atlanta	81	81	.500	16
Pittsburgh	80	82	.494	17
Los Angeles	76	86	.469	21
Philadelphia	76	86	.469	21
New York	73	89	.451	24
Houston	72	90	.444	25

Most Valuable Player — B.Gibson, StL
Cy Young — B.Gibson, StL
Rookie of the Year — J.Bench, CIN

League Leaders

Batting	P.Rose, CIN	.335
Runs	G.Beckert, CHI	98
Home Runs	W.McCovey, SF	36
RBI	W.McCovey, SF	105
Steals	L.Brock, StL	62
Wins	J.Marichal, SF	26
Saves	P.Regan, CHI, LA	25
ERA	B.Gibson, StL	1.12
Strikeouts	B.Gibson, StL	268

1969

American League East Division	W	L	PCT	GB
Baltimore	109	53	.673	—
Detroit	90	72	.556	19
Boston	87	75	.537	22
Washington	86	76	.531	23
New York	80	81	.497	28½
Cleveland	62	99	.385	46½
West Division				
Minnesota	97	65	.599	—
Oakland	88	74	.543	9
California	71	91	.438	26
Kansas City	69	93	.426	28
Chicago	68	94	.420	29
Seattle	64	98	.395	33

Most Valuable Player — H.Killebrew, MIN
Cy Young — M.Cuellar, BAL, D.McLain, DET (tie)
Rookie of the Year — L.Piniella, KC

League Leaders

Batting	R.Carew, MIN	.332
Runs	R.Jackson, OAK	123
Home Runs	H.Killebrew, MIN	49
RBI	H.Killebrew, MIN	140
Steals	T.Harper, SEA	73
Wins	D.McLain, DET	24
Saves	R.Perranoski, MIN	31
ERA	D.Bosman, WAS	2.19
Strikeouts	S.McDowell, CLE	279

Championship Series Results
NL — New York (East) def. Atlanta (West) 3-0
AL — Baltimore (East) def. Minnesota (West) 3-0

World Series
New York (NL) def. Baltimore (AL) 4-1

All-Star Game
July 23 at Washington — NL 9 - AL 3

Record Setters
Most home runs by a shortstop, season, AL — 40, R.Petrocelli, BOS
Most bases on balls, season, NL — 148, J.Wynn, HOU (tied with E.Stanky)
Most times stealing home, season — 7, R.Carew, MIN (tied with P.Reiser)
Most consecutive wins at the start of a season, AL — 15, D.McNally, BAL (tied with J.Allen)
Most strikeouts in a nine-inning game, NL — 19, S. Carlton, StL (tied with C.Sweeney and T.Seaver)
Most team strikeouts, pitching staff, season — 1,221, HOU

National League East Division	W	L	PCT	GB
New York	100	62	.617	—
Chicago	92	70	.568	8
Pittsburgh	88	74	.543	12
St. Louis	87	75	.537	13
Philadelphia	63	99	.389	37
Montreal	52	110	.321	48
West Division				
Atlanta	93	69	.574	—
San Francisco	90	72	.556	3
Cincinnati	89	73	.549	4
Los Angeles	85	77	.525	8
Houston	81	81	.500	12
San Diego	52	110	.321	41

Most Valuable Player — W.McCovey, SF
Cy Young — T.Seaver, NY
Rookie of the Year — T.Sizemore, LA

League Leaders

Batting	P.Rose, CIN	.348
Runs	B.Bonds, SF	120
	P.Rose, CIN	120
Home Runs	W.McCovey, SF	45
RBI	W.McCovey, SF	126
Steals	L.Brock, StL	53
Wins	T.Seaver, NY	25
Saves	F.Gladding, HOU	29
ERA	J.Marichal, SF	2.10
Strikeouts	F.Jenkins, CHI	273

Records listed in **Record Setters** still stand as of publication date.

PICTURE CREDITS

Front cover: Brooks Robinson and Max Alvis by Walter Iooss, Jr./*Sports Illustrated*

Back cover: Roberto Clemente by Focus on Sports

Front Matter, Back Matter
4-5 Malcolm W. Emmons; 182 (top) National Baseball Library, Cooperstown, New York; 182 (bottom) Ron Menchine Collection/Renée Comet Photography; 183 (top) Ron Menchine Collection/Renée Comet Photography; 183 (bottom) National Baseball Library, Cooperstown, New York; 184 Ron Menchine Collection/Renée Comet Photography; 185 (top) Ron Menchine Collection/Renée Comet Photography; 185 (bottom) Ron Menchine Collection/Renée Comet Photography; 186 Ron Menchine Collection/Renée Comet Photography

The Greatest Sacrilege
6 AP/Wide World Photos; 7 Walter Iooss, Jr./*Sports Illustrated*; 9 (left) Fred Kaplan; 9 (right) UPI/Bettmann Newsphotos; 10 Focus On Sports; 11 (left) Louis Requena; 11 (right) AP/Wide World Photos; 12 New-York Historical Society; 13 (left) National Baseball Library, Cooperstown, New York/World Telegraph & Sun/Wm. Greene; 13 (right) UPI/Bettmann Newsphotos; 14 Marvin E. Newman; 15 (left) UPI/Bettmann Newsphotos; 15 (right) AP/Wide World Photos; 16 Ron Menchine Collection/Renée Comet Photography; 17 (top) National Baseball Library, Cooperstown, New York; 17 (bottom) UPI/Bettmann Newsphotos; 18 (top) Robert Riger; 18 (bottom) UPI/Bettmann Newsphotos; 19 (left) Herb Scharfman/*Sports Illustrated*; 19 (right) AP/Wide World Photos; 20 Marvin E. Newman; 21 Louis Requena; 22-23 Marvin E. Newman; 23 (right) National Baseball Library, Cooperstown, New York/Courtesy of Carl Seid; 24 AP/Wide World Photos; 25 Walter Iooss, Jr./*Sports Illustrated*

Squeezing the Sluggers
26 Richard Darcey; 27 Fred Kaplan; 28 (left) Fred Kaplan/*Sports Illustrated*; (right) Fred Kaplan; 30 Marvin E. Newman; 31 (left) Fred Kaplan; 31 (right) UPI/Bettmann Newsphotos; 32 © 1949 Time Inc. All rights reserved. Reprinted by permission from Time.; 33 (top) *The Sporting News*; 33 (bottom) Fred Kaplan; 34 (left) AP/Wide World Photos; 34 (right) Malcolm W. Emmons

Year of the Pitcher
36-37 Malcolm W. Emmons; 38 Herb Scharfman/*Sports Illustrated*; 39 (top) Fred Kaplan; 39 (bottom) Malcolm W. Emmons; 41 (left) UPI/Bettmann Newsphotos; 41 (right) Focus On Sports; 42 James Drake/*Sports Illustrated*; 43 UPI/Bettmann Newphotos; 44 Long Photography; 45 Walter Iooss, Jr.; 46 (left) National Baseball Library, Cooperstown, New York; 46-47 Lewis Portnoy/Spectra-Action, Inc.; 47 (right) Lee Balterman/*Sports Illustrated*; 48 Ron Menchine Collection/Renée Comet Photography; 49 Peter Read Miller/*Sports Illustrated*; 50 Marvin E. Newman; 51 (left) Marvin E. Newman; 51 (center) Fred Kaplan; 51 (right) Malcolm W. Emmons; 52 (left) Malcolm W. Emmons; 52 (center) Malcolm W. Emmons; 52 (right) Focus On Sports; 53 (left) Malcolm W. Emmons; 53 (center) Malcolm W. Emmons; 53 (right) Malcolm W. Emmons; 54 Herb Scharfman/*Sports Illustrated*; 55 Robert Riger; 56 (left) AP/Wide World Photos; 56 (right) Focus On Sports; 57 Walter Iooss, Jr./*Sports Illustrated*; 58 Herb Scharfman/*Sports Illustrated*; 59 (left) AP/Wide World Photos; 59 (right) AP/Wide World Photos; 60 UPI/Bettmann Newphotos; 61 (left) AP/Wide World Photos; 61 (right) AP/Wide World Photos; 62 National Baseball Library, Cooperstown, New York; 63 (top) UPI/Bettmann Newsphotos; 63 (bottom) Cranston & Elkins/Photofest

Expansion Theater
64 John Zimmerman/*Sports Illustrated*; 65 Ron Menchine Collection/Renée Comet Photography; 67 (left) National Baseball Library, Cooperstown, New York; 67 (right) © 1960 Fleer Corp./Gershman Collection; 68 Ron Menchine Collection/Renée Comet Photography; 69 Walter Iooss, Jr./*Sports Illustrated*; 70 Neil Leifer/*Sports Illustrated*; 71 (left) UPI/Bettmann Newphotos; 71 (right) AP/Wide World Photos; 72 (left) National Baseball Library, Cooperstown, New York; 72 (right) AP/Wide World Photos; 73 Paul Thomas/Seattle Times © 1961; 74 Ron Menchine Collection/Renée Comet Photography; 75 (left) National Baseball Library, Cooperstown, New York 75 (right) National Baseball Library, Cooperstown, New York

The Astrodome
78-79 Neil Leifer/*Sports Illustrated*; 80 Robert Riger © 1963; 81 (left) Ron Menchine Collection/Renée Comet Photography; 81 (right) AP/Wide World Photos; 82 Robert Riger © 1963; 83 (left) Robert Riger © 1963; 83 (right) Bob Gomel © 1965; 84 (left) AP/Wide World Photos; 84 (right) Marvin E. Newman; 85 AP/Wide World Photos; 86 (left) AstroTurf Industries Inc./Renée Comet Photography; 86 (right) AP/Wide World Photos; 87 Focus On Sports; 88 National Baseball Library, Cooperstown, New York; 89 Bob Straus, Jr.

Pennant Race Parity
90 Malcolm W.Emmons; 91 Courtesy of The Minnesota Twins; 92 Walter Iooss, Jr.; 93 Malcolm W. Emmons; 94 Marvin E. Newman; 95 (left) Herb Scharfman/*Sports Illustrated*; 95 (right) Malcolm W. Emmons; 96 (left) National Baseball Library, Cooperstown, New York; 96 (right) Bob Gomel © 1965; 97 (left) Herb Scharfman/*Sports Illustrated*; 97 (right) Malcolm W. Emmons; 98 (left) Marvin E. Newman; 98 (right) Marvin E. Newman; 99 UPI/Bettmann Newsphotos; 100 Eric Schweikardt/*Sports Illustrated*; 101 (left) Marvin Newman/*Sports Illustrated*; 101 (right) National Baseball Library, Cooperstown, New York; 102 National Baseball Library, Cooperstown, New York; 103 (left) AP/Wide World Photos; 103 (right) Malcolm W. Emmons; 104 Neil Leifer/*Sports Illustrated*; 105 (left) Marvin E. Newman; 105 (right) Marvin E. Newman

Sandy Koufax
106 John Zimmerman/*Sports Illustrated*; 107 (left) Ron Menchine Collection/Renée Comet Photography; 107 (right) Ron Menchine Collection/Renée Comet Photography; 108 (left) Malcolm W. Emmons; 108 (right) Fred Kaplan; 109 AP/Wide World Photos; 110 Neil Leifer/*Sports Illustrated*; 111 UPI/Bettmann Newsphotos; 112 Courtesy of *The New York Post*

The Hold-Out
114 AP/Wide World Photos; 115 Ron Menchine Collection/Renée Comet Photography; 116 AP/Wide World Photos; 117 (left) Neil Leifer/*Sports Illustrated*; 117 (right) Long Photography; 118 Malcolm W. Emmons; 119 Malcolm W. Emmons; 121 (left) UPI/Bettmann Newsphotos; 121 (right) National Baseball Library, Cooperstown, New York; 122 (left) Dick Raphael/*Sports Illustrated*; 122

Return of the Running Game

Billy, Ted, Earl and the Lip

The Amazin' Mets

FOR FURTHER READING

Jim Brosnan, *The Long Season*. Penguin, 1983.

Robert W. Creamer, *Stengel: His Life and Times*. Simon & Schuster, 1984.

Orlando Cepeda and Robert Markus, *High & Inside: Orlando Cepeda's Story*. B & L Publishers, 1984.

Glenn Dickey, *The History of American League Baseball*. Stein & Day, 1982.

_____The History of National League Baseball Since 1876. Stein & Day, 1982.

Ralph Houk and Robert W. Creamer, *Season of Glory: The Amazing Saga of the 1961 New York Yankees*. Putnam, 1988.

ACKNOWLEDGMENTS

Jim Murray's column on page 26 was originally published in the *Los Angeles Times* on April 15, 1967, and is reprinted with permission.

The author and editors wish to thank:

Harry Naiman of Oxford, Maryland; Ron Menchine of Baltimore, Maryland; Patricia Kelly, Peter Clark, Tom Heitz, Bill Deane and John Blomquist of The National Baseball Library, Cooperstown, New York; Paul Dickson of Garrett Park, Maryland; Philip J. Lowry of San Diego, California; Early Wynn of Nokomis, Florida; Colin Ruh of Falls Church, Virginia; Chuck Stevens of Garden Grove, California; Dave Kelly of the Library of Congress, Washington, D.C.; Tal Smith of Houston, Texas; Tom Mee and Wendie Erickson of the Minnesota Twins, Minneapolis, Minnesota; Dick Johnson of the New England Sports Museum, Boston, Massachusetts; Lloyd Johnson of SABR, Kansas City, Missouri; Connie Barthelmas of the Cincinnati Reds, Cincinnati, Ohio; Rosa Gatti of ESPN, Bristol, Connecticut; Andy Esposito of New Hyde Park, New York; Helen Bowie Campbell and Gregory J. Schwalenberg of the Babe Ruth Museum, Baltimore, Maryland; Steven P. Gietschier of *The Sporting News*, St. Louis, Missouri; Karen Carpenter of *Sports Illustrated*, New York, New York; Nat Andriani of Wide World Photos, New York, New York; Sarah Goodyear of Bettman Newsphotos, New York, New York; Renee Comet of Washington, D.C.; Sy Berger of The Topps Company, Inc., New York, New York; Ellen Hughes of the National Museum of American History, Smithsonian Institution, Washington, D.C.; Jo Ann Palmer of Focus on Sports, New York, New York; Thomas Carwile of Petersburg, Virginia; Allen Reuben of Camera 5, New York, New York; Ed Milner of AstroTurf Industries, Inc., Dalton, Georgia; The Fleer Corporation, Philadelphia, Pennsylvania; Walter Iooss, Jr., of New York, New York; George Gunia of East Brunswick, New Jersey; Greg Rhodes and Linda Bailey of the Cincinnati Historical Society of Cincinnati, Ohio; Michael Gershman of Westport, Connecticut; Jenny E. Ramsey of the City of Blue Ash Municipal & Safety Center, Blue Ash, Ohio.

Illustrations: 8, 10, 35, 40, 49, 66, 76–77, 89, 113, 120 Dale Glasgow; 29 Sam Ward.

World of Baseball is produced and
published by Redefinition, Inc.

WORLD OF BASEBALL

Editor	Glen B. Ruh
Design Director	Robert Barkin
Production Director	Irv Garfield
Managing Editor	Larry Moffi
Picture Research	Rebecca Hirsh
	Louis P. Plummer
Design	Ruth Burke, Randy Cook,
	Monique Strawderman
Staff Writer	Jonathan Kronstadt
Copy Editor	Anthony K. Pordes
Editorial Research	Ed Dixon, Victoria Salin
Editorial Assistants	Elizabeth D. McLean
	Janet Pooley
Production Assistant	Kimberly Fornshill
Picture Assistant	Dana Wolf
Copy Preparation	Gail Cerra
Index	Lynne Hobbs

REDEFINITION

Administration	Margaret M. Higgins,
	June M. Nolan
Fulfillment Manager	Karen DeLisser
Marketing Director	Harry Sailer
Finance Director	Vaughn A. Meglan
PRESIDENT	Edward Brash

Library of Congress Cataloging-in-Publication Data
The explosive sixties/William B. Mead.
    (World of Baseball)
    Includes index.
    1. Baseball—United States—History.
I. Title. II Series.
GV863.A 1m43 1989   89-3548
796.357 0973—dc19
ISBN 0-924588-01-2

Printed in U.S.A.
10 9 8 7 6 5 4 3 2

CONTRIBUTORS

William B. Mead, author of *The Explosive Sixties*,
has worked as a reporter and bureau manager for
United Press International, as a prize-winning
writer for *Money Magazine*, and as a writer and
editor for *Washingtonian* magazine. Mr. Mead
splits his writing time between two diverse special-
ties: baseball and personal finance. He is the
author of *Baseball Goes to War, The Official New
York Yankees Hater's Handbook,* and the forthcom-
ing *Two Spectacular Seasons.* His books on finance
include *American Averages: Amazing Facts of
Everyday Life* (with Mike Feinsilber) and *Strassels'
Tax Savers and Money Matters: The Hassle-Free,
Month-by-Month Guide to Money Management,*
both authored with Paul N. Strassels. The closest
Mead ever came to the major leagues was as an
eager participant in a Baltimore Orioles fantasy
camp.

Henry Staat is Series Consultant for World of
Baseball. A member of the Society for American
Baseball Research since 1982, he helped initiate
the concept for the series. He is an editor with
Wadsworth, Inc., a publisher of college textbooks.

Ron Menchine, an advisor and sports collector,
shared baseball materials he has been collecting
for 40 years. A sportscaster and sports director for
numerous radio stations, he announced the last
three seasons played by the Washington Senators.

This book is one of a series that celebrates
America's national pastime.

Redefinition also offers World of Baseball Top
Ten Stat Finders.

For subscription information and prices, write:
Customer Service, Redefinition, Inc.,
P.O. Box 25336,
Alexandria, Virginia 22313

The text of this book is set in Century Old Style;
display type is Helvetica and Gill Sans. The paper
is 70 pound Warrenflo Gloss supplied by Stanford
Paper Company. Typesetting by Darby Graphics,
Alexandria, Virginia. Color separation by
Colotone, Inc., North Branford, Connecticut.
Printed and bound by Ringier America, New
Berlin, Wisconsin.